THE UNCONSCIOUS IN ITS
EMPIRICAL MANIFESTATIONS

THE PSYCHOLOGY
OF C. G. JUNG

Volume I

THE UNCONSCIOUS IN ITS
EMPIRICAL MANIFESTATIONS,

WITHDRAWI

With Special Reference to the Association
Experiment of C. G. Jung

by C.A. MEIER

With 2 plates and 11 illustrations in the text

Translated by Eugene Rolfe

SIGO PRESS
BOSTON

SIGO PRESS
77 North Washington Street, 201
Boston, Massachusetts 02114

Publisher and General Editor: Sisa Sternback-Scott
Associate Editor: Becky Goodman

Translation originally funded by the Jung Foundation, New York.
Subsequent funding was provided by Sigo Press.

Library of Congress Cataloging in Publication Data

Meier, C. A. (Carl Alfred), 1903–
    The unconscious in its empirical forms.

    (The Psychology of C.G. Jung ; v. 1)
    Translation of: Die Empirie des Unbewussten.
    Bibliography: p. 215
    Includes index.
    1. Jung, C. G. (Carl Gustav), 1875–1961. 2. Sub-
consciousness. 3. Association of ideas. 4. Association
tests. I. Title. II. Series: Meier, C. A. (Carl Alfred),
1903–   . Lehrbuch der komplexen Psychologie
C.G. Jungs. English ; v. 1.
BF173.J85M43513   vol. 1   150.19'54 s [150.19'54]   85–13996
ISBN 0–938434–10–1

Set in English Times.
Printed in the United States of America.

TABLE OF CONTENTS

LIST OF ILLUSTRATIONS

Figures

Plates

FOREWORD

Only gods are born miraculously full-grown from trees, mountains or the head of Zeus. Every science possesses its own phylogeny and ontology, just as it possesses its own postulates and its own conclusions. We epigones are therefore only deceiving ourselves if we disregard the position of a school or doctrine in the history of thought or the personal history and development of its founder. If we do so, our assimilation of our subject will remain, as it were, at the epiphenomenal level.

Carl Gustav Jung was always aware of the need to take into account the historical background of psychology. On the other hand, he never stressed the motivations that arise from an individual's own personal history. For him, such considerations were *too* personal and ephemeral—they were, in fact, not important. Yet for anyone who is, as it were, not exactly born and bred in the same milieu, this deficiency must inevitably exact its revenge. All too easily, it can give rise to another illusion, which would have us believe that Jung's point of view is a relatively closed and completed structure, whose origins are to be found in the prehistory of psychology at the turn of the century and whose end coincided with the death of its founder.

In contradistinction to this standpoint, we remain firmly convinced that Jung is a figure who far transcends—and will always transcend—both these particular boundaries. Physically, of course, the beginnings of his career date back to his first scientific publications (i.e., to 1902); in the realm of ideas, on the other hand, we must seek them among his personal forebears and intellectual precursors, who, in turn, are also our own. The establishment of contexts of this nature was one of Jung's own principal concerns in the work of analytical education, since the survival of these "dominants," as he called them, was never more clearly in evidence than here. It was in this way that the collaboration between master and pupil became a creative contribution toward the development of personality and outgrew "analysis" in the strict sense of that term, just as the "Zurich School" outgrew the "Vienna School." It is true that the term "analytical psychology," which was originally chosen by Jung to distinguish his own therapeutic method from the "psychoanalysis" of Sigmund Freud, still bears witness to the relationship between the two schools. Yet the term can really only be justified if we reserve its use strictly to the therapeutic situation.

Many years ago, when I had the privilege of taking over the task of lecturing on Jung's psychology at the Swiss Federal Institute of Technology at Zurich, it was clear to me that I could not limit my theme to the popularization of the problems of the analyst's consulting room. Jung himself, my predecessor, had lectured on psychology in quite general terms—although he naturally did so from his own specific viewpoint. It was therefore by no means without hesitation that I took up the pupil's time-honored task of representing his teacher as faithfully as possible—although to some extent my appointment could be justified on the grounds that I had been Jung's assistant and at times his deputy for many years. On the occasion of the establishment of the Psychology Fund at the Swiss Federal Institute of Technology, Jung had outlined a characteristic program for his own work as a lecturer there:

> The treatment of psychology should in general be characterized by the principle of universality. No special theory or special subject should be propounded, but psychology should be taught in its biological, ethnological, medical, philosophical, cultural-historical and religious aspects.
>
> The aim of this stipulation is to liberate our teaching about the human soul from the narrowing effects of specialization, and to give the student who is burdened by his specialist studies an overall breadth of view and a summary grasp of the whole field which will make it possible for him to achieve an orientation in spheres of life for which his specialist training does not prepare him. It is the aim of these lectures to offer the student, within the broad framework of general psychology, an opportunity to acquire psychic cultivation.

At the same time, it struck me that the founder of our school, as he poured forth the full tide of his wisdom and experience, was inclined to take too much for granted the context and development of his own point of view, so that not infrequently the unprepared student was credited with a knowledge he did not possess. In any case, I think I may say that my contacts with students in my own lectures and seminars have taught me the kind of unspoken nuances involved in any attempt which we may make to arrive at a real understanding of the many subtle issues in modern psychology. As an expression of my gratitude for the stimulation and the many fruitful suggestions which I have received, I should like to dedicate this volume to the Extramural Department and the students of the Swiss Federal Institute of Technology.

Perhaps the subsequent volumes of this "textbook" will also make it clear why I prefer to use "complex psychology" as the title of my subject. It is true that this term has at times been opposed, among "Jungians" of all people, on the grounds that it is difficult to translate. Yet German is, after all, a civilized language, and anyone who doubts the truth of this statement might do worse than consult the collected edition of Jung's own works in the original. "Analytical psychology" is in any case an inadequate and superficial description of our science, particularly as contrasted with psychoanalysis, even if the emphasis is transferred in this way from "analysis" to "psychology." Complex psychology (a term we owe to a suggestion made by the late Toni Wolff[1]) is far less restricted by the pathological associations of the analyst's consulting room. It stresses the point that the major concern of our discipline is with the complex, rather than the elementary, human phenomena in the world, and this brings us back once again to the historical antecedents of psychology.

Since in any discussion of a problem Jung's psychology always takes into account the unconscious, there is a certain analogy between this method and problems connected with complex numbers in mathematics. These are numbers composed as a result of additions between real and imaginary quantities. In terms of psychology, the real quantities would be conscious, and the imaginary components of the psyche unconscious. In this sense, it can be said that psychology is exclusively concerned with complex psychic phenomena. Jung, it is true, did on two occasions concern himself exclusively with psychological questions which were at least relatively simple: (1) his research into the nature of complexes (not to be confused with the sense of the word *complex* in complex psychology) and (2) in typology, the functions of orientation of the conscious mind.

Yet here again, we immediately notice how he goes on to consider the more comprehensive and complex functions, as for instance in his *general* theory of complexes, with its applications in psychotherapy, parapsychology, folklore and mythology, and in the examples he gives of the impact of typological phenomena and differences on the history of civilization, e.g., in the medieval controversy about universals and in religion and mysticism.[2] Thus complex psychology embraces both the simpler psychic phenomena whose roots, as Freud has shown, are to be found immediately in the instincts, and also those other, less obvious phenomena to which we can only attribute a mental origin. When the *Codex Jung* was presented to him, the founder of this "complex psychology" confessed his faith in the following terms:

> If we really wish to arrive at a psychological understanding of modern man, then we *must* have a knowledge of the history of his mind. We *cannot* reduce him simply to biological phenomena, since he *is* not in fact a purely biological or "natural" creature. He is also a product of his mental antecedents.

One of the onerous tasks which this textbook sets out to perform is to provide a conscientious account of the empirical elements in Jung's psychology in terms of their historical origins. That is why I quote only first editions in the Bibliography. My aim is to make it possible for every reader to follow the original course of development. At the same time, this method places Jung's ideas in the context from which they are actually derived and to which they logically belong—a process that should supply us with the perspective we need if we are to understand their true significance.

It is also my intention to try to leave open those questions which are still in fact really open and not to give the impression that Jung's psychology is some kind of "doctrine." Even in his most detailed, strictly scientific work, Jung's ideas still retain their stimulating quality and in most cases their productiveness has by no means been exhausted. The complexity of psychological phenomena is in fact unlimited, and it is precisely here that Jung's completely open approach has proved its value as an aid in the most various disciplines; at the same time, it lays no claim to final completeness. Its frontiers are as complicated as those of Switzerland itself, and it touches many different spheres of culture.

We need only call to mind the fact that for no fewer than three members of the academic staff of the Swiss Federal Institute of Technology Jung's knowledge has been fruitful in their completely different fields. I am referring to Wolfgang Pauli (in theoretical physics), Eugen Boehler (in political economy) and Karl Schmid (in

Germanic studies). Jung also made a significant contribution to sinology (through Richard Wilhelm), to Indian studies (through Heinrich Zimmer), to mythology (through Karl Kerényi) and to Iranian mysticism (through Henry Corbin). This many-sided productiveness is probably the most graphic justification we could find for our use of the term *complex psychology*.

When I said that Jung's psychology was not a closed system or doctrine of any kind, I was implicitly admitting that an account of it in textbook form is in the nature of things a hopeless undertaking. Yet experience has shown that there is in fact a need for summary treatments of this kind, and there are people who actually wish to learn Jung's psychology. However, in contrast to previous attempts at a systematic account—beginning with Joan Corrie's *ABC of Jung's Psychology*[3] and continuing with subsequent essays of this type—we shall do our best to avoid giving the impression that such an open "system" as this could be completely covered by any "account." If we succeed in discussing only a few of the many issues which are still quite undecided, the aim of this textbook will have been amply fulfilled.

Jung himself never produced a systematic treatment of his own work. He possessed, it is true, neither the aptitude nor the inclination for such a task. Yet there is, I believe, a more important reason. He knew that such a treatment could never do justice to the essential nature of his discoveries. The only two systematic works he produced (*Psychological Types* in 1921[4] and "On Psychic Energy" in 1928[5]) were never taken up by him again or continued in any way, although they both contain insights which are extremely useful, particularly from the point of view of psychological practice.

I hope that the readers of this textbook will accept this attempt at a treatment which is far from systematic and will bear with me if in places I am obliged to say things or to introduce concepts which will only become clearer subsequently, in another context. The same applies logically to occasional unavoidable repetitions. I shall do my best not only to state clearly whatever is empirically well-founded, but also to give appropriate emphasis to the problems still outstanding. That many things, in fact too many things, will be omitted in the process is inevitable, although the reasons for this will necessarily be in part subjective. In particular, I refrain from giving any account of the therapeutic side of Jung's psychology, since this can only be learned or rather experienced in the practical work of a personal analysis. I should also like to make clear that the clinical material I cite is derived from exceptional cases. In practice, "miraculous cures" of this kind are as rare in psychology as they are at Lourdes.

As we know, Jung experienced only too fully the truth expressed by Wieland in the lines

> He that has dared to break new ground
> A nest of scholarly wasps has found.

I refrain in this book from entering into polemics. This is not because we cannot learn from them, but because they can only become profitable if the individual, true to the spirit of analysis, tackles the task of coming to terms with this own wasps' nest in a calm and dispassionate manner. I sincerely hope that the present volume will provide him with abundant opportunities for this experience.

It only remains for me to thank the late Professor Arthur Rohn, former Chairman of the Swiss Educational Council, for inviting me to deliver lectures on Jung's psychology at the Swiss Federal Institute. Without the lessons which I myself learned as a direct result of this opportunity, the present volume could never have been written. I should also like to express my appreciation to all those students who attended my lectures or took part in my seminars for their many stimulating comments and suggestions. A quite special word of thanks is due to the late Chairman, Professor Hans Pallmann, for his unfailing interest and encouragement. It was owing to his good offices in the first place that I received grants from the Dr. Donald C. Cooper Fund and the Esther T. Taylor Legacy to the Swiss Federal Institute. As a result I was able to leave my psychological practice for a time and devote myself to the task of writing. A final expression of gratitude is due to my friend, the late Wolfgang Pauli. My discussions on physics and Jungian psychology with him ranged over a period of a quarter of a century, and I had the privilege of his invaluable criticism and stimulation.

INTRODUCTION

It is the best of news that, with this volume, the English-speaking world will at last be introduced to Dr. C. A. Meier's unique work on C. G. Jung. Dr. Meier has long been known for his book on incubation and healing in ancient Greece, as well as for the published accounts of the many lectures he has given in America on Jungian psychology and religion. In a world hungry for a more comprehensive approach to healing, it is strange that after the impact of his work on incubation the translation of his four volumes on Jung, long available in German, was not immediately undertaken, since they render psychology a service which no others have done. This could easily sound like an exaggeration: there has been no shortage of books on Jung and his psychology.

These books have ranged from the eminently valuable and distinguished, each throwing a light on some significant aspect of the life and work of one of the greatest liberators of the human spirit, right down to the slanted, the trivial, and the unashamedly false and destructive. Even the best of these have tended to deal with some particular part of Jung's work; none have yet adequately encompassed its totality. Despite the numerous books already published on Jung, the signs are that we are only at the beginning of what promises to be a flood.

As is their nature, human beings might gather after this flood of books like some Tower of Babel, and become so smitten by the confusion of tongues that they would lose the unity and meaning of what Jung achieved against incredible odds of the mind, the spirit, the scientific and religious establishments, and the trends of the day. What seemed lacking and urgently needed to prevent this confusion was something much more comprehensive and far-sighted than what

1

had been written. It seemed to people like myself a danger from which the study of Jungian psychology could be delivered only by an almost inspired textbook. One which, in the full classical sense of the term, would describe, explain, evaluate, interpret and verify incontrovertibly, the immense totality that is Jung, and the psychology associated with his name. Without such a work the student seeking after knowledge of Jung could, one fears, stray like a sailor without a compass on the as yet inadequately charted sea of the collective unconscious.

The trouble always was, of course, that a work of that kind required someone of unusual gifts and stature. For one thing, Jung travelled fast and travelled far beyond the horizons of his and even our own day. He himself always claimed that he was an introverted, intuitive type, using the terms which are such significant signposts in his far-reaching book on the functions of the human mind and spirit. Introverted he was, certainly, but I always thought that he should have put intuition first as his own superior function, followed by thinking. His whole life proved for me that only a person of the most inspired and steadfast intuition could have enabled him to go the unknown and fashionably discredited way he did, against all the powerful vested interests of the mind and spirit of the modern world. Indeed he pressed on with such courage and speed in the manner true intuitives do, that his tendency was to linger with one visionary leap forward into the dark only long enough to establish it empirically, pack up as fast as possible, and then press on with the next intuitive vision. The danger for all intuitives, I imagine, is always that the blessing of having intuitions is almost enough, and leaves them inclined to neglect the dreary work, the exacting detail and long, hard confrontation with the relevant facts necessary for establishing their perception in the heart and dust of the imperative here and now.

It is to Jung's everlasting credit that he had the scientific and moral discipline to pay in full his empiric dues to his intuitions. Nonetheless the various stages of his own swift progression into the unknown remain in need of enlargement. I mention this aspect of the nature of Jung's achievement because it has a bearing on the qualifications which were essential for the sort of comprehensive work needed on Jung and which, happily, Dr. Meier brings to the writing of these volumes. Obviously someone who could write with authority on the totality of Jung the man and his exploration would need some of his pioneering passion and share his abundant and many-sided interests. It would not have been enough, for instance, to have been the devoted student, who, after sitting at Jung's feet and acquiring all the academic background which such an experience demanded, then went on merely to repeat what he had acquired in book form. Dr. Meier, of course, possesses all the elementary qualifications. He knew, studied and trained with Jung and found the whole experience so tailor-made to his own seeking and the demands of his nature that he went on to work closely with Jung. For a generation or more, he was, as it were, in a kind of psychological partnership with Jung. Besides being one of Jung's closest collaborators, he was designated to found the C. G. Jung Institute in Zurich. Once that was firmly established, he went on to take C. G. Jung's old chair of psychology at the E. T. H. in Zurich, so that in general, and then more and more in his own independent and individual way, he made a highly significant contribution to the evolution of analytical psychology. When Jung died, Dr. Meier established his own clinic in Zurich for broadening and deepening scientifically the fundamentals of Jung's work. At this clinic for many years now, for instance, he has been conducting an intensive investigation into the nature of sleep and dreams and carried on into new dimensions the uses of Jung's association method. Engaged in such active continuation and not just the teaching of Jung's findings, his appraisal of the vast field of Jungian psychology is unshackled from the past, dynamic and forward-moving, with the sense of the future that was implicit in all Jung accomplished, with the consciousness more and more acute, as he grew older, of how much more still remained to be done. Undaunted, Dr. Meier has also maintained his own work as a psychiatrist. He continues to promote understanding of ourselves as one of the most urgent tasks of the day, knowing that only an increase of individual awareness could prevent the grim neglected and unrecognized forces, building up in the collective unconscious of an entire world from overwhelming humankind as it nearly overwhelmed and destroyed us in the great totalitarian tyrannies of a generation ago. And the battle, now more insidious and tenacious, is far from over yet. As a result, Dr. Meier brings to his view of analytical psychology much urgency and immediacy, as well as an unusually wide grasp of the history of healing and its religious and philosophic implications, starting from far back in the Greece of Epidauras and Eleusis, and reaching from thereon through this desperate day forward to the new frontiers of the natural sciences.

He can claim indeed to stand on the furthest frontier where the depth psychiatrist and the physicist can recognize each other at last, not as embittered antagonists but as long-lost partners who must take each other by the hand before they can continue, whole, the work that has been only half-done until now. Jung's breakthrough into the collective unconscious of man and its revelation of the metaphoric power latent in the individual there, matches the breakthrough into the nuclear heart of the atom, so that on this far perimeter of human awareness they appear strangely undivided, as if the one were but life and creation from within as the other is seeing it from without. It is not for nothing, therefore, that the concluding volume of this series should be dedicated to Wolfgang Pauli, the great Swiss physicist and Nobel prize winner.

Though initially qualified as a doctor, surgeon, and research biologist, Dr. Meier came to psychology unusually well-protected against the dangers of becoming a prisoner of the orthodox medical and psychiatric specialists of the day. Educated both in Switzerland and France, his imagination always has been unusually open and alive to all the rainbow diversity and abundant potential of the European culture he inherited. History for him lives in the present. He is the only person I know who travels in Greece with a classic Baedeker compiled in Greek before the birth of Christ. He has a profound gift for and love of music, of literature, of art, and overall an abiding sense of the pattern of metamorphosis and the pentecostal nature of his calling, knowing that analytical psychology has meaning and succeeds only in the service of a transcendent religious design in the life of man and the universe. With it all, Dr. Meier has a gift of expressing the most complex concepts and issues simply, instead of making the simple and obvious complex and obscure as so many writers on scientific subjects have the unhappy habbit of doing. Even a lay person like myself finds him always easy to follow and a delight to read. I am convinced that these books of his will not only enrich the natural scientist but act as an unfailing guide to the increasing hordes of lost people in search of a soul, in a world that has forfeited its meaning.

This, then, in English at last, is the first of four books without which no school, university, seminary or public library conscious of their duty, can do without.

Sir Laurens van der Post
London
July, 1984

CHAPTER I

CRITICAL HISTORICAL
INTRODUCTION

Cobbler, stick to your last! [1]

Scarcely more than sixty years have passed since Freud began his great pioneer work. [2] He was the first to draw our attention to those psychic phenomena whose occurrence can only be explained on the hypothesis of the existence of an unconscious psyche. He arrived at his point of view as a result of his experience as a doctor with mentally sick patients, and for this reason the phenomena he observed were mainly of the nature of psychic disturbances, i.e., they related to undesirable and usually most unpleasant effects of the unconscious. When it became clear to what a tremendous extent the psychic life of everyone, including the normal, was affected by mechanisms of this kind, a storm of indignation arose. It is in fact remarkable how soon this storm subsided, and indeed to what a degree the public today has actually assimilated Freud's concepts (although not necessarily his point of view). His concepts have not only found acceptance among the general public; there is no doubt that they now dominate the broad field of academic and applied psychology, especially in the United States. The reason for this dominance is alleged to be the scientific clarity and precision with which Freud's teachings were formulated, the result being, it is claimed, that they can actually be taught and learned.

Yet here psychologists would do well to remind themselves of the well-known saying of Niels Bohr, the physicist, to the effect that

5

there is an inverse relationship between the clarity and the truth of a concept. Yet is it not possible that Freud's concepts are by no means so clearly defined? If, as is said, their applicability is universal, is it not likely that they are often simply applied in the wrong way? I should prefer, in the present context, not to pursue this question; instead, I should simply like to make the point that it is, in principle, perfectly possible to consider the unconscious from a point of view quite distinct from that of the analyst's consulting room. In that case, the unconscious may also be credited with more gratifying effects, and this should make it easier for us, not merely to accept its evidence, but actually to acknowledge it with gratitude.

It is the aim of this volume to demonstrate the part played by the unconscious in the genesis of human utterances and actions of every conceivable kind. In particular, the point of view of the Complex Psychology of C. G. Jung will be shown to be relevant in this context. Actually, it was the introduction of the concept of the unconscious which first enabled psychology to do justice to the true motives and dynamism of human life and action, so that our whole contemporary picture of man can no longer be conceived without the unconscious dimension.

If our theme in what follows is to be the manifestations of this "unconscious," I must make it clear at the outset that our treatment of it will be subject to two qualifications.

In the first place, there is absolutely no human activity in which the unconscious does not play some part. This means that we shall have to be selective and to concentrate on phenomena in which these effects can be clearly demonstrated and which positively demand the hypothesis of the unconscious if they are to be understood at all. So we shall have to restrict our scope and abandon any claim to complete comprehensiveness, if only for this reason.

In the second place, we shall have to refrain from offering a definition of the unconscious, however appropriate this might appear to be at the beginning of our inquiry. Such an omission is in fact desirable both on educational and scientific grounds. Before we decide any theoretical questions about the unconscious, we need to establish and investigate its phenomenology. For this purpose, we shall adopt a skeptical and empirical standpoint, and I should like these terms to be understood in the sense given them by the later Greek sophists.

Let us recall, for example, the philosophical doctor Sextus Empiricus (c. 200 A.D.), who taught in Alexandria and at Athens. The Greek *empeiria* (ἐμπειρία) means experience and is the exact equivalent of the Latin *experientia*. The attitude adopted by Sextus

Empiricus is skeptical and antirationalistic. He divides philosophers into three classes: the Dogmatists, who assert that they know the truth; the Academics, who affirm that the truth is absolutely unknowable; and the skeptics (his own school), who are undecided about the essential nature of things. For the sake of ataraxia, or tranquillity of mind, they prefer to suspend judgment about the real nature of things, since they are seriously persuaded of the inherent uncertainty of our knowledge. They call this suspension, in which they take great pride, ἐποχή (*epochē*), and they justify it on the grounds that, in their view, our logical reasoning is invariably circular. They use the following syllogism, based on Aristotle, to illustrate this argument[3]:

> Men, horses and mules are long-lived.
> Men, horses and mules have no gall-bladder.
> Therefore all animals that have no gall-bladder
> are long-lived.[4]

Of course, this example is not a logical proof at all, but an easily recognizable *petitio principii*. Sextus Empiricus makes this the occasion for a criticism of *all* Aristotelian syllogisms, on the grounds that the major premise, on which the conclusion is based, always implies the truth of the latter. He therefore gives living experience (ἐμπειρία) a decisive preference over logic. Doctors—especially when they have had a philosophical training—would be bound, no doubt, to concede without grudging that in medicine experience is more valuable and important than logic. In any case, it was medical experience that led to the discovery of the phenomenology of the unconscious, and if scientists such as Freud and Jung had had a purely rationalistic outlook, we should probably still be unconscious of the unconscious today. In the case of the two great pioneers of the unconscious, however, the abandonment of pure rationalism demanded an unusually high degree of that moral courage which is an essential qualification of every responsible scientist. Their first discoveries consisted of nothing but the uncomfortable, objectionable and forbidden aspects of the psyche—in a word, all those things that are happily forgotten and repressed, and that have fallen a victim to the good intentions of our educational system. Freud's discoveries in particular were painful in the way Wilhelm Busch had in mind when he wrote:

> When with grass an ancient wound
> Is covered in the plain,
> Sure as fate a camel comes
> And gnaws it bare again.

Jung understood the unconscious in a much wider sense than Freud. The unconscious is not simply the threshold and matrix of the conscious mind; it remains essentially unfathomable, like the soul itself. "You will never discover the frontiers of the psyche, not even if you wander through all the ways in the world; so deep is its meaning."[5] Once, in a discussion, Jung made a bon mot in this connection; he said, "The exciting thing about the unconscious is precisely the fact that it *really is* unconscious!" So he too understood "the unconscious" not in terms of a definition, but negatively, as that which is not conscious. In the first place, then, it is a "limitative conception" in the sense in which Kant[6] employs that term, and "only of negative use."

Clearly, Kant's definition of the borderline concept agrees quite well with Jung's pithy saying quoted above. He calls it, "A conception . . . connected with the limitation of sensibility, without, however, being capable of presenting us with any positive datum beyond this sphere."[7] This "positive datum" is something transcendental, namely the "noumenon" or "thing-in-itself."

Such questions, however, belong to the realm of the philosophers. We doctors, as I have said, must remain content with experience. Yet we too cannot experience the unconscious as such. This would involve a contradiction in terms. We can only experience its *effects*. We shall have to confine ourselves, therefore, to a discussion of certain examples of such effects, which cannot be explained on the basis of the conscious mind alone, but which simply "happen" to us, as it were.

It is characteristic of the general attitude of humankind that these phenomena first became the subject of scientific interest in their *negative* form, i.e., as *disturbances* of the normal functioning of the psyche. Once again, it was the doctors, and in particular the psychiatrists, who first observed them. Psychotic disturbances are essentially bizarre exaggerations or lapses which occur in the daily life of normal people. That common sense shares this point of view was made clear to me by the following incident. I once had to show a Zurich magistrate, who had originally been a master locksmith, around the psychiatric clinic at the University,[8] and in so doing, I made a point of demonstrating to him some of the most serious cases. At the end of the visit, I asked him about his impressions. He replied promptly, "That is a concentrated collection of Zurich oddities!"[9]

CHAPTER II

CREATIVE EFFECTS OF THE UNCONSCIOUS

I begin my account of the empirical basis of a psychology of the unconscious by citing some more agreeable examples, which show quite clearly that this unconscious of ours can also produce positive achievements—i.e., that it can also function in an entirely normal manner. I have selected the phenomenon of "bright ideas" to illustrate this point.

"Bright Ideas"

When we are dealing with pictorial expressions, it is always interesting from a psychological point of view to investigate the meaning of the word concerned. The German word *Einfall*, or bright idea, means literally *infall* and presumably refers to something which falls into us from above, in the form of a finished product or even of a foreign body. It is a kind of procreation or conception (e.g., the "conception" of ideas), and it therefore stands in a certain relationship of antithesis-cum-identity with the mythological motif of "birth from the head" (e.g., Zeus and Pallas Athene). The fact that it "falls" upon us from above contains a reference to its suspected origin in an unconscious regarded as existing at a higher level. This should warn us against the use of such a derogatory expression as "the *sub*conscious."

I interpret the expression "bright idea" very widely, that is to say as a very frequent phenomenon—and it is an interesting fact that in contrast to the disturbances which we noted above, it is precisely the absence of bright ideas which strikes us as unpleasant. As a function, bright ideas are operative, for example, when a speech "flows" instead of going stickily; here again, the metaphor gives us to understand that we have to assume the existence of a spring that bubbles up of its own accord—and this, of course, is the unconscious.

Thus our ordinary use of language shows us that a *vis a tergo* of this kind is naively assumed as something given. When things are going well, its functioning is quite undramatic and we do not notice it at all. If, however, we happen to have "a good idea," we do not want to hear any more about the autonomous working of this function; in that case, we call it a "thought," and we flatter ourselves that we ourselves have produced it. And yet, from the point of view of psychological hygiene such an attitude has little to recommend it. It may amount to hubris, and in that case it conceals within itself the danger of a psychological inflation, in the sense in which Jung employs that term.[1]

As a perfect example of the opposite of this condition, I should like to cite the case of the orator Aelius Aristides of Smyrna, who lived from 129 to 189 A.D. He belonged to the so-called "Second Sophistic" school of Greek philosophers and was a pious adherent of a pantheistic form of syncretism. True to this creed, he thanked the gods for all the creative ideas in his speeches and paeans, with which he had achieved triumphant successes throughout the ancient world; by so doing, he protected himself against the danger of succumbing to megalomania.[2] An attitude of this kind had in fact been traditional since the earliest days of Greek poetry. The poet would invoke the muse for inspiration; and he would also thank her. I need only recall the poet's invocation of the Muse in the opening lines of the Odyssey: "Tell me, O Muse, the tale of the man of many wanderings. . . ."[3]

The polar opposite to this attitude is to be found in the rationalism of a much later period—for example, in the French rationalism which coined the phrase "J'ai *fait* un rêve" ("I have made a dream"), where the ego actually claims to be the author of the dream, although there is not the slightest doubt that in fact the dream provides us with a classic example of a spontaneous product of the unconscious. The same attitude is expressed by the proverb "Tout songe tout mensonge" ("All dreams are lies"), although in this case dubious mendacious tendencies are ascribed to the same ego.

The Role of Bright Ideas in Artistic Creation

Some bright ideas can only be described as creative. They are unusually vivid and compelling; in fact, they may make us practically drunken or possessed. In what follows, I should like to describe a number of such cases, which are derived from the lives of exceptionally creative people.[4] These can perfectly well be allowed to speak for themselves, and all I shall attempt in the commentaries that accompany them is to discuss certain details typical of the relationship of the subject with his unconscious and of his productive intercourse with it.

1. Mozart (in a letter which was lost until 1931):[5]

> This kindles heat in my soul—that is, if I am not disturbed—; and it gets bigger and bigger, and I spread it out and make it wider and brighter; and the whole thing is almost finished in my head, even if it is a long piece, so that afterwards I can see it in my mind *at a single glance, as if it were a beautiful picture or an attractive person*, and similarly, when I rehearse it over in my imagination, I do this *not at all in sequence*, as it will have to be produced later, but I hear it *all together, at the same moment*. That is a feast, if you like! The whole process of finding and making the music only takes place in me as it were in a *lovely, vivid dream*; but the best part about it is hearing everything all together like that! (K) [Author's italics]

As we see, a musical work of art constitutes a whole, which may therefore quite appropriately be anthropomorphized ("an attractive person"); at the same time, the musical "sequence" is fused into an "all-together"—i.e., the time factor is practically nullified. This feature is really a characteristic of unconscious processes in general, and it gives rise to a problem with which we shall have to concern ourselves more than once later on. The expression "lovely, vivid dream" might actually be recommended as an extremely apt technical term for conditions of this kind; not only does it testify to their unconscious nature, but it also helps us to realize that the content which is "rehearsed over" actually appears in the form of a *finished product*, with which Mozart is confronted as a subject meets an object. This explains the feeling which we have in such cases that "something is thinking inside us," or that "we are being thought" and *not* that we ourselves are making these products.

2. Goethe:

(a) *Tame Epigrams*, III (circa 1820):

All our most honest and sincere endeavours
Only succeed in the unconscious moment.
How dearly would the rose adore to blossom
Could she but *see* the sun in all his splendour!

(K)[6]

(b) *Tame Epigrams*, VIII (circa 1823)

The philosopher whose views I like to share[7]
Teaches—unlike most, if not all, the rest—
That we *unconsciously* produce our best.
I think so too—and live without a care.

(K)[8]

(c) Eckerman, "Conversations with Goethe," 11th March 1828:

"No productiveness of the highest kind," said Goethe, "no remarkable discovery, no great thought that bears fruit and has results, is in the power of anyone; such things are above earthly control. Man must consider them as an unexpected gift from above, as pure children of God which he must receive and venerate with joyful thanks. They are akin to the daemon, which does with him what it pleases, and to which he unconsciously resigns himself whilst he believes he is acting from his own impulse. In such cases, man may often be considered an instrument in a higher government of the world—a vessel worthy to contain a divine influence. I say this when I consider how often a single thought has given a different form to whole centuries, and how individual men have imprinted a stamp upon their age which has remained uneffaced and operated beneficially for generations." (K)[9]

Some observations which throw a great deal of light on our subject are to be found in the correspondence between Goethe and Schiller. I have selected only the following representative example:
3. Schiller to Goethe (27th March 1801):

Only a few days ago I attacked Schelling about an assertion he makes in his Transcendental Philosophy, that, "in Nature one starts from the Unconscious in order to raise it to the Conscious; whereas, in Art, one proceeds from the Conscious to the Unconscious." Here, it is true, he speaks only of the contrast between the product of Nature and that of Art; in so far he is quite right. I fear, however, that idealists, such as he is, take too little notice of experience, and in experience the poet too only starts with the Unconscious; nay, he may consider himself fortunate if, by being most clearly conscious of his operations, he gets to that point where he meets again in the work he has completed, with the *first, obscure total-idea* of his work, and finds it unweakened. There can be no poetic work without an *obscure, but mighty total-idea* of this kind, which precedes all technical work; and poetry seems to me, in fact, to consist in being able to express and communicate that Unconscious state—in other words, to transfer it to some object. (K)[10]

In his reply to Schiller (4th April 1801), Goethe writes:

With regard to the questions contained in your last letter, I not only agree with your opinion, but go even further. I think that everything that is done by genius as genius, is done unconsciously. A person of genius can also act rationally, with reflection, from conviction, but this is all done as it were indirectly. No work of genius can be improved, or be freed from its faults by reflection and its immediate results, but genius can by means of reflection and action be gradually raised, in so far as in the end to produce exemplary works. *The more genius a century possesses* the more are individual things furthered. (K)[11] [Author's italics]

Clearly Schiller's "obscure but mighty total idea" represents an experience which is extremely reminiscent of the statement by Mozart that we quoted above. But it also directs our attention to what is probably the crucial problem in all creative achievement—the question, that is, as to *how* what has been envisaged and conceived within the human mind can be delivered into the outside world without damage at birth, or as Schiller puts it, how the idea can be "transferred to an object." The extent to which Goethe's "genius of the century" can be compared with Jung's collective unconscious is a matter which must be left to a later stage in our inquiry. The religious ardor with which the Romantics gave themselves up to the unconscious is of course proverbial. However, in view of the fact that a great deal of material has already been collected on this topic,[12] I shall confine my attention to two examples which seem to me to be particularly noteworthy.

4. Jean Paul (1763–1825), in "Vorschule der Ästhetik" (Introduction to Aesthetics) Abt. I, § 13:

Man's Instinct[13]
The most powerful force in the poet's mind, which is responsible for the inspiration of his works by the spirits of both good and evil, is

precisely the unconscious . . . If we were entirely conscious of ourselves, we should be *our own creators* and therefore *unbounded* . . . If we have the *audacity* to speak about what is unconscious and unfathomable, we can only presume to determine its *existence*, not its depth. [Author's italics]

We shall select three points for emphasis from the text of this quotation:

(a) The danger of hubris, which arises as soon as we refuse to recognize the boundary between the ego (i.e., the conscious mind) and the unconscious, is clearly recognized by the author when he speaks of a state of identification with the Creator (on inflation, cf. p. 10 of the present volume).

(b) This danger expresses itself in a fear of the unconscious, so that even to speak of it is described by the author as audacity. From time immemorial an attitude of caution has been adopted toward the unconscious—a kind of superstitious awe, as it were—and this attitude has by no means been confined to primitive peoples. Unknown quantities should always be treated with respect, and we should be well advised to have recourse to euphemism (εὐφημισμός) in our dealings with them.

The Greeks always spoke of the "Eumenides" ('Εὐμενίδες), "the Kindly Ones," when they meant the Erinyes ('Εριννύες), the wrathful huntresses who track down every evil deed, the Furiae (furies) of the Romans. They also thought it more prudent to speak of the dreaded, inhospitable Black Sea (πόντος ἄξεινος) as the πόντος Εὔξεινος or Friendly Sea.

Today, the reverential awe of the ancients has given place to a secularized form of euphemism, which we use when we say, for example, as if to reassure ourselves, "It was *only* a complex," or "*only* a dream." It is open to question whether this attitude is any better than that other reaction—equally widespread—which is encountered among scholars in arts subjects whenever psychology presumes to indicate certain connections between phenomena of special interest to these experts and qualities of the unconscious psyche. In such circumstances, the charge of psychologism is very quickly raised, though it has to be admitted that it is often provoked by the free-and-easy way in which the psychologists often employ their own jargon. This only too easily gives rise to the suspicion that the psychologists are know-alls or even materialists—which in turn only aggravates the resistances that are to be found among the experts in any case. Yet it is obvious that in the realm of fairy tales or myths, for example, a language is being spoken which only relates to the conscious mind in the second instance, and which does not address it directly at all. At all events, respect for the unconscious is associated with a positive attitude: resistances, on the other hand, put us rather in mind of tilting at windmills.

(c) Jean Paul contents himself with establishing the existence of the unconscious. His attitude is empirical, and his warning against any attempt to determine the *depth* of the unconscious, distinctly recalls the fragment of Heraclitus which we quoted above (where "deep" corresponds to the Greek βαθύς). And yet, scarcely a century later, Freud was driven by the modern spirit of research to attempt to plumb those selfsame depths; and since Olympus proved unfavorable to such an undertaking, he was obliged to invoke the assistance of Acheron (one of the rivers of Hades), as we can see from the epigraph to his "Interpretation of Dreams" (Flectere si nequeo superos, Acheronta movebo = "If I cannot sway the Gods, I will move Acheron").[14] He is unlikely to have been fully aware of the fact that by quoting this verse he was putting himself into the position of the jealous goddess Juno!

As a second example from the history of the Romantic movement I should like to use the following passage.

5. E.T.A. Hoffmann (1776–1822), in his "Rat Krespel":

> I did not doubt for one single moment that Krespel had gone mad. But the Professor denied this. "There are people," he said, "from whom nature or some strange fatality has removed the covering under which we ordinary mortals carry on our private lunacies without fear of discovery. They resemble those thin-skinned insects which appear misshapen when we watch the vivid play of their muscles in full view, although everything soon reassembles again and assumes its proper form. What in ourselves remains a thought, is all translated by Krespel into action. The bitter scorn which he feels at the way in which the spirit encapsulated in our earthly doings seems to dominate his life is acted out by Krespel in crazy gestures and skilful caperings like a rabbit. But this is actually his lightning conductor. What arises out of the earth he returns to the earth; yet he knows how to cherish the divine spark. And so, as I see it, his inner consciousness is really in excellent shape, in spite of the apparent craziness which is so obvious to the outside observer."

Here, as before (see p. 8), the psychopathological is seen as the normal, from which, however, the "covering" has been "removed," so that the underlying unconscious processes become visible. Seen from outside, they appear to be crazy; yet it is admitted that they contain much that is divine. This reminds me of a case which takes me back to the days when I worked at the Psychiatric Clinic (it was in 1932). I should like quite briefly to tell you about it.[15]

The patient was a youngish man who had for years been confined to the clinic on account of a severe catatonic condition. When I took over the department for violent patients in which he was confined, I was specifically warned by my predecessor to beware of this patient, who was widely feared in the hospital because of his supposed aggressiveness. I found him standing in a practically cataleptic state in a corner of the dayroom.

Next morning, I took a closer look at this patient. I noticed that, in contrast to his general attitude, there was a gleam of something unusually lively, warm and human in the expression of his eyes. I went up to him and held out my hand to greet him. To my astonishment, he returned my greeting and pressed my hand very cordially, though without speaking. On the following day, I took him along to my room—a gesture which caused quite a commotion among the nursing staff. When he was with me, the patient immediately started talking, and in the course of the ensuing sessions he explained to me his entire delusory system, which I do not propose to discuss further in this context.

Within the next two weeks the patient returned to psychic normality, and after another two weeks it was possible to discharge him from the clinic. Nine years later, I happened to meet him in the street in Zurich, and he introduced me to his fiancée. He said that since his discharge from the hospital he had worked successfully and continuously and that there was scarcely any risk that he would suffer a relapse. His parting words to me were, "You know, doctor, if I hadn't experienced it myself, I should never have believed what a blessing such an illness can bring!" The expression on his face as he said that was unmistakable and left no possible doubt that the years he had spent in the Burghölzli had been transformed into a deep and genuine religious experience which had healed this man, i.e., had made him whole.

6. Charles Lamb (1775-1834), who is best known for his "Tales from Shakespeare," once said—according to Max Schulz[16]—that "the true poet dreams being awake."

7. Robert Louis Stevenson (1850-1894), the Scottish writer, who is probably best known to us as the author of *Treasure Island* and *The Strange Case of Dr. Jekyll and Mr. Hyde*,[17] is one of the few men of letters who have provided us with ample opportunities for gaining an insight into their creative processes. "A Chapter on Dreams" in his book *Across the Plains* (1892) must be regarded as a locus classicus for those creative effects of the unconscious with

which we are concerned in this chapter. In it, he describes how for a long time he suffered from an inability to write, till at last he discovered that his dreams often contained interesting motifs. He then succeeded, in a meaningful way such as is only possible to an artistically gifted personality, in opening up a relationship with his own unconscious material which led to a genuine cooperation, so that finally he was able to dream and record completely connected stories and thus to achieve an extremely fruitful output as a writer.

Very much in the spirit of Aelius Aristides (cf. p. 10), he now gave the entire credit for his creative work to his dream figures; in the course of time these had become stereotyped, and Stevenson, following the usage of Scottish folklore, called them his "Brownies" or "the Little People." How far he was prepared to take this metaphor can be seen from the following passage:

> And for the Little People what shall I say—they are but just my Brownies, God bless them! who do one-half of my work for me while I am fast asleep, and in all human likelihood, do the rest for me as well, when I am wide awake and fondly suppose I do it for myself. That part which is done while I am sleeping is the Brownies' part beyond contention; but that which is done when I am up and about is by no means necessarily mine, since all goes to show the Brownies have a hand in it even then. Here is a doubt that much concerns my conscience. For myself—what I call I, my conscious ego, the denizen of the pineal gland unless he has changed his residence since Descartes, the man with the conscience and the variable bank-account, the man with the hat and the boots, and the privilege of voting and not carrying his candidate at the general election—I am sometimes tempted to suppose he is no story-teller at all, but a creature as matter-of-fact as any cheesemonger or any cheese, and a realist bemired up to the ears in actuality; so that, by that account, the whole of my published fiction should be the single-handed product of some Brownie, some Familiar, some unseen collaborator, whom I keep locked in a back garret, while I get all the praise and he but a share (which I cannot prevent him getting) of the pudding. I am an excellent adviser, something like Molière's servant; I pull back and I cut down; and I dress the whole in the best words and sentences that I can find and make; I hold the pen, too; and I do the sitting at the table, which is about the worst of it; and when all is done, I make up the manuscript and pay for the registration; so that, on the whole, I have some claim to share, though not so largely as I do, in the profits of our common enterprise.[18]

As my final example from the literary field, I should like to quote two passages from Nietzsche.

8. Friedrich Nietzsche (1844–1900):

(a) *Ecce Homo*, 1888 (the reference in this passage is to the composition of *Thus Spake Zarathustra*, III):

Has any one at the end of the nineteenth century any distinct notion of what poets of a stronger age understood by the word "inspiration"? If not, I will describe it. If one had the smallest vestige of superstition left in one, it would hardly be possible to set aside the idea that one is a mere incarnation, mouthpiece or medium of an almighty power. The idea of revelation, in the sense that something which profoundly convulses and shatters one becomes suddenly visible and audible with indescribable certainty and accuracy, describes the simple fact. One hears—one does not seek; one takes—one does not ask who gives; a thought suddenly flashes up like lightning, it comes with necessity, without faltering,—I never had any choice in the matter.[19]

(b) *Antichrist*, 14 (1888):

We deny that anything can be made perfect so long as it is still made conscious.[20]

The first example makes it clear that instead of "bright ideas" we could equally well speak of inspiration or illumination ("lightning"). In the extreme terms in which (b) is formulated, on the other hand, we find that "transvaluation of all values" which is so characteristic of Nietzsche. Unfortunately, he was himself too little aware of the perilous nature of this extreme position, as was proved by the sequel, shortly afterwards.

The Role of "Bright Ideas" in Scientific Discoveries

In the realm of science, we are fortunate enough to possess at least *one* first class testimony to the importance of a "bright idea" in the genesis of a great discovery.

1. August Kekulé von Stradonitz (1829–1896):

Kekulé's great achievement is frequently cited as an illustration of the part played by the unconscious in creative work. Unfortunately, however, almost all the writers who have dealt with this subject have either not read Kekulé's own autobiographical account, or if they have read it, their own unconscious has played tricks on them in the form of mnesic delusions or of a petitio principii. The one honorable exception which is known to me is H.E. Fierz-David,[21] in his communication in *Gesnerus*[22] and in his book on *Die Entwicklungsgeschichte der Chemie.*[23]

Whenever, in the following account, we allow Kekulé to speak for himself, his remarks are taken from the speech which he made in the Town Hall of Berlin on 11th March 1890, on the occasion of the celebration organized by the German Chemical Society in honor of the twenty-fifth anniversary of his discovery of the formula for benzene in 1865. The attitude of this scientist toward his own brilliant achievement is so exemplary that I cannot refrain from including in my quotation those passages which prove that genuine achievement makes its originator modest—provided, of course, that he does not identify himself with it.

In this context it should be borne in mind that Kekulé's discovery of the ring formula for benzene was the first occasion on which the concept of a ring formation had been applied to any chemical compound, so that the importance of this discovery for aromatic chemistry and for the tremendous development of organic chemistry as a whole since that time can scarcely be overestimated.[24]

At the present moment, I am simply incapable of thanking the speakers as is their due, or indeed of making any reply to all the kind things which have been said about me. One point is absolutely clear in my mind: my own modest merits have been praised far beyond their due. In all the speeches and addresses which have been made I hear the same tone of exaggeration . . . You have organized a really incredible and magnificent celebration without any adequate cause and you have associated this celebration with my name. And so, very much against my own inclination, I am constrained to speak about myself and to consider the question as to whether my own modest merits have deserved such homage, and indeed whether they have deserved any homage at all . . .

My dear colleagues, we all stand on the shoulders of our predecessors: is it strange, then, that we can see further than they could? If we travel along the routes opened up by them or at least tread the paths which they trod before us and so, quite effortlessly, reach positions which they only attained after overcoming innumerable difficulties and which to them represented the utmost limits of their advance—in these circumstances is it any credit to us if we still have the strength to press on further into the realm of the unknown than they did?

Certain ideas are in the air at certain periods; if they are not given expression by one thinker, another will do so shortly afterwards. It has been said that the benzene theory appeared suddenly, like a bolt from the blue—that it was absolutely new and unprecedented. Gentlemen! the human mind does not work like that! No absolutely new idea has ever been conceived by man—least of all in the realm of chemistry . . .

It is not true, as has often been maintained, that our present ways of thinking are built on the ruins of past theories. None of these earlier theories has in fact been rejected by later generations as totally erroneous; stripped of certain unsightly curlicues, it has always been found possible to incorporate them into the later structure, and they have blended with it to form a harmonious whole.

It has been said that the benzene theory sprang, fully-armed, like Pallas Athene from the head of a chemical Zeus. Perhaps it did look like that from outside. But I can assure you that the reality was very different. I am in a position to give you inside information on this subject . . .

It may perhaps be of some interest to you if I make some very indiscreet disclosures about the actual workings of my mind, and show you how I arrived at certain ideas.

During my period of residence in London (in 1854), I lived for some time in Clapham Road, in the neighbourhood of Clapham Common. But I often spent my evenings with my friend Hugo Müller in Islington, at the opposite end of the great city. We used to talk about various things, but mostly about our beloved chemistry. 'One fine summer evening, I was returning by the last omnibus, "outside" as usual, through the deserted streets of the metropolis, which are at other times so full of life. I fell into a reverie and lo! the atoms were gambolling before my eyes. Whenever, hitherto, these diminutive beings had appeared to me, they had always been in motion; but up to that time I had never been able to discern the nature of their motion. Now, I saw how, frequently, two smaller atoms united to form a pair; how a larger one embraced two smaller ones; how still larger ones kept hold of three or even *four* of the smaller; I saw how the larger ones formed a chain'[25] and dragged smaller ones along at the ends of it.

[The point at issue here was the quadrivalence of carbon and its implications for chain formation.]

I saw what Kopp, the Grand Old Man of chemistry and my own revered teacher and friend, describes so enchantingly in his "Molecular World"; but I saw it long before he did. The voice of the conductor calling out "Clapham Road" awakened me from my reveries, but 'I spent part of the night putting on paper at least sketches of those dream forms.' That was how the *structural theory* came into being.

[And here, as we can see, the question at issue is the ring structure of benzene in the narrower sense:]

The benzene theory had a similar origin. During my stay in Ghent (1865) I lived in fashionable bachelor quarters in the High Street. But my study was in a narrow side street and during the daytime it had no light. For a chemist, who spends his daylight hours in the laboratory, this was not really a disadvantage. I simply sat there and wrote away at my textbook. And yet somehow I couldn't get it going properly. My mind was on other things. 'I turned my chair to the fire and *dozed*. Again the atoms were gambolling before my eyes. This time the smaller groups kept modestly in the background. My mental eye, rendered more acute by repeated visions of this kind, could now distinguish larger structures, of manifold conformation; long rows, all twining and twisting in snakelike motion. *But look! What was that? One of the snakes had seized hold of its own tail, and the form whirled mockingly before my eyes. As if by a flash of lightning I awoke.*' This time, too, I spent the rest of the night working out the implications of the hypothesis.

Let us learn to dream, gentlemen; then, perhaps, we shall discover the truth:

"And if to think you cannot shift
She'll come to you as a gift
No need for care or sorrow" (Goethe)

—but let us take care not to publish our dreams before they have been examined by our waking intellect. "Countless germs of mental life fill the spaces of the universe, but it is only in a few rare chosen spirits that they find the soil they need for their development; in such spirits the idea which comes from nobody knows where is brought to life in the creative act."[26] [Author's italics]

We have here a most carefully formulated description by a scientifically trained intellect which has clearly acquired a certain skill in the observation of semiconscious or unconscious processes (cf. the case of Robert Louis Stevenson, pp. 16–17 above), and it is therefore only fair to him that we should take his account seriously. The phenomena which he is describing relate to dozing or reverie, and not to sleep and dreaming (as is often carelessly stated).

Today we should probably be reminded in the first place of a trick film or, in the technical language of psychology, of *hypnagogic visions.*[27] Although the phenomena take the form of "images" of atoms, they behave quite anthropomorphically, like independent living creatures engaged in a peculiar kind of "round dance" which is reminiscent of folklore or even mythology. At all events, if account is taken of the conclusions which Kekulé was able to draw from them, their activities must be regarded as highly meaningful.

But when, finally, the snake seized hold of its own tail, a new psychological element appeared; this was a tremendous *emotion,*[28] which startled Kekulé into full waking consciousness. The "mocking whirling of the form" was also a part of this emotionality, and so, too, was the exclamation "But look! What was that?" The simile of the "flash of lightning" also points to a moment of illumination (cf. the case of Nietzsche, pp. 17–18 above), and if we wished to describe the way in which the idea of the ring-structure was actually conceived, this is the figure of speech we should inevitably use.

It need hardly be said that much remained to be done before the theory was finally formulated, and that a great deal of work still had to be put in at the conscious level; the same was true of the period leading up to the occurrence of the "historic moment." Yet the decisive image was "given" to Kekulé, as he himself admits in that quotation from Goethe. So the chemist H. E. Fierz is justified in claiming that "The symbol of the benzene ring could not have been discovered by rational scientific thought."[29] At all events, this statement holds good if we qualify it by adding "at the level of the scientific knowledge and experimental technique which prevailed at the time"; there were, of course, no Laue and Debye-Scherrer Diagrams at that period.

Yet if we are to do justice to the text of Kekulé's autobiographical description, we must still make some attempt to explain the origin of the image of the *snake biting itself in its own tail*. We learn from the biography of Kekulé that as a student he was involved in a murder trial in which the crucial piece of evidence was a finger-ring that "consisted of two intertwining circlets, one of gold and the other of white metal, in the form of two snakes biting themselves in the tail."[30] Yet, as we have seen, this fact is not mentioned by Kekulé in the passage quoted here.

If we look up the other contexts in which this peculiar image occurs, we discover that it plays a significant part in an almost forgotten sphere of culture, which is in fact historically related to chemistry, and that is in the old natural philosophy of the alchemists. The Greek alchemists called this snake ouroboros (ὀυροβόρος),[31] the tail-eater, and very often made it their central symbol. One of the oldest pictorial representations of it is to be found in the *Codex Marcianus* 299, f. 188 V. (Library of Saint Mark, Venice). Here the circular area enclosed by the snakes bears the inscription ἕν τὸ πᾶν (the One, the All), which is based on the ancient interpretation of the ouroboros as a symbol that unites the opposites.[32]

The ouroboros can be regarded as hermaphroditic: the tail end is then masculine, while the mouth which receives it is a feminine symbol. This makes it a conjunctio oppositorum, while at the same time the motif of self-devouring is a symbol of death culminating in rebirth, a much older idea which probably dates back to the Egyptian conception of the identity of the Father God with Pharaoh, the representative of God and the Son. So too it is frequently interpreted as a symbol of the circulation of the alchemical opus, which is repeatedly described as an *opus circulare* (circular work) or *rota* (wheel). As serpens Mercurii or serpent of Mercurius (quicksilver), the ouroboros also unites the opposites solid metal—liquid metal, cold—fiery, poison—remedy and matter—spirit. In this connotation it became extremely popular and appeared in countless variations.

It is undoubtedly an archetypal image in the sense in which Jung used that term. In his last great works Jung assembled the material relating to this image.[33] In certain people whom we call "creative," the tension between what we know and what we do not know is resolved in such a way, that, in Goethe's words, (cf. example (a), pp. 11–12), "in the unconscious moment" a synthetic uniting achievement is attained. Often, as here in the case of Kekulé, an archetypal symbol appears at the same time—and this, in turn, is accompanied by the emergence of an additional quantum of emotion, as we can see very clearly from Kekulé's account. At this stage, there is no point in speculating about causal relationships; we must content ourselves with noting the presence of this triad of components— tension, symbol or archetypal image, and emotion—out of which, if all goes well, the solution of the problem will emerge as the fourth element. In the history of science there are also instances in which the emotion seems to have appeared as a result of the solution, as for example in the well-known case of Champollion.

2. Jean François Champollion (1790–1832), the decipherer of the Egyptian scripts and the father of modern Egyptology:

The decisive insight which enabled Champollion to fight his way through to the discovery that the hieroglyphic, hieratic and demotic scripts were all essentially phonetic, came to him on September 14, 1822, at the end of a severe crisis, during which he had to fight a battle inside himself against the claims of other hypotheses. His biographer, H. Hartleben,[34] describes the scene as follows:

And so September 14th dawned, the day that was to witness the outbreak of nothing short of a revolution in that old house, which even then looked gloomy and inhospitable, but which nevertheless offered to the nascent science of Egyptology a modest shelter. Together with Figeac [his brother] and his son, Ali, Champollion occupied the second storey of the house, but had established his "arsenal" one floor above, in an airy and bright room, surrounded by a gallery, where before him Horace Verney had had his studio for a while . . . It was approaching midday when Champollion finally worked his way through to the ultimate incontrovertible certainty;

then, gathering together the whole mass of the evidence which he had collected, he left his desk and hurried away, just as he was, to tell the news to his brother. His brother was working, as usual, at the Institut,[35] and he was not a little astonished when François rushed up to him, flung a pile of papers onto the table and cried, "I've got it!" He was completely beside himself with joy, but scarcely had he begun to stammer out the reason for his extraordinary statement than he suddenly collapsed and fell like a dead man to the ground.

For a moment Figeac was petrified with horror. But he quickly realized that it was not death but a fainting-fit which almost counterfeited the rigidity of death that had stricken his overwrought brother. They carried him into the flat nearby and left him undisturbed in the complete peace which he needed so desperately in both mind and body.

And he remained in this lethargic condition for five whole days. Yet Champollion had scarcely opened his eyes, on the evening of 19th September, when he was back again like a flash of lightning in the midst of his intellectual preoccupations. But his tired body still needed rest.

On 27th September, 1822, at a meeting of the Académie Royale des Inscriptions et Belles-Lettres, Champollion delivered his first report on his discovery of the key which was to open the door at a single stroke to more than thirty centuries of texts and inscriptions from what has been described as one of the richest cultures in the world. H. Hartleben has this to say about it:

Champollion's report made no mention of the *illumination which had come to him so suddenly* on 14th September, and which at a single stroke had demonstrated the phonetic basis of the script used in Egypt in the middle of the second millenium B.C. His audience— and, subsequently, his readers—had the impression that the realization had come to him quite gradually.

There was great excitement among those present, since, in addition to the theoretical and practical use of the hieroglyphic alphabet, a basis was now suggested for the dating of a large number of the great monuments of Ancient Egypt; a point of special interest was the information relating to the royal titles of the son of Julius Caesar and Cleopatra (Ptolemy-Caesarion) on the temple at Dendera, since they provided a new element of historical certainty. Above all, the age of the Zodiac had now been determined; in fact, Champollion was driven to suppose, on the basis of the material in his possession, that the Zodiac itself had now spoken. It was also possible to identify other monuments of this type as Egyptian work carried out under Roman emperors; the actual names of these emperors were given.[36]

This passage shows once again that an unusually powerful emotion must have been involved, which, however, revealed itself *post eventum*—as in the case of the "Rider over Lake Constance."[37] This displacement of phases is probably connected with the fact that the full realization of an achievement of this kind inevitably takes quite a considerable time; so, too, it is well known that the emotional reaction, or psychic pain, which is caused by severe strokes of misfortune is often only experienced later, and that students who have taken an examination may afterwards fall into a so-called "examination hole" or period of emotional desolation.

We cannot here examine the extremely interesting problem of how image, symbol, archetype and emotion are interrelated; we shall only recall Jung's suggestion that image and emotion may be interpreted in terms of form and dynamism—in such a way that they would represent different aspects of one and the same transcendent psychic phenomenon[38]; in that case the question of causality would become irrelevant. It should be remembered that the process which we have described in relation to Kekulé has a very common counterpart in the most banal situations of everyday life. When our train of thought refuses to flow properly, i.e. when our ideas insist on remaining vague and indistinct, we quite automatically take refuge in figurative expressions and say something like "It's *as if* . . . ."; and this is followed, not by a concept but by an *image*. It is far simpler to find and to formulate the right concept on the basis of some such pictorial expression.

Phenomena of this kind can probably be explained as exemplifications of the well-known axiom that figures of speech have their roots in archetypes, and that consequently, like every true symbol, they perform a synthetic function, which makes it possible for us to continue to spin the thread of our thought to a successful conclusion. This means that a positive solution to the conflict between the conscious mind and the unconscious which had previously been disturbing us has now been achieved.

My attention was drawn by my late friend Wolfgang Pauli to another case in which the unconscious played a significant part in a major discovery. The case in point is the periodic system of the elements, which was elaborated by Mendeleev.

3. Dmitri Ivanovich Mendeleev (1834–1907):

Our account is based on P. Walden's essay in *Das Buch der grossen Chemiker*.[39]

> When he was 35 years old (in 1868–69), Mendeleev constructed his "periodic system of the chemical elements," and in so doing pro-

vided the clearest possible evidence of his vision and capacity as a true man of science. This system has won a permanent place in the history of the human mind as an example of bold perspicacity in action. From the point of view of the biology of scientific discoveries or just in simple human terms, it may be interesting to reconstruct the *genesis* of this system, all the more so since we can do this in Mendeleev's own words. The external causes were relatively unimportant.

Mendeleev himself wrote as follows: "When (in 1868) I undertook to write a manual entitled 'Elements of Chemistry,' I had to decide on some regular system for the classification of simple bodies [he distinguishes between elements and simple bodies], so that when I was arranging them I should not fall back on random or instinctive suggestions, as it were, but should make use of some specific, precisely defined principle."

Now we know that, throughout all changes in the properties of simple bodies, their atomic weight remains the still pole or constant factor. So Mendeleev continues, "I therefore decided to try to base my system on the size of the atomic weights . . ." (1869). He goes on to say, "We have to find a functional relationship between the *individual* properties of the elements and their atomic weights.

"But to find anything—whether it be mushrooms or a relationship of some kind—we can only proceed by observation and experiment. So, after I had written down the elements with their atomic weights and basic properties on small separate cards, I began to collect elements which resembled one another and atomic weights which were closely related to one another in magnitude—and this quickly led me to the conclusion that the properties of the elements stood in a periodic relationship to their atomic weights . . ."

The process of selecting the most appropriate arrangement involved trying out a large number of alternatives; afterwards, Mendeleev described how one evening he experimented once again with different methods of grouping his element cards, and then later, when he was asleep and unconsciously still working on his problem, he had suddenly caught sight of the right system, which he wrote down as soon as he woke up. The exhaustive testing of this system from every possible point of view in chemistry and in physics was a task which absorbed him till the day of his death. . . .[40]

We are dealing here with a dream in the strict sense of that term; at the same time, however, we are also told that the preoccupation of the conscious mind with the problem of the periodic system was carried over into sleep, so that this is obviously a very clear case of cooperation between the conscious mind and the unconscious which directly produced a creative result.

It is possible that the examples which we have quoted above may give rise to misunderstandings of three different kinds:

- It may be supposed that it is our intention to represent *every* creative "bright idea" as due to the cooperation of the unconscious.
- It may be held that the view which we have taken only holds good in exceptional cases.
- It may be imagined that we are claiming that the meager hints which we have given "explain" the mystery of creative achievement.

In order to dispel these possible misconceptions I should like to make the following points.

Dogmatism and generalization are nowhere more out-of-place than in psychology. Unfortunately, however, both are eagerly practiced in this field. All that we are concerned to suggest in this context is that room should be left in our thoughts for the unconscious and that we should be aware of the part it plays in our lives. On the whole, artists and scientists do still realize that—although work, knowledge and ability are obviously indispensable—we still need now and then to sleep over our problems. Unfortunately for us psychologists, this means that in most cases we are not able to supply conclusive evidence of the cooperation of the unconscious; this of course does not disturb creative people. It is, however, precisely the authors of quite exceptional achievements who are most in need of that prudent counsel which suggests that in the interests of psychological hygiene we should express our gratitude to the kairos.[41] Exactly where *the unconscious* comes in, especially when we are dealing with *team work*, is likely to be a difficult question to answer. My own remarks do not claim to be more than a point of view which merits consideration.

The choice of exceptional cases was dictated entirely by their heuristic value, though a further argument in its favor is the fact that the mental discipline practiced by great thinkers and scientists makes them more critical and honest than others in their self-appraisal, and this gives their evidence greater authority.

Outstanding achievements such as those we have mentioned provide us with unusually vivid exemplifications of the great riddle of the human spirit. To understand more about this is a pleasure of a very special kind, and all creative people, whether they are aware of it or not, indulge in this pleasure in their own fashion. In the spirit of our introductory chapter, and in the absence of more positive knowledge, we call this great enigmatic factor simply the unconscious; by so doing we neither impair nor diminish its stature in any way. It would not disturb us if anyone were to prefer a more frankly religious terminology, even though we ourselves, as psychologists, feel it is our duty to stick to our last.

We now come to our final example from the history of science. This will, however, oblige us to go beyond the subject of the present chapter in certain respects.

4. Julius Robert Mayer (1814–1878), the discoverer of the principle of the conservation of energy:[42]

This case—for it is a case in the strict psychiatric sense of that term—aroused the most violent emotional reactions at the time it occurred. Contemporary opinion was divided by two distinct controversies. In the first place, there was the dispute, which raged for years, over the question of Mayer's priority in making the discovery. This was finally settled in Mayer's favor by the magnanimous intervention of Clausius and Tyndall. And secondly, Mayer's supporters and biographers carried on an indignant campaign against the alleged defamation of their hero by his psychiatric diagnosis; in this cause, they did not even shrink from falsifying the historical record. Such a reaction illustrates in the most graphic way the strong social prejudice which attaches itself to anyone who at times becomes a plaything of the unconscious; this prejudice is of course intensified if the condition of the unfortunate sufferer makes hospitalization necessary.[43]

Mayer came from Heilbronn, where he also practiced as a doctor. He came from a district in which manic depressive insanity may be said to be practically endemic. Ever since his student days, his life had been overshadowed by the symptoms of this disease. We have an excellent description of his personality, which we owe to Rümelin, the friend of his youth who—without himself being a doctor—possessed an extraordinarily sensitive understanding of his friend's strange yet characteristic psychology. He explains that even as a boy Mayer had been subject to flights of ideas, and that he often produced "a regular firework display, in which thoughts jumped about like crackers." His brilliant and bizarre notions actually earned him the nickname of "the Brain." At school and university he was known as "a whimsical fellow" and "a dreamer."

At Schönthal training-college, where he lived between the ages of 14 and 18, he went through agonies of self-reproach which were quite unfounded; at the same time, he suffered from fits of hypochondriacal depression, which were accompanied by feelings of world-weariness and a fear of going mad. He also experienced hypomanic phases. In 1832 he was expelled from the University of Tübingen for belonging to a forbidden students' association. He was put in the students' lock-up and went on hunger strike for six days, with the result that he had to be released. The doctor who was called in was of the opinion that "he could not be regarded as completely insane, but was in a condition which could easily develop into insanity. This view was shared by all those who had known him for any length of time; they were all agreed that if an incident occurred which he found objectionable in any way, Mayer was always liable to become extremely agitated, and that he could easily pass into a borderline state."

After he had completed his medical studies, Mayer experienced an irresistible urge to become acquainted with the world, and in particular with the tropics. He obtained a post as a ship's doctor on a Dutch sailing vessel bound for the East Indies. While awaiting instructions to join his ship, he visited Paris with his friends Wunderlich and Griesinger.[44] There he suffered an unmistakable, slightly manic phase, in the course of which he spent a great deal of money. On February 22, 1840 he left Rotterdam on board the Java. Fortunately, we possess his diary, written during the journey out, which lasted three months, and some letters dating from the same period. In one of these he wrote,

And now farewell, for a time, my dear, dear parents; my child's thanks for the innumerable kindnesses which you have constantly shown me, and please, please forgive me for being so often ungrateful to you and accept my most fervent prayers for your well-being. In tears I throw myself into your arms and kiss you.
—Your grateful son Robert

Here already we can see the first signs of an endogenous depression; this gradually deepened, and finally revealed itself quite openly in a number of entries in the diary. Thus on April 4 he writes:

Today was not too terribly hot. The thermometer on deck registered 24°. The evening was brightened by a beautiful sunset, with a romantic afterglow. This had a soothing effect on my mind, which since the beginning of this month has been oppressed by troubled forebodings.

On April 10 we read:

Today gloomy thoughts and leaden cares, which center around the hallowed head of my father, weight more heavily than ever upon my soul . . .

At such times I look out more than anything else for my father's favourite constellation, the Great Bear, and think that perhaps he himself is gazing at it this very moment; then I call out friendly greetings to it for my dear ones in the home country.

On May 30:

Father's birthday. Gloomy cares oppress me on this festival day, which I have often spent so happily in the bosom of my family; it was only after a struggle that I managed to fight my way out of them at last.

On June 8, the day on which the southwestern tip of Java emerged into view above the sea, the "peripeteia"[45] of the illness can be seen very clearly. Mayer writes:

The breakers which seethed against the rocks and cliffs of the southern coast with furious energy, the splendid spectacular green of the tremendous trees which cover the mountain face as it rises sheer out of the water, the arrow-swift path of our ship through the waves, and the glorious weather—all this aroused a tempest of the most blissful feelings within me . . .

On June 12:

Yesterday evening at 11 o'clock we arrived safely at the roadstead of Batavia. O God! Your world is beautiful! The strait of Sunda is surely one of the most beautiful places in the world; . . . Admittedly the heat is pretty intense—25° to 27° or 28° Centigrade at midday; so far, however, I am bearing it without the slightest discomfort—in fact, I have never been more healthy in my life—though at the same time I am taking every possible care of myself. [Here his hypochondriacal side comes out.] My mind is so peaceful, and the only thing I need to complete my happiness is news about my dear ones. With thousands of greetings and kisses to you, dear parents, brothers and aunts and all my loved ones; I can see you all in my mind's eye as I write.

—Your obedient son Robert

On June 22, 1840 he writes once again from Batavia to his parents:

As a firm faith in God and a glad heart are my constant companions you can imagine that I look to the future with a quiet mind; like the past, its parade of dark and sunny hours will soon be over. My health, which is in any case sound, is still further sustained by self-control, a habit in which I am well-advanced.

In a letter home dated July 25, he gives a summary description of his stay in the East Indies, and I quote the following passages which are relevant to our subject:

The days fly past me like hours and are pleasantly and usefully occupied in study. Mental activity and physical rest are all I look for in this climate; it is astonishing how much effort a little letter costs me, and I am amazed, too, at the way in which my thoughts—otherwise so free, freer than ever before, in fact—become so stupid when I touch the beastly paper . . .

This was the historic moment at which Mayer conceived the idea of the conservation of energy. He wrote about this to his friend Griesinger, the psychiatrist, on June 16, 1844:

This theory was by no means hatched out at my writing desk. I had occupied myself, eagerly and continuously, on my journey to the East Indies, with the physiology of the blood, and my observation of the changed physical condition of our crew in the tropics, and of the process of their acclimatization, provided me with a great deal of food for thought; the types of illness from which they suffered, and particularly the state of their blood, drew my attention over and over again to the generation of animal heat in the body as a result of the process of respiration. But we cannot gain an insight into physiological matters if we know nothing of the corresponding physical processes—unless indeed we prefer to approach the subject from a metaphysical angle, a prospect which fills me with infinite distaste. So I concentrated on physics and pursued this subject with such enthusiasm that many people might be inclined to laugh at me, since I asked very few questions about the strange part of the world in which I found myself, but preferred to remain on board, where I could work uninterruptedly, and where I quite often felt like a man inspired—in fact I cannot remember having experienced anything similar, either before or since that time. I had a number of *flashes of insight*—this happened on the roadstead at Surabaya—which I followed up assiduously, without delay, and these in turn led me on to new themes. Those times are now past, but the calm testing of what I experienced at that period has convinced me that it was truth—not merely something which was felt subjectively, but something which can also be objectively substantiated—though whether this can be done by a man so little versed in physics as myself is a question which must remain undecided for the present. What is certain is that the day will come when these truths will be the common property of science; by whom, and when, this development will be brought about, who can tell?

It is a well-known fact that an old-style sea-voyage is always liable to activate the background of the human psyche. This makes it possible for us to understand how it came about that on two occasions during the voyage to the East Indies Mayer fell a victim to inexplicable fits of depression. We should express this in our terminology by saying that during these periods of relative introversion,[46] libido (i.e., psychic energy) flowed backwards, in such a way that the subject's interest now concentrated on certain contents belonging to his inner reality and turned away from the outside world; this process is also known as regression.

We saw from Mayer's correspondence that one special object of his interest at this time was "the hallowed head of his father." This image is an excellent symbol for the "patris potestas,"[47] that is to say for the man who, by virtue of his dominant position, served as an example to his son in his primary task of mastering his own powers—a task in which Mayer had so significantly failed. As usually happens in such cases, the image activated by the regression of the libido had a fascinating effect upon Mayer. It appeared to him in projected form in the heavens; he was fascinated by the sun as a center of energy.[48] Whenever a fascination of this kind occurs, we can take it that a *primordial image*, or—in Jung's terminology—an *archetypal image*, is at work. Once such an image has been activated, it will obtrude itself upon the conscious mind with elemental power.

Meanwhile, Mayer's depressive fits died away and gave place—particularly on his arrival in Java—to a manic mood disorder. Mayer was now possessed by "the most blissful feelings"—and suddenly we find him working away like mad at scientific problems. He even forgets the conscious purpose of his laborious journey—to learn about the tropics in the Far East, and only sets foot on land once, for a brief visit to Madura. The automatic onset of the progressive movement of the libido, which is a well-known feature of *manic* depressive insanity, had brought about a projection of the emergent archetype, and in view of Mayer's outstanding scientific endowment, it is not surprising that the entire progressive movement of the libido flowed over into the concept of energy and the principle of the conservation of energy—two concepts which in fact may very well represent the father-archetype at the conscious level.

The quantum of energy which is invariably inherent in archetypal images gave an added impetus to the forward movement of the libido, with the result that the manic excitement was intensified and began to assume threatening forms. We know from oral communications subsequently made by Mayer to his friends that he suffered from "acute attacks of delirium" on the voyage home, and it is clear from all the evidence that this was in fact one of the worst manic phases in his entire career.

On returning from his trip to the East Indies, Mayer devoted himself almost exclusively, and with incredible concentration, to the development of his concept of the conservation of energy. From that time on he regarded it as *the* result of his journey. I do not believe that we shall be far wrong if we take it that the energy which he employed for his purpose derived from the archetype which he had encountered in Surabaya Bay. I should like to take this opportunity to forestall another objection which may easily be raised in this context. We may be told that any attempt to explain the outstanding achievement of the discovery of the principle of the conservation of energy as "nothing but" the product of an essentially pathological phenomenon amounts to "professional defamation." Nothing could be further from my thoughts than that. It would, in fact, reduce me to the level of the anecdotal psychiatrist who is said to have replied to Robert Mayer, when the latter wished to explain to him his physical theory, "Well, well, my dear Mayer, still the same old crazy idea?"

As I have already remarked, Robert Mayer had worked intensively on his "idea." After his first publication[49] had been received with a certain amount of surprise by the experts, who found his formulations too far removed from the language of physical science, he, a layman in physics, did not shrink from the task of familiarizing himself with the higher ranges of the calculus and of mathematical analysis, a purpose in which he was assisted by his friend Baur, who was at that time professor of mathematics at Stuttgart.

There is no doubt that these studies and the new wording of his paper,[50] which was more adequate to the level of knowledge in physics at that period, represented a tremendous achievement in terms of Mayer's work on himself. To a considerable extent he had succeeded in *objectivizing* the original, largely subjective content of his idea and had transformed it in such a way that it constitutes a universally valid truth. It is, in fact, nothing less than the *First Law of Thermodynamics*. Not only did he give the world a great new idea, which secured his fame alike as a genius and an enricher of civilization[51]; he had also, at the same time, redeemed his own soul. This is substantiated by a passage from a letter dated August 16, 1841, in which he writes to his friend Baur (the reference is to this second publication): "Dixi et animam salvavi" ("I have spoken and

I have saved my own soul"). In our terminology, we should say that the work put in here by Robert Mayer can only be described as a piece of self-analysis. The point at issue was the assimilation of an exceedingly potent content of the collective unconscious, namely the archetype of the father.

We may be tempted to suppose that this magnificent performance of Mayer's was equivalent to an analysis of the causes of his disorder, and that as a result of it he would have been restored to health. However, this was not to be. During the period 1845 to 1853 we find him involved in extremely severe manic phases and depressions. During one of these episodes (in 1850) he made a really dangerous attempt at suicide, and in the ensuing years he voluntarily entered a mental hospital whenever he was threatened with the onset of a manic or depressive phase.

Unfortunately, no detailed notes or medical histories are available to us from this period, and I am by no means certain that reports of this nature would in fact provide us with any real information about the content of Robert Mayer's psychosis. We do know, however, that in the years after 1871 he was again compelled to enter a psychiatric institution. The manic and depressive attacks became less and less pronounced, however, and we find that, as the emotional fluctuations ebbed away, their place was increasingly taken by a rising tide of deep religious feeling.

In 1869, when the controversy over the significance and priority of his achievement which had agitated the entire scientific world had been finally settled in his favor, he was invited to give a lecture at Innsbruck to the Forty-Third Conference of German Scientists and Doctors on the subject of "The Necessary Consequences and Inconsequences of Heat Mechanics." To the great surprise of all those present, he concluded his otherwise impeccably scientific dissertation with the following remarks:

> Let us now leave the realm of nature as it is known to physics and approach the living world. Where the former is governed by necessity and the unvarying clock of law, we now enter a realm of purposive adaptation and beauty—a realm of progress and freedom. And the boundary between the two is marked by *number*. In physics, number means everything, in physiology it means very little, and in metaphysics nothing at all. From the bottom of my heart I must proclaim this truth! A sound philosophy can and must be nothing less than a preparatory school for the Christian religion!

It can easily be imagined what a "shaking of heads" was produced by this outburst among the scientific audience of this lecture.

Yet what we have here is an inevitable psychological consequence of Robert Mayer's basic problem. We could actually use the very wording of the title of his lecture in a figurative sense and speak of "a necessary consequence of heat mechanics"!

Act I of his illness had confronted Robert Mayer with the idea of the principle of energy. It approached him in a form which enables us to recognize the characteristics of an archetypal content of the imagination in the midst of his severe psychotic symptoms. This content is in fact a genuine symbol, i.e., it is an image of a psychological state of affairs which could not be better or more completely expressed in any other way than by this precise image. We can see quite distinctly that this expression includes both a rational and a nonrational factor. The first, purely scientific treatment of this content by Robert Mayer remained entirely within the confines of the rational dimension; and in fact he believed, very much in the old Kantian spirit, that his mathematical-cum-physical treatment of the subject had exhausted its entire significance. However, it was inevitable that this one-sidedness would take its revenge on a mind as deep as Mayer's. Almost without intermission the primordial image tore him once again from the most exalted heights and plunged him into the most abysmal depths, till as a result of these repeated grievous experiences he realized and accepted their ultimate *nonrational* residue.

Now at last he gave an impression of genuine balance, so that, for example, his friend Heinrich Rohlfs could say of him in 1876: "At the same time Mayer developed a dazzling wit and a delightful sense of humor which—though often sharp—was always at the same time good-humoured, and of such an engaging childlike and lovable quality that I was quite carried away."[52] It was not until now, in Act II of the tragedy of his fate, that Mayer's dictum, *"Dixi et animam salvavi"* was completely verified.

To explain and clarify what I had in mind when I chose Robert Mayer as an example, I should like to add the following remarks:

The idea of the conservation of energy was in the air at that period (cf. W.R. Grove[53], Joule, Colding, Carnot, Clausius, Tyndall, Helmholtz etc.), and it took possession of a mind that was scarcely capable of comprehending it in strictly scientific terms by first assuming the form of an image of an archetypal nature (cf. Kekulé's ouroboros or Schiller's "obscure but mighty total idea"). Subjective reasons why this idea should have fastened on Mayer, a mental patient, of all people, are to be found, we believe, in the nature of his illness, manic depressive insanity, a disease in which the *dynamic* nature of the psyche manifests itself in a particularly obtrusive form—to the extent, in fact, that the patient becomes a defenseless plaything of emotional forces. This oscillation between manic and depressive mood disorder is related to such concepts as the "progression" and "regression" of the psychic energy known as libido, and also to the two opposite habitual attitudes of that energy (extraversion and introversion), which we shall be examining later on.

In the realm of folklore the phenomenon of powerful emotional fluctuations was personified in the figure of the Low German folk hero Till Eulenspiegel; quite generally, too, fools, buffoons and court jesters (cf. Rigoletto) exhibit these marked oscillations of mood. Another equivalent of Goethe's "One moment exulting, the next quite cast down" (*Egmont*, Act III) in the realm of normal psychology is provided by Goethe's own "diastole" and "systole." However, when the amplitude of the oscillations is as great as it was in the case of Robert Mayer, the need is felt for a regulating or governing principle, and at the same time we are faced with the urgent problem of finding an energic equivalent on the unconscious side of the equation—a question which arises owing to the fact that although the psychic manifestations of the manic phase are plain to see on every hand, during depressive episodes such evidence will only be forthcoming if an active search is made for it. A brief example from clinical experience may serve to illustrate this point:

A primary schoolteacher about 50 years old entered the psychiatric clinic on account of an acute attack of melancholia, as endogenous or psychotic depression is also called. He gave an impression of complete mental paralysis and apathy. All the same, when I visited him I gave him little lectures on the dynamics of the psyche, along the lines of the theory set out above. In essence I told him, "It is necessary to assume that in this condition extremely crucial developments are taking place within the psyche. It would be most useful from a therapeutic point of view if you would be on the lookout for any development of this kind; the best source of information about such things is dreams; you should make a point of remembering your dreams, etc." In spite of the apparent inapproachability of patients of this type, my powers of persuasion were so far successful that one morning ten days later this patient came up to me of his own accord in a completely transformed state of mind; whereas previously he had been practically mutistic, he now told me that on the previous night he had dreamed that someone had been singing very beautifully in the courtyard outside, under his bedroom window; he had got up and had discovered that the song was in fact intended for him and that it was a radiantly beautiful girl who had serenaded him in this fashion. The patient was virtually

restored to health from that moment, and it was possible for him to
be discharged and sent home a few days later.[54]

However, since Mayer was fascinated by natural science, he
devoted himself to the question of the balance of energy in terms
of the contemporary level of knowledge on that subject—at first
with little success and many disappointments, but later with increasing objectivity, until at last he won the highest degree of scientific
recognition. This whole course of development toward a rational
formulation of the principle of energy in terms of physical science
was not accompanied by any improvement in his psychic condition.
On the contrary, a nonrational element, which can probably be best
described as a god-image, asserted itself with increasing effec-
tiveness. And it was in fact not until this stage had been reached
that Mayer too attained a healing balance in the emotional sphere,
so that his scientific achievement was finally crowned by its
psychological counterpart.

To sum up Mayer's case in simplified terms, we could say that in
the course of a sea voyage (sea = unconscious) and during a
depressive phase (introversion + regression of the libido), in conditions of tropical heat (sun = energy), at the moment of landfall
(= consciousness), after 98 days at sea and in stormy weather (wind
= spirit), the image of the father (patris potestas) and the idea of
the conservation of energy had obtruded themselves on the attention of our author. At the same time the depressive episode gave
place to a manic phase, since the libido was fascinated by these images, and under the influence of this attraction it moved forward
and became available for intellectual work. The subsequent history
of Mayer's life shows that, in addition to the solution of the problem on the scientific level, another solution, complementary or compensatory to the first, is required on the metaphysical level, so that
the mind can occupy a central position between the two of them.
Perhaps the process can be represented by the following equation:

$$\text{Sun} = \text{Father} = \text{``Force''} \begin{cases} \longrightarrow \text{First Law of Thermodynamics} \\ \longrightarrow \text{God-Image} \end{cases}$$

Incidentally, this scheme would exemplify Jung's concept that
every archetypal image and every commonplace emotion alike contain two aspects: (a) dynamism and (b) form, content or image—
both of which have to be taken into account.

To conclude this chapter, I should like to add one or two further
qualifications. We have dealt with certain notable cases, wherever

possible quoting the accounts given by the subjects themselves, which make it clear that the collaboration of the unconscious has been an essential factor in the outstanding achievements of unusually gifted creative personalities.

If we are inclined to accept this finding, we are immediately confronted by a number of questions. For example, is this positive cooperation of the unconscious with the conscious mind confined to men of genius and in fact does this constitute the nature of genius, quite independently of any specific gifts or endowment? It is clearly not my responsibility to examine this problem here. I should like simply to ask a counter question. Are examples of this kind really exceptional? Is it not really far more probable that they do not differ in kind but only in degree from productive achievements which are to be found in the realm of the normal or of the average? In such cases the only difference would be that both the achievements themselves and the components of the unconscious involved in them would be less spectacular.

In saying this it is not my intention to detract in the slightest degree from the respect that is due to genius; I simply wish to give us ordinary mortals some share in the opportunities of life. Psychological experience teaches us that a creative quality is in fact involved in all kinds of problem solving, and that fortunately for us this spark of creativity is often successful. And if ever we have a chance to observe the natural genesis of this process under laboratory conditions, as it were, in such a way that we are able to form a general picture of at any rate the major factors involved in its working, we regularly find that—to paraphrase Nietzsche (see p. 18)—nothing succeeds perfectly without the assistance of the unconscious—and that in any case this principle invariably holds good when we are dealing with a problem which is *psychic* in the narrower sense. This qualification should destroy the force of the charge of psychologism, and one possible cause of irritation to which our particular point of view might give rise would—at any rate in theory!—be eliminated.[55]

CHAPTER III

THE DISTURBING EFFECTS
OF THE UNCONSCIOUS

It was Freud[1] who first drew our attention to those phenomena which since that time have been known as faulty actions or parapraxes, and it was he who, by applying his psychoanalytical point of view, succeeded in explaining the mechanism by which they are brought into being. In connection with the concluding remarks of Chapter II, this raises yet another question: What is the factor that decides whether the interference of the unconscious with the conscious mind results in a creative effect, or in a parapraxis? Before I attempt to answer this question, I should like to suggest that we should approach it from a new angle.

When we are dealing with a successful positive synthesis, let us assume that it has come about because the subject has a positive *attitude* to the unconscious, i.e., an attitude of acceptance; in the opposite case, however, let us suppose that the subject's attitude is negative, i.e., an attitude of *rejection*, so that the unconscious has to exert its right to express an opinion by force, as it were, in diametrical opposition to the will of the subject.

Admittedly, a conception of this kind involves something approaching an anthropomorphism of the unconscious, since it seems as if the unconscious behaves well when we are friendly toward it— as in fact we expect civilized human beings to do. But analytical experience has shown that this hypothesis stands the test of practice. Every analyst knows that even those people who at first are firmly convinced that they never dream can remember dreams, and that this happens when the analysand concerned succeeds in cultivating a more friendly attitude toward the unconscious. It looks exactly as if the unconscious wants to show its appreciation for a gesture of this kind. Such experiences encourage a frame of mind which is far removed from modern rationalism and which in fact seems much closer to superstition; attention has already been called to this point in our commentary on Example 4 in Chapter II. We are not afraid of this kind of "superstition"; in fact, we are actually encouraged in our positive attitude by the fact that the results of an exaggerated "resistance" to the unconscious, as Freud has also shown, can assume grotesque forms which are really far more deserving of the epithet "superstitious" than anything we are advocating.

Here too it was psycho*pathology* that gave us the clue. Owing to the conspicuous nature of pathological symptomatology, we had entirely lost sight of the fact that similar resistances are to be found in the defense mechanisms *of healthy people*, which may then command unquestioning respect as evidence of genuine superiority or virtue, so that any attempt to expose or "unmask" them would itself incur the penalty of social disapproval. Our purpose here, however, is not to conduct iconoclastic campaigns of this kind, since the only thing we could possibly establish is that enlightenment applied to human nature leads to rank absurdity.

1. Parapraxes

Parapraxes are almost always represented in German by the use of the pejorative prefix *ver-* (English *mis-*), as for instance in *ver-sprechen* (slips of the tongue), *ver-lesen* (misreadings), *ver-schreiben* (slips of the pen), *ver-gessen* (forgetting), *ver-lieren* (losing), *ver-legen* (mislaying), *ver-wechseln* (confusing) etc.; or else by *zer-*, e.g., *zer-brechen* (breaking to pieces), *zer-schlagen* (smashing) etc. These inadvertent happenings—though at times comic—may be exceedingly awkward and embarrassing.

(a) Slips of the Tongue

Many of us have known what it is to have the experience of congratulating someone on somebody's death instead of expressing our regret or sympathy. It can be decidedly illuminating to do a little research into the truth concealed behind such happenings; for the saying *lingua lapsa verum dicit* (slips of the tongue tell us the truth) embodies a very ancient insight, although I have not been able to establish the age of that particular proverb.

At all events, this motif is displayed quite transparently in the story about the aspiring young academic who, as the successor of his former teacher, had the task of pronouncing a laudatory address in his honor, and who began as follows: "I am not *inclined* (G. *geneigt) to pay a tribute to the outstanding merits of my predecessor.*" Of course, he should have said that he was not *qualified* (G. *geeignet*), but his unconscious was not in agreement with this proposition, since it would have involved an excessive, hypocritical display of modesty (quoted from Freud).[2]

In the world of public administration, a situation once arose that necessitated a committee of inquiry. A member of this committee who was not exactly a paragon of moral courage was appointed to report on the findings. He began by saying, "But then facts came to 'Vorschwein'. . . ."[3]

These anecdotal examples should suffice. At best, such slips have the advantage that they appeal to the audience's sense of humor. But they can, of course, be exceedingly embarrassing, as can be seen from the following example quoted by Freud, which has achieved classic status:

A year later another speaker in the same place was not so fortunate. He wished to appeal for a demonstration *with no reserves* (*rückhaltlos*) in support of the Emperor, and in doing so was warned by a bad slip of the tongue that other emotions were to be found within his loyal breast. "*Lattmann* (German National Party): On the question of the Address our position is based on the standing orders of the Reichstag. According to them the Reichstag is entitled to tender such an address to the Emperor. It is our belief that the united thoughts and wishes of the German people are bent on achieving a *united demonstration* in this matter as well, and if we can do this in a form that takes the Emperor's feelings fully into account, then we should do so *spinelessly* (*rückgratlos*) as well." (Loud laughter which continued for some minutes.) "Gentlemen, I should have said not *rückgratlos* but *rückhaltlos* (unreservedly)" (laughter), "and at this difficult time even our Emperor accepts a manifestation by the people—one made without reserve—such as we should like to see."

The social democratic paper "*Vorwärts*" of November 12, 1908, did not miss the opportunity of pointing to the psychological significance of this slip of the tongue: "Probably never before in any parliament has a member, through an involuntary self-accusation, characterized his own attitude and that of the parliamentary majority towards the Emperor so exactly as did the anti-Semitic Lattmann, when, speaking with solemn emotion on the second day of the debate, he slipped into an admission that he and his friends wished to express their opinion to the Emperor *spinelessly*. Loud laughter from all sides drowned the remaining words of this unhappy man, who thought it necessary explicitly to stammer out by way of apology that he really meant 'unreservedly'."[4]

Another example from the same source illustrates very clearly the resistances against the process of becoming conscious and the various symptoms which they may call up.

I went for a walk one evening with Dr. Frink and we discussed some of the business of the New York Psychoanalytic Society. We met a colleague, Dr. R., whom I had not seen for years and of whose private life I knew nothing. We were very pleased to meet again, and on my invitation he accompanied us to a cafe, where we spent two hours in lively conversation. He seemed to know some details about me, for after the usual greetings he asked after my small child and told me that he heard about me from time to time from a mutual friend and had been interested in my work ever since he had read about it in the medical press. To my question as to whether he was married he gave a negative answer, and added, "Why should a man like me marry?"

On leaving the cafe, he suddenly turned to me and said: "I should like to know what you would do in a case like this: I know a nurse who was named as co-respondent in a divorce case. The wife sued the husband and named her as co-respondent, and *he* got the divorce." I interrupted him, saying "You mean *she* got the divorce." He immediately corrected himself, saying: "Yes, of course, *she* got the divorce," and continued to tell how the nurse had been so affected by the divorce proceedings and the scandal that she had taken to drink, had become very nervous, and so on; and he wanted me to advise him how to treat her.

As soon as I had corrected his mistake I asked him to explain it, but I received the usual surprised answer: Had not everyone the right to make a slip of the tongue? It was only an accident, there was nothing behind it, and so on. I replied that there must be a reason for every mistake in speaking, and that, had he not told me earlier that he was unmarried, I would be tempted to suppose he himself was the hero of the story; for in that case the slip could be explained by his wish that he had obtained the divorce rather than his wife, so that he should not have (by our matrimonial laws) to pay alimony, and so that he could marry again in New York State. He stoutly denied my conjecture, but the exaggerated emotional reaction which accompanied it, in which he showed marked signs of agitation followed by laughter, only strengthened my suspicions. To my appeal that he should tell the truth in the interests of science, he answered: "Unless you wish me to lie you must believe that I was never married, and hence your psychoanalytical interpretation is all wrong." He added that someone who paid attention to every triviality was positively dangerous. Then he suddenly remembered that he had another appointment and left us.

Both Dr. Frink and I were still convinced that my interpretation of his slip of the tongue was correct, and I decided to corroborate or disprove it by further investigation. Some days later I visited a neighbor, an old friend of Dr. R., who was able to confirm my explanation in every particular. The divorce proceedings had taken place some weeks before, and the nurse was cited as co-respondent. Dr. R. is today thoroughly convinced of the correctness of the Freudian mechanisms.[5]

(b) Misreadings

Misreading is one of the most frequent and commonplace parapraxes. They were wittily exemplified in an example given by the well-known physicist Georg Christoph Lichtenberg of Göttingen (1742-1799):

> For *angenommen* (G. = accepted, supposed) he always read Agamemnon—so thoroughly had he studied his Homer.

The victim of this satire by Lichtenberg must obviously have been a classical scholar, in whose mind that particular grouping of the letters which resembled the name of a Homeric hero had automatically been "homerized," so as to conform with the subject of his conscious preoccupation.[6]

The analytical interpretation of the following example quoted by Freud is particularly illuminating:

> A close acquaintance of mine had repeatedly declared to me that when his turn came to be called up he would not make any use of his specialist qualifications, which were attested by a diploma; he would waive any claim based on them for being found suitable employment behind the lines and he would enlist for service at the front. Shortly before the call-up date in fact arrived, he told me one day in the curtest way, and without giving any further reason, that he had submitted the evidence of his specialist training to the proper authorities and as a result would shortly be assigned to a post in industry. Next day we happened to meet in a post-office. I was standing up at a desk and writing; he came in, looked over my shoulder for a while and then said: "Oh! the word at the top there's *Druckbogen* (printed sheet)—I'd read it as *Drückeberger* (shirker)."[7]

(c) Slips of the Pen

It is not difficult to understand how the conscious intention of a writer may be disturbed by an unconscious intention—very much along the lines of Lichtenberg's example of misreading *angenom-men* as Agamemnon, and the introduction of mechanical writing techniques such as the typewriter has provided even greater opportunities for "typing errors." We already knew that these could be annoying, but we owe to Freud the insight that occasionally something really "worth reading" can be deduced from them. So, as *pars pro toto*, I am quoting one of his best examples:

> An American living in Europe who had left his wife on bad terms felt that he could now effect a reconciliation with her, and asked her to come across the Atlantic and join him on a certain date. "It would be fine," he wrote, "if you could come on the *Mauretania* as I did." He did not however dare to send the sheet of paper which had this sentence on it. He preferred to write it out again. For he did not want her to notice how he had had to correct the name of the ship. He had first written "Lusitania."
>
> This slip of the pen needs no explanation: it is perfectly plain. But a happy chance enables a further point to be added. Before the war his wife paid her first visit to Europe after the death of her only sister. If I am not mistaken, the *Mauretania* is the surviving sister-ship of the *Lusitania*, which was sunk in the war.

Printer's errors, too—so dear to the hearts of humorous periodicals ("Unconscious humor, as we know, In funny papers loves to grow")—obviously belong to the same category, since they are in fact nothing but "typing errors" of the compositor compounded by misreading on the part of the proofreader ("negative misreading," as it were, an interesting problem in gestalt psychology); here again the occasional unconscious motivation shows through all too transparently.

(d) Forgetting

It is characteristic of all parapraxes that they occur more frequently when the subject is in a state of exhaustion or of distraction and preoccupation; however, this is especially true of forgetting. *Resistances*, too, of which we are insufficiently conscious take a delight in playing tricks on us, as for example when we leave at home the most important documents required for a meeting to which we are not particularly looking forward—in which case a protest that we have not been able to express in any other way is probably finding an involuntary outlet.

A more sardonic analysis of forgetting was given by Nietzsche:

> "I have done it" says my memory. "I cannot have done it," says my pride and remains inexorable. Finally, my memory gives way.[8]

Here, long before Freud, the mechanism of *repression* is clearly exposed. According to Nietzsche, the prime mover in repression is the complex psychological phenomenon we know as pride; this is then reduced by Freud to the so-called instinctual fate of the individual in the Oedipal situation. We must guard against oversimplification in the realm of psychology; let us only recall that there is scarcely anything of importance that we do which is not accompanied by a negative component that also makes its presence felt. This basic *ambivalence* (Bleuler's term) in our emotional makeup belongs to the essential nature and dignity of man; without it, no decision—whether free or unfree—would be conceivable. However, there are also other aspects of the question of repression. We return to these later.

(e) Mislaying

In this type of faulty action, we are confronted with something that works in a far more "mysterious" way than those we have previously considered, so that the impression we receive is one of an exceedingly subtle "arrangement"—which once again invites us to "anthropomorphize" the unconscious. A senior colleague once told me that whenever his mother was looking for some article which had clearly been mislaid, she used to say, three times over, in the Swiss dialect, "Tüfel tue de Tooppe drab" ("devil take your paws off it"), whereupon she invariably found the missing article. Here the act of mislaying is construed as the machination of a daemonic power, which can be "dis-covered" by magical means. An example quoted by Silberer, in which the unconscious motivation is clearly indicated, may be apposite in this context:

> I happened to be at Ischl, and I remembered with distaste that I should have to break off my very pleasant stay there because I had promised to pay an irksome visit to someone I knew at Aussee. How then does chance contrive to detain me for two more whole days at Ischl? All of a sudden I find that my ring, a valuable piece of jewelry, has vanished. I cannot possibly leave without trying to find it. Was it stolen? Had I lost it? I advertise, offer a reward, take all possible steps—and two days later I discover my ring peacefully reposing under a hollow candlestick in my room! The circumstances make it clear that my own hand was responsible for playing this prank—which could not conceivably have been carried out in a simpler or more unobtrusive manner. And that this incident really had the meaning I ascribed to it is further substantiated by the fact that this particular ring was actually connected in a certain way with the person at Aussee.[9]

(f) Losing

I do not wish to give the impression that we deny the existence of purely statistical "accidents." In many cases, we shall remain content with an acausal interpretation; where, however, such an interpretation leaves us with a feeling of *relief*, it is probably just as well to suspect a psychological etiology and to search our consciences accordingly.

After all, the question as to whether we do, or do not, know the course destiny will take cannot be a matter of complete indifference to us. But if we really do want to know this, we shall have to make an effort, and this is something we are generally only too glad to avoid, since resistance and repression—not to mention intellectual indolence—are deeply ingrained in our nature. And moreover, a careful examination will always reveal that there is a peculiar kind of "dottiness" which invariably plays a part in these cases, and which must always be taken into account since it is a precondition of faulty actions. In contrast to the exhaustion or distraction which we have already mentioned, this kind of "dottiness" is specific— i.e., it is already determined by the basic unconscious "intention" which is to be found at the roots of the parapraxis and which represents exactly what Pierre Janet called "abaissement du niveau mental."[10]

As we shall show later, Jung proved experimentally that this "dottiness" is strictly localized; it is to be found in the region of a so-called complex.[11] An example from Silberer's instructive paper may serve to illustrate this point:

My friend Paul is engaged. He is wearing an engagement ring.[12] Recently, this ring seems to have fallen under the influence of an unlucky star. Paul visited me and told me that the day before yesterday he had pulled it off along with his glove and nearly lost it, and that just now he must have been playing with it on the tram-car and have let it drop, all quite unconsciously, since the passenger sitting opposite him had suddenly bent down to pick up something, and to his astonishment had handed him his ring. Paul then left me, and sure enough I found the ring, which he had taken off in order to show it to me, still on my table. Are we to suppose that all this was happening purely by accident? Isn't it more probable that Paul himself played a part in the production of this "accident"? Isn't it possible that there was an unacknowledged impulse inside him which wished to be rid of this ring—or rather of the emotional commitment which it represented? In actual fact, the engagement was broken off shortly afterwards.

(g) Confusing

Maeder devoted an article to a special form of this.[13] We are standing before the door of a particularly dear friend, and we take out the key to our own front door. It is not difficult to decipher the meaning of this. We feel very much at home in this house—or at any rate, we should very much like to feel so. Many doctors who visit patients at home must have had the same experience, especially in the case of patients—whether male or female—toward whom their feelings are not entirely indifferent. Freud has contributed two cases in which he himself was involved, to the discussion of this phenomenon, and he has analyzed his own unconscious motives at the time.

There is a house where twice every day for six years, at regular hours, I used to wait to be let in outside a door on the second floor. During this long period it has happened to me on two occasions, with a short interval between them, that I have gone a floor too high— i.e. I have *"climbed too high."*[14] On the first occasion I was enjoying an ambitious daydream in which I was "climbing ever higher and higher." On this occasion I even failed to hear that the door in question had opened as I put my foot on the first step of the third flight. On the other occasion, I again went too far while I was deep in thought; when I realized it, I turned back and tried to catch hold of the phantasy in which I had been absorbed. I found that I was irritated by a (phantasied) criticism of my writings in which I was reproached with always "going too far." This I had now replaced by the not very respectful expression "climbing too high."[15]

(h) Smashing

There are people (and they are not only domestic servants!) who have a special gift for "sacrificing" or "punishing" crockery and also more valuable objects that are fragile. However often this may be due to simple carelessness or clumsiness, there are still reasonable grounds for further reflection, at least in cases involving the destruction of valuable objects. At all events, the proverb *Scherben bringen Glück* (Broken crocks bring good luck) has an apotropaic origin— unless indeed it is simply a euphemism (see p. 14 above). In the light of considerations such as these, which are intended to "explain" faulty actions, we may be tempted to adopt a superstitious attitude. With the process of inner transformation already at work inside him, Faust sought to force himself from such an attitude: It looms, it warns us, lies for us in wait.[16]

So we will confine ourselves to innocuous examples, such as the following mischance, which happened to Freud himself. He describes how an "accidental clumsy movement" rid him of an object he no longer cared for. On his desk, surrounded by a ring of delicate, precious statuettes, was a rather inferior inkwell. One day, his sister drew his attention to the fact that this inkwell did not match its surroundings; he really ought to obtain a nicer one, she said. Soon afterwards, he sat down to write, and unexpectedly made a sweeping movement with his hand forward in such a way that the lid of the inkwell was swept to the floor and smashed. In reality, this "clumsy" movement was exceedingly adroit and well-directed, since the execution of the condemned inkwell was carried out in such a way that the statuettes which surrounded it were miraculously spared.—"The unconscious can often manage things better than we are able to do on the conscious level."[17]

One of my women patients produced a faulty action which provided an almost incredible corroboration of Silberer's concluding sentence.

This rather elderly lady had been given by her even more elderly husband four little bottles of expensive scent, three of which he had brought home from *Morocco* and one from *Paris*. These were set out by her with military precision on a bracket which was above and behind a sofa; she arranged them in the following order

M   M   P   M

One evening, the family circle were sitting together; my patient was on the sofa and her husband was describing his trip to Morocco. The lady felt chilly and threw on a shawl; her aim was so deadly accurate that the Paris perfume was knocked onto the floor and the little bottle was smashed. The explanation of the mystery is that the lady entertained vivid fantasies about the unfaithfulness of her husband. According to her traditional notions Paris (not Morocco!) is the place which is notorious for infidelity; that is why the scent from Paris annoyed her. The unconscious could claim the credit for a direct hit.

According to the proverb, there is a close connection between luck and glass, so that it is advisable to treat pieces of broken glass with respect.[18] I know an artist who carefully collects all the pieces of broken glass which are to be found in his household and every now and again uses them—just as they are—to make a mosaic of considerable artistic merit, thus building a temple to broken glass and the destructive forces in general.

Of course, a great many more examples could be given of parapraxes with the German prefix *ver-* and *zer-*, since as Faust put it—

Now fills the air so many a haunting shape,
That no one knows how best he may escape.[19]

However, the examples already quoted should provide a sufficiently clear indication regarding the kind of factors which encourage the occurrence of these "impish tricks." In what follows, we shall concentrate on investigating phenomena which proved, and still prove, less easy to recognize for what they are—faulty actions.

(i) Symptomatic Actions

This expression is derived from Freud,[20] and he illustrates it as follows: "Symptomatic actions are completely at home in autobiographical novels by writers with a gift for introspection." Silberer quotes Strindberg's *Inferno* in this context:

Strindberg was reproaching himself because he had deserted his wife and child. Then he made the acquaintance of a charming Englishwoman, who captivated him and reminded him of his wife; in fact he called her a "luxury edition" of his wife. To please Strindberg, an artist friend invited the lady to his Thursday night soirees. I will let the poet tell the story in his own words: "I went to the party but kept myself in the background, since I had no desire to expose my feelings to an audience who would make fun of me. Towards eleven o'clock the lady got up and gave me a signal of secret understanding. I got up rather awkwardly and made my farewells, offered to accompany the young lady and went out with her, while the shameless young people laughed." And he went on to make himself impossible to the lady herself by his clumsy behavior. It is clear that his conscious intention was to make advances to the charming Englishwoman, but that obstacles arose from the depths of his wounded conscience which took the form of clumsy actions that made excellent use of external incidents (which I need not describe here) for their purpose. Strindberg had sufficient insight to grasp the underlying connection, and he writes: ". . . I was a beggar, who had not fulfilled his obligations to his own family, and yet I was attempting to enter into a relationship which would inevitably have compromised an innocent girl. That was quite simply a crime—and I imposed the proper penance on myself for it."[21]

Freud cites the following passage from *The Life and Opinions of Tristram Shandy*, a largely autobiographical work which is still extremely popular. It was written between 1760 and 1767 by the Irishman Lawrence Sterne (1713–1768), who was a kind of precursor of James Joyce:

> . . . And I am not at all surprised that *Gregory* of *Nazianzum*, upon observing the hasty and untoward gestures of *Julian*, should foretell he would one day become an apostate;—or that St. *Ambrose* should turn his *Amanuensis* out of doors, because of an indecent motion of his head, which went backwards and forwards like a flail;—or that *Democritus* should conceive *Protagoras* to be a scholar, from seeing him bind up a faggot, and thrusting, as he did it, the small twigs inwards.—There are a thousand unnoticed openings, continued my father, which let a penetrating eye at once into a man's soul; and I maintain it, added he, that a man of sense does not lay down his hat in coming into a room,—or take it up in going out of it, but something escapes, which discovers him.[22]

Clearly, what we have here amounts to a special subsection of the art of physiognomy or the understanding of expressive movements.

In cases of losing and smashing, and also in the incident from Strindberg's life which we have just quoted, we can often easily recognize certain traits of self-punishment, self-execution or self-sacrifice which are probably to be found to some extent in all types of faulty action. Freud has already shown us that the complex configurations involved in symptomatic actions and parapraxes often reveal a whole series of determining factors; they are, as he says, "overdetermined." One particular aspect of this "overdetermination" comes out quite clearly in the well-known fact that bad luck and misfortune generally only come about as the result of a whole chain of circumstances which form a causal nexus that is interlinked and connected with a positively diabolical consistency. If a single link in this chain were missing, the whole happening would never occur at all, so that every time it looks very much as if a hidden purpose were trying to get its own way at all costs. Once again, there is a temptation here to anthropomorphize the unconscious.

Just as there are people who smash things with the greatest of ease, so, too, there have always been people who seem simply to have been born unlucky. Strangely enough, it only dawned on the psychologists of the Anglo-American world a few years ago that the same principle applies to accidents; this led them to coin the expression "accident proneness."[23]

The examples of faulty actions we have considered so far have been of a more or less innocuous nature. Accidents, on the other hand, may raise questions of more far-reaching significance. And if it is true that accidents have to be interpreted in the same way as parapraxes of the kind we have described, our whole approach to the subject will be made so exceedingly uncomfortable, that, retrospectively, the resistances it provoked are in human terms only too understandable. Also, in the case of most accidents, we are so impressed and preoccupied by the facts of the case, which are generally very complicated, that we naturally forget the psychological aspects of the problem; nor need our forgetfulness on this occasion be interpreted as a parapraxis in the sense we have just considered. Yet there are certain enigmatic accidents in the face of which we find ourselves literally compelled to review the situation from the point of view of a possible hidden psychological background.

So long as it is only we ourselves who are the injured party in an accident, the question of our guilt may not even arise. Let us suppose, for example, that we have a fall while skiing which involves the fracture of a limb. Many of us would pass this over without experiencing "moral scruples" of any kind. Yet we know of many cases in which people of robust health in body and mind have found themselves wondering, at the very moment when they fell, whether there wasn't perhaps some guilty situation for which the accident might be a punishment. That in most cases there was some uncertain, clumsy "false" step or maneuver is obvious enough; but was there not something which "distracted" our attention (cf. distraction in the Association Experiment, Chapter IV)—something that preoccupied our minds and left us no peace, something which we ought perhaps to have attended to earlier? If this is so, the "punishment" may then seem to us to go too far, and we may dismiss the thought as "morbid brooding."

But this tendency may not triumph quite so easily if we are involved in an accident in which other people are injured and in which we ourselves—apparently quite innocent people—have in fact been partially or even wholly responsible for the death of another—equally innocent—person. The question as to our guiltiness will then be determined along strictly judicial lines. Let us take the extreme case, in which the legal inquiry comes to the conclusion that the injured or deceased party was not guilty, and in which the verdict is not contested. The fact remains that from the psychological point of view the question may, and in some cases must, be raised as to whether the complete innocence of the "victim" (the one that was sacrificed) is not in fact a rather credulous assumption, since we know nothing about any possible "accident proneness" or suicidal tendencies he may have had. If we think of inquiring into the nature of the relationship between the "victim" and the person of the "agent," we are likely to receive a dusty answer; this is a consideration which our modern legal system no longer takes into account in any shape or form. However, I myself happen to know of a case in a so-called "underdeveloped country," which made a great impression on me.

A man of blameless reputation had quite simply killed another man, of equally blameless reputation, with whom he had no quarrel and in fact no relationship of any kind. When he was asked by the court about the motive for his action, he replied "He was standing there in such a way that you simply had to kill him." The man was then acquitted by the court. It seems, then, that in certain quarters provocation, in the sense suggested by our previous question, is taken far more seriously than it is by ourselves.

Accidents in which we are involved without any conscious intention of our own, have in fact two aspects—to which the legal assessment of the case adds a third. To take the unconscious—i.e., the psychological, subjective aspect—into consideration is admittedly most uncomfortable; but it does, after all, comply with the injunction *et altera pars audiatur* ("let the other side also be heard"). And it has to be admitted that the subtlety with which such situations are arranged by the unconscious can scarcely be surpassed by the conscious mind—nor would the conscious mind in fact be morally capable of this kind of performance.

The special use which Alfred Adler made of such "arrangements" by the unconscious for the purpose of his theory of the neuroses may be recalled in this context.[24] In such cases, the judge will always act rightly, in accordance with the existing law, if he denies the responsibility of the agent, admits the involuntary nature of his conduct, and to a large extent exonerates him from blame. In fact the agent was acting literally under a compulsion which was stronger than the blameless ego, so that the responsibility and criminality of the agent are very considerably diminished.

Here, too, a chain of circumstances is involved, and this recalls the notorious "series-formation" tendency of chance, by which, for example, doctors are impressed when they speak of a "law of the duplication or multiplication of cases." Schopenhauer racked his brains over this problem, since serial chains of circumstances may play a fateful part in the lives of both "perpetrator" and "victim."[25] At all events, the examples quoted should be sufficient to suggest to our minds the advisability of treating the powers of the unconscious with caution and respect and of cultivating a relationship of peaceful cooperation with them.

2. Déjà vu, déjà entendu, déjà raconté, automatisms, fausse reconnaissance and cryptomnesia

Related to faulty actions are a number of peculiar phenomena which are to be found in everybody and which imply some form of unconscious activity. The heading to this section only names some of these. Freud[26] treated them quite cursorily, and, in fact, an explanation of them along the lines found suitable for faulty actions is not really satisfactory.

We have all at some time or other had the experience of having heard or seen something and of having at the same time the distinct impression that we had already seen or heard this something before; but then, on sober reflection, we have come to the conclusion that this was simply not possible. Such experiences cannot always be dismissed as commonplace mnesic delusions and have in fact already given rise to many psychological, philosophical and epistemological speculations. In the case of *déjà vu* or *fausse reconnaissance*,[27] the outer perception must have been preceded by an inner perception, the memory image of which is so powerfully resonated by the outer image that it imposes itself as a real memory. Resonance is only possible when there is a high degree of congruence, i.e., when even the smallest details correspond. Even if the "resonance theory" is not correct, we must at any rate assume that *one* quite specific individual trait of the corresponding memory image is so powerfully stimulated by the real situation that the rest is then assimilated by confabulation of memories and in this way made to coincide. This motif is in fact a popular device in belles-lettres. We shall only quote one example, from Charles Dickens' *Pictures from Italy*.

> At sunset, when I was walking on alone, while the horses rested, I arrived upon a little scene, which, by one of those singular mental operations of which we are all conscious, seemed perfectly familiar to me, and which I see distinctly now. There was not much in it. In the blood-red light, there was a mournful sheet of water, just stirred by the evening wind; upon its margin a few trees. In the foreground was a group of silent peasant-girls leaning over the parapet of a little bridge, and looking, now up at the sky, now down into the water; in the distance, a deep bell; the shadow of approaching night on everything. If I had been murdered there, in some former life, I could not have seemed to remember the place more thoroughly, or with a more emphatic chilling of the blood; and the real remembrance of it acquired in that minute, is so strengthened by the imaginary recollection, that I hardly think I could forget it.[28]

The subjective impression here is quite incontrovertible—all the more so because, up to the present, it has never proved possible to establish to what reality the experience of the obviously preexistent inner image corresponds. As we have seen, Dickens immediately has recourse to the hypothesis of reincarnation. Far from providing an explanation along lines acceptable to Western science, this hypothesis can apparently also be applied to other phenomena with a Western ambience.

In recent years an American hypnotist has caused considerable stir because one of the subjects he used for his experiments developed a second personality who identified herself as Bridey Murphy, an Irishwoman born in Cork in 1798.[29] She spoke a language similar to that current in Ireland at that period, and mentioned quite a number of topographical details which could perfectly well have been true of that locality at that time. So far, the most rigorous and competent investigators have not been able to find either evidence of deception or immediate sources for the information which this subject gave under hypnosis. Nor, on the other hand, has it proved possible to provide conclusive evidence identifying the material produced by the subject with objective reality. Thus as often happens in such cases, the positive and negative evidence seems to be evenly balanced between the two positions. Also, of course, no single case can ever be statistically significant, since it always remains a single case, even though quite an impressive number of cases involving phenomena of this kind have already been subjected to careful investigation. On the other hand, the fact that a large number of similar elements seem to occur in all these cases is interesting from a psychological point of view. This suggests that what Jung would call an archetypal configuration has been at work. Photographic accuracy in the reproduction of historical settings is very difficult to verify, in any case, nor does it lend itself to evaluation in quantitative terms.

The phenomenon of *split personality*, which is essentially what we are dealing with here, has long been known and is not the exclusive preserve of psychopathology. Every normal person has two or more sides to his nature, and each of these aspects occupies the foreground in turn as the claims of the situation require. It is even possible to produce a *multiple* personality experimentally, as the experiments of Morton Prince have convincingly demonstrated.[30] The membranes dividing the part personalities vary widely in thickness and can even seal off their contents hermetically. If, then, there is a natural tendency in the mind to produce a number of these "compartments," it can be readily understood that, for example, *fausse reconnaissance* may be due to a leak in the dividing membrane. But the preceding inner perception may be derived from quite other sources. For example, it may come from:

1. *Subliminal perceptions*, i.e. sense perceptions which are too weak to appear in consciousness above the threshold (L. *limen* = threshold), but which are nevertheless registered somewhere in a sensory form.

2. *Dreams* which are forgotten, but specific elements of which are reactivated by a corresponding external situation and are then falsely recalled (as suggested by the above-mentioned theory), not in the form of dreams but as concrete experiences. Theoretically, this source can never be entirely excluded, for understandable reasons.

3. *Fantasies*, which have remained forgotten in the interim. The same applies to these as to dreams.

However, in the case of both these last two sources, we still have to confront a thorny problem. How is it possible for a dream or a fantasy to anticipate a situation which only appears in outer reality later on? The discussion of this problem belongs quite clearly to the realm of parapsychology.

In general, it can be said that experiences of this kind have a strong emotional coloring, or perhaps even that they actually occur in moments of extreme emotional excitement. At all events, they do tend to appear in connection with passionate love experiences, as may be seen from the following examples:

(a) Richard Wagner, *Tristan and Isolde*, III/1
    Tristan:
    I was
    Where I have been for ever,
    Where I for aye shall go:
    The boundless realm
    Of night's domain.[31]

(b) Hugo von Hofmannsthal/Richard Strauss, *Der Rosenkavalier*
    Octavian/Sophie, II/32:
    Where did I taste, of old,
    Such heavenly rapture?
    Though death await me there,
    To that fair scene I must betake me once again.

    Octavian, II, 124:
    Say, seems it not that once, in far-off days,
    In some dear magic dream,
    We loved each other thus?[32]

In all three examples the motif of death and rebirth is sounded. We have already encountered this in Dickens, and Bridey Murphy also seems to be convinced of its existence. So far as psychology is concerned, Jung has set down in summary form the essential points that can be made about it.[33] Here I should only like to recall that this motif is exceedingly ancient—that, for example, the Bodhisattva (Buddha) in the *Jātakas* recalls over 500 prenatal existences and that many others are to be found in the *Pancatantra*.[34]

There are also parallels with the well-known phenomena of spiritualistic seances, in which, it is maintained, verbal contact may be made with the departed. I do not wish in any way to imply that I accept the objectivity of these phenomena; but the very fact that such conceptions exist is of psychological interest in this context.

It should not be necessary to provide examples of all the forms of mnesic delusion mentioned in our heading; yet something should be said about *automatisms* and *cryptomnesia*. We all know how obsessive certain tunes can be; we find it almost impossible to get them out of our heads, and we are under a compulsion to hum them all the time. Often this happens so unconsciously that it is necessary for someone else to draw our attention to it. If the tune is associated with a written text, it may be comparatively easy to discover the reason for the obsessive automatism of the tune. Jung has given us some convincing examples of this.[35]

1. A young colleague who had just finished his dissertation was impelled to whistle for half the day Handel's "See, the con-quering hero comes."

2. An acquaintance who was pleased with his new and lucrative position betrayed his feelings by singing the obsessive melody "Are we not born for glory?"

3. On his rounds, a colleague met a nurse who was supposed to be pregnant, and immediately afterward found himself whistl-ing: "Once there were two royal children, who loved each other so dear."

Such often highly revealing utterances of the unconscious are encouraged by a lowering in the level of attention and inhibited by purposive activity at the conscious level.

Cryptomnesia. In *fausse reconnaissance* something is interpreted as a memory which cannot in fact be a memory. In cryptomnesia, the situation is reversed: something which impresses us as a genuine spontaneous idea turns out to be a content which had in fact been consciously acquired earlier on, but which had since that time been completely forgotten and was actually not recognized as such at the moment of recall. Normally the discovery takes place by accident, through the medium of third parties, generally after the event; this is most likely to happen when we think we have had a spontaneous idea, which we proudly parade as our own intellectual property, and which subsequent investigation by others proves to have been an example of unconscious plagiarism.

Of this, too, Jung has left us an impressive example, from Nietzsche's *Zarathustra*[36]:

Nietzsche, *Thus Spake Zarathustra.*
("They say . . . that through the volcano itself the narrow path leads down to the gate of the underworld".)

Now about the time that Zarathustra sojourned on the Happy Isles, it happened that a ship anchored at the isle on which the smoking mountain stands, and the crew went ashore to shoot rabbits. About the noon-tide hour, however, when the captain and his men were together again, they suddenly saw a man coming towards them through the air, and a voice said distinctly: "It is time! It is highest time!" But when the figure drew close to them, flying past quickly like a shadow in the direction of the volcano, they recognized with the greatest dismay that it was Zarathustra . . . "Behold", said the old helmsman, "Zarathustra goes down to hell!"

Kerner, *Blätter aus Prevorst*

"An Extract of Awe-Inspiring Import from the log of the ship *Sphinx* in the year 1696, in the Mediterranean."

The four captains and a merchant, Mr. Bell, went ashore on the island of Mount Stromboli to shoot rabbits. At three o'clock they mustered the crew to go aboard, when, to their inexpressible astonishment, they saw two men flying rapidly towards them through the air. One was dressed in black, the other in grey. They came past them very closely, in the greatest haste, and to their utmost dismay descended amid the burning flames into the crater of the terrible volcano, Mount Stromboli. They recognized the pair as acquaintances from London.

Nietzsche's sister, Elisabeth Förster-Nietzsche, told me, in reply to my inquiry, that Nietzsche had taken a lively interest in Kerner when staying with his grandfather, Pastor Oehler, in Pobler, between the ages of 12 and 15, but certainly not later. It could scarcely have been Nietzsche's intention to commit a plagiarism from a ship's log; had this been the case he would surely have omitted that extremely prosaic and totally irrelevant passage about shooting rabbits. Obviously, when painting the picture of Zarathustra's descent into hell, that forgotten impression from his youth must have slipped half or wholly unconsciously into his mind.

This example shows all the peculiarities of cryptomnesia: a quite unimportant detail which only deserves to be forgotten as quickly as possible is suddenly reproduced with almost literal fidelity, while the main point of the story is, one cannot say modified, but recreated in an individual manner. Around the individual core—the idea of the journey to hell—there are deposited, as picturesque details, those old, forgotten impressions of a similar situation. The story itself is so absurd that the young Nietzsche, a voracious reader, probably skimmed through it without evincing any very profound interest in the matter. Here, then, is the required minimum of associative connections, for we can hardly conceive of a greater jump than from that stupid old tale to Nietzsche's consciousness in the year 1883. If we realize Nietzsche's state of mind at the time when he wrote *Zarathustra*, and the poetic ecstasy that at more than one point verges on the pathological, the abnormal reminiscence will appear more understandable.

If we pause for a minute and consider all these parapraxes as a whole, we shall not feel inclined to blame anyone who comes to the conclusion that such nonsense as this is simply not worth discussing seriously. Such a person will argue, and not without reason, that what we have here is simply a tendentious collection of chance incidents which is lacking in all scientific credibility; that anyone who is impressed by it is indulging in superstition; that even if the *inci*dent happens to be a serious *ac*cident, it is well within the range of statistical "normality"; that it would be absurd to believe that there is an intention or meaning underlying a statistical series of causal factors.

In the face of arguments of this kind we have really no defense, and we gladly admit that the idea that the unconscious behaves like gnomes or demons constitutes a regression from the point of view of the contemporary scientific picture of the world—but we do so subject to the minor reservation that this particular regression is quite conscious and deliberate.

And here we are confronted by an inevitable weakness in the account we have given of our case up to the present. The conviction that the unconscious plays a part in so many of our human affairs was not originally derived from the examples we have quoted, but from clinical experience of the material produced by patients. The phenomena which we observe in that context have, as it were, much larger amplitudes, and are therefore far more vividly and immediately convincing. However, they cannot be used for our present purpose, for a variety of reasons. In particular, we cannot convey in theoretical terms the experience which we have with a patient. And even if we could do this, the fact remains that there are still numerous psychiatrists among us who have the benefit of such object lessons in their daily work but for whom the unconscious remains a negligible quantity. Obviously, then, it is possible in all good faith to remain aloof from ideas such as those we are considering.

Evidence such as this constrains us to admit that the phenomenon of the human psyche can also be investigated purely from the standpoint of natural science, and that incontestable and assured results can be obtained in this way. On the other hand, the same logic should constrain the natural scientist or doctor who thinks along these lines to concede that his approach, too, only accounts for a *segment* of the total reality. But this in no way justifies the assumption that whatever is omitted, more or less intentionally, from this segment is nonexistent or even unimportant. From our own point of view we are equally entitled to stake out a claim to another segment of reality as our particular province, simply because we find it equally, or more, interesting.

While another investigator prefers chemistry and physics as the reality he proposes to study, we choose the psyche, and as a working hypothesis we are then entitled—and in fact obliged—to ascribe an equally independent reality to this field, subject always to the same proviso or limitation. With reference, then, to the purpose we set before us in this chapter, we propose to subject the concept of "chance," considered as a psychological reality, to a closer scrutiny and evaluation.

3. Chance

As we have already pointed out, the meaning and history of words can be an illuminating adjunct to psychological research. Most probably the German word *Zufall* (chance) is a translation of the Latin *casus* (lit. = "fall"; casu = "by chance"); the German prefix *zu-* corresponds (1) to the Latin *oc-* in *oc-casio* (e.g., occasio *temporis* = favorable opportunity) and (2) to L. *ac-* in *ac-cidens* (per accidens or ex accidenti = by accident, accidentally), and the latter then in German, Italian and English comes to mean an "accident" in the sense of an *unfavorable* opportunity (= "*Unfall*"). *Accido* means "happen to," "befall," and is related in meaning to the Greek σύμπτωμα (symptoma) (see p. 167). *Coincido* means "happen to fall upon," "befall" and reminds us of the meaning of "Einfall" which we stressed earlier (p. 9). But the classic Greek term for chance is no doubt τύχη (tychē).

This originally connoted the act of a god; later on it stood for an abstract cause beyond our control, and finally it became personified as the Goddess τύχη, who was invoked, for example, by those who wished to consult an oracle, and in fact in mantic practices of all kinds. At Delphi, she was actually invoked first, before all other "numina." In Rome, she became Fortuna Romana or Fortuna Panthea, and the great center of her cult was at the Roman "Delphi," i.e. Praeneste (the modern Palestrina).[37] Her prestige there is indicated by the fact that she was described as Fortuna Primigenia (πρωτογόνη), i.e., as the first-born daughter of Jupiter, and was even represented as the mother of the infant twins Juno and Jupiter (puer) himself.

And I am tempted to believe that she did manifest herself once again in the selfsame place during the Second World War, when the Americans bombed Palestrina in 1944. We can scarcely suppose that there was a conspiracy on the part of archaeologists in the Allied Air Command, but it is a fact that the area bombing cleared exactly, to the square yard, the site of the ancient sanctuary of Fortuna, opening it up to archaeological excavation. As is well-known, this oracle was dedicated to the task of ascertaining the divine will, and was thus the final authority on questions relating to the policy of the State. This conception is still quite distinctly to be found in the scholastic philosopher, Duns Scotus (1266–1308); he equates Tychē with the absolute will of God.

As we have already observed, Schopenhauer in his later period was particularly interested in the role of chance. In the passage quoted earlier, he says, "To ascribe an intention to chance is a thought which is either the height of absurdity or the depth of profundity—according to the way in which we understand it." He accordingly makes a distinction between (1) a demonstrable fatalism, which applies to blind or ordinary chance, to that which is "pure chance" and behind which no meaning is hidden, and (2) a transcendental fatalism, which is not blind but arranged or intentional. Previously, he had still defined chance quite simply as "lack of the connection which is expressed by the principle of causality."[38] This implies that chance may be divided up genealogically, as it were, into two or more causal series, which intersect one another "accidentally" at a specific point, and this is what we call the accident (cf.

symptoma!). Yet his later *Transcendental Speculations*, as is already evident from the above quotation, brought him to a distinctly more profound view of the subject. Jung dealt with this question very thoroughly, and in what he described as "synchronicity," he introduced a new way of looking at the problem; we shall be considering this later on.

At this point I should like to mention one or two additional authorities, who do not prejudice our psychological approach to the subject.

Goethe leaves the question entirely open in "Primal Words. Orphic" under τυχη, Chance:

> The rigid barrier tactfully evades
> The shifting flux of change within and round us.

Voltaire humorously complains: "His Sacred Majesty King Chance decides everything"—a saying which Frederick the Great was fond of quoting.

L.A.J. Quételet (1796–1874), the Belgian astronomer, who is regarded as the founder of modern social statistics, and who, largely on the basis of his research into the statistics of crime became convinced that he had discovered the work of a natural law which overruled the freedom of the human will, came to the following conclusion: "Le mot hasard sert officieusement à voiler notre ignorance." It would be tempting to inquire whether the quantities subsumed under Quételet's natural law do not correlate with certain aspects of the qualities of the unconscious.

Novalis makes it the responsibility of the individual to seek a deeper meaning in chance and to profit by such a meaning, or otherwise, when he writes: "All the chances of our life are materials, out of which we can make what we will; the more intelligence we possess, the more we will make out of our lives."

This saying seems to me to bear a remarkable resemblance to a saying of the poet Ion (5th Century B.C.) which is recorded by Plutarch: "Though chance is something very unlike wisdom, in their actual effects the two are very similar."[39]

Since, as we have said, from the point of view of statistics, the significance of an individual case is precisely nil, the decision as to whether we shall make much or nothing out of experiences of this kind rests entirely with our own free will as individuals, as Novalis said. But that considerations relating to a secret intention or a hidden deeper meaning or purpose in such chance events may in certain cases be exceedingly valuable to the subject has been established and confirmed by innumerable examples. Moreover, it corresponds to a consensus of the human race, which has always stood in awe of such coincidences.

Another interesting subject for research would be the kind of superstition which might be supposed to occur by way of compensation among scientists of the strictly rationalistic school, who have no place for a final or teleological approach.

Niels Bohr used to love to tell the following story. Once when he went to visit a colleague in the United States he discovered a horseshoe fixed above his front door. He was astonished and asked him ironically, "My dear colleague, you surely don't believe in this nonsense?" "Nothing of the sort," was the reply, "but I have heard it said that it works even if you don't believe in it."

A history of man's conception of the function of chance in human life has still to be written. In this context the following modes of apprehension of this function would have to be taken into account.

1. A *second will* or *alter ego* is distinguished in both animate and inanimate objects in the outside world. It is by virtue of this will that these objects can play an agreeable or disagreeable part in our lives. This conception corresponds to a kind of *animism* (Tylor) and is to be understood in purely psychological terms as a *projection* (literally a "throwing outwards") of unconscious contents onto the objects. As one form of this we may recall the proverbial notion of the *cussedness of the object*, which was portrayed with inimitable good humor by Fr. Th. Vischer in his novel *Auch Einer*.[40] The distance separating this notion from imaginary beings such as goblins and demons is really not very great. And Brownies and angels, particularly guardian angels,[41] have a similar pedigree—from a strictly psychological point of view, that is.

2. On the other hand, we find the emergence of a conception according to which chance occurrences are instruments of destiny which give us hints that enable us to recognize our own fate and to adjust our attitude accordingly. This represents a distinctly more psychological level than (1). To have a right attitude to fate is in itself a most finely attuned religious attitude. Yet a perfunctory assessment would decry it as superstition.

A typical example of this attitude is the scrupulously religious observation of omens, which is familiar to us from our knowledge of the ancient Romans. The proverbial expression *Un Romain retournerait* ("A Roman would turn back") has a psychological meaning. It implies that anyone who leaves his house intent on some specific project and then stumbles over the threshold must have inner resistances against the plan he has in mind and would be better advised to return home and sleep once more upon his project.

An example of the violation of this principle is provided by the case of C. Flaminius, who, at Lake Trasimene in the Second Punic War, fell from his horse as he was setting out for the battle and encountered a further bad omen when his standard could not be pulled out of the earth. However, C. Flaminius did not "behave like a Roman" but in the modern fashion. He launched an attack in spite of the omens, was devastatingly defeated by Hannibal and was himself slain in the battle.[42] In these cases it is already assumed that the unconscious, manifesting itself in physical signs, represents a source of superior knowledge. But when we say that the unconscious, particularly when it forms chains or series of chance occurrences, can have "fatal" effects, that is only our contemporary way of putting it. The ancient tragedians were well aware of these relationships and they portrayed in an extremely dramatic way the formation of nexus which persisted through successive generations (cf. the curse of the Atridae). The Eleatic philosophers and the Stoics turned this insight into a genuinely religious attitude, which was far removed from vulgar superstition. Seneca[43] quotes Cleanthes in this context:[44]

> O Father and Ruler of Heaven, do Thou guide me
> Where e'r Thou willest: I will gladly follow.
> Did I not so, with groans I'd *have* to follow
> And suffer as evil what I could have accepted as good.
> Fate leads the willing, drags the unwilling, man.

Jung, too, chose *Ducunt volentem Fata, nolentem trahunt* as the motto for his essay on "The Significance of the Father in the Destiny of the Individual."[45] The passage recalls Euripides:

> The man who knows how to submit to fate's decrees,
> By us is accounted wise: he knows the divine.[46]

This is also quoted by Epictetus.[47] Finally, we should do well to remember that there are certain interventions of the unconscious which we too revere as judgments of God, as the example of Schiller's ballad, "The Walk to the Forge,"[48] shows us.

3. As a final reflection which is, perhaps, in equal measure absurd and thought-provoking, I should like to add that occurrences of this kind imply that the unconscious can have effects upon the

object as well as upon the subject, even if the former should happen to be inanimate (for example, in the case of C. Flaminius's standard). At this point, however, there can be no doubt at all that we are entering the sphere of parapsychology.

To sum up, it can be said that the question as to whether a meaning is to be attributed to the intersection of two or more causal series which are not causally related to one another is, in a sense, an arbitrary matter. The criterion of meaning first arises when man becomes involved in events of this kind. But then the decision may be of fateful significance.

CHAPTER IV

THE ASSOCIATION EXPERIMENT
AS DEVELOPED BY C. G. JUNG

Our scientifically orientated contemporaries find it necessary to subject the phenomena they study to an experimental, quantitative examination. If the effects of the unconscious are to be made the subject of experiments of this kind, we shall first have to find a suitable measuring instrument for this purpose or, alternatively, we shall have to construct such an instrument. The conditions under which the experiment is held should be kept as simple as possible, so that the factors which have to be taken into account in the analysis are not too difficult to handle. They should also be reproducible at any time and by anybody, so that the greatest possible number of scientists will be able, within a brief period, to produce the largest possible number of results that are comparable and susceptible to statistical treatment.

As it happened, the association experiment which had been put forward by Wilhelm Wundt (of Leipzig, 1832–1920) to a large extent fulfilled these conditions. However, when in 1903 Jung introduced this experiment with certain modifications into psychiatric research, it was not with any intention of using it to record the manifestations of the unconscious psyche. His aim was rather to improve the accuracy of diagnosis in psychiatry by introducing a psychological test technique.

These hopes of a refinement of diagnostic technique were not, in fact, destined to be realized. Instead, the way in which the results of the experiment were evaluated changed under Jung's hand, and he began to concentrate more and more on the *disturbances* which appeared here and there during the course of the experiment. Previous investigators had regarded these lapses simply as mistakes and had ignored them, but Jung very soon recognized that they occurred with a greater degree of probability at certain favored spots in the experiment. "Spooks" of this kind in the "psychic spectrum" resembled in many ways the disturbances being reported by Freud at the same time (cf. Chap. III, 1.), and their explanation on the basis of the principles proposed by him was altogether convincing. It was this more than anything else that prejudiced Jung in favor of Freud's ideas and which led to the meeting of the two scientists and to the long friendship between them.

At this point I should like to introduce a brief excursus into the intellectual history of the period. Freud's *Interpretation of Dreams* had appeared in 1900 and his *Psychopathology of Everyday Life* in 1904; Jung's first contribution to the "Diagnostic Studies in Word Association" also appeared in 1904. In physics during these same years we find the works of J.W. Gibbs on *Elementary Principles in Statistical Mechanics* (1902), Ludwig Boltzmann's fundamental work on statistical heat mechanics, Max Planck's discovery of the quantum (1900), and Einstein's special theory of relativity (1905). The essential point about the accomplishments of these physicists was that they took the statistical description of natural laws seriously; this led Planck, for example, to conclusions which certainly shocked their originator (I am referring here to the quantum theory). Einstein, too, can be understood in the same way—i.e. he took the findings of Lorentz, Fizeau and Michelson seriously.

In the field of psychology, *at the same time*, the two outsiders Freud and Jung were engaged in a serious analysis of disturbances of the normal (i.e., of discontinuities) and in so doing enriched the "description of nature" with nothing short of a new dimension—which was quite a shock for the human race. As Fierz pertinently remarks, the theory of relativity and the quantum theory were a universal topic of conversation contemporaneously with psychoanalysis.[1] Such a striking parallelism in intellectual history can scarcely be overlooked; it puts me in mind of Goethe's "Genius of the Century," which encourages the development of the individual.

In any event, the turn of the century (plus or minus five years) can be regarded as a very special *kairos* from the point of view of the history of the natural sciences.

When in 1933, after an interval of 20 years, Jung resumed his university teaching at the Swiss Federal Institute of Technology, he held regular seminars in addition to his lectures. And the first subject he dealt with was the Association Experiment, to which he devoted an entire semester. He repeated these seminars periodically, and regarded them as a basic preparation and precondition for any further study of the psychology of the unconscious. So we realized that practical experience of the Association Experiment is exceptionally important from a didactic and educational point of view; and in fact I myself have carried on Jung's tradition right up to the present day, with great benefit to my students and myself.

Unfortunately, we still possess no systematic account of this method, so that the task of familiarizing students with it is made unnecessarily difficult.[2] I should like, then, as part of my inquiry into the empirical manifestations of the unconscious, to give a condensed account and evaluation of the association experiment; this may serve at the same time as a pocket manual for students. I propose to deal with this subject in the following order: (1) the previous history, (2) the set-up of the experiment, (3) the results of the experiment, (4) questions which remain open and (5) theoretical conclusions. This final section is designed to lead up to a general theory of complexes.

In any psychological experiment, the subject is confronted with a specific external situation, in the form of a stimulus. The effect of the stimulus is to evoke in the subject a reaction to these external conditions, and this of course constitutes the object of the experiment. The conditions represent a defined, objective constant; the reaction, on the other hand, is to a large extent uncertain and subjective. The subjective element is based in the first place on the individual way in which the complex stimulus is apprehended by the subject—or, as we say, is assimilated by him. In this sense the association experiment is a projective technique similar, for example, to the Rorschach Test. It asks the subject the question, "If it's like that outside, what is it like inside yourself?"

This correspondence between the outer and the inner world should never be confused with a relation of causal dependency, since it is, in fact, by no means rational. The complication arises from the interposition between stimulus and response of a third reality—the psyche of the subject. On an average, however, the psyche functions in a similar way in the most widely differing subjects, and this makes it possible for the results of the experiment to be evaluated statistically, especially when lengthy runs are available. From the mean values obtained in this way, we can identify and measure the statistical dispersions and from them infer, e.g., that a disturbance of the known functioning of the conscious psyche has been produced by interference with the unconscious.

1. The Previous History

We cannot estimate the significance of any new advance in knowledge unless we are aware of its historical antecedents. But this general rule has a quite specific relevance in the case of the association experiment, since the point at which Jung left the beaten track in this field in fact marks the historic parting of the ways between theoretical, abstract "academic" psychology and "psychology with a soul." We have already drawn attention to the chronological coincidence between this point and the epoch-making discoveries of Freud. But it was the accession of Jung which first provided an experimental foundation for any kind of psychoanalytical approach and which therefore represents Jung's first basic achievement on behalf of analysis of all schools. The discovery, the naming and the clinical evaluation of complexes, in association with quantitative measuring techniques, is and remains Jung's great contribution; however, this can only be convincingly demonstrated if we first briefly sketch the position of scientific psychology *before* this period.

There is no doubt at all that the problem of the human soul has been one of the great preoccupations of humankind in all historical periods; this emerges very clearly from the account given by von Siebeck in his book on the history of psychology.[3] The psyche was always seen as a living being and a phenomenon very close to reality. When they heard the word ψύχη, the Greeks also thought of a butterfly[4] (one of the oldest meanings of the word). For the same reason, they also described the soul as άίολος (iridescent or fleet-footed). Hippolytus, one of the Church Fathers (c. 165–235 A.D.) was no doubt still thinking of this connotation when he wrote: "The soul is hard to understand; in fact, it seems impossible to capture her." Yet if we are to treat an object scientifically, we *must* capture it, i.e. we must subject it to conditions which enable us to obtain results which go beyond our own purely personal opinions. In other words, we need the aid of scientific methods.

It is only too easy to forget that psychology in the strict sense of the word is an exceedingly young science; historically, until very recent times, it was simply a part of philosophy. However, it has been clearly shown, and not least by the research of Jung himself, that its real forbears are to be found in the world of alchemy, astrology, mythology and religion. This statement is not intended to establish the kind of equation between religion and psychology that was attempted, for example, by Freud.[5] What Jung unearthed was simply a most remarkable parallelism or even identity between the formal and dynamic contents of these realms, and what we ourselves, especially in the analytical situation, discover as spontaneous contents of the unconscious in our "subjects." On the basis of these findings we psychologists today feel justified in submitting them to psychological examination, without necessarily detaching them from the purview of religion, claiming them exclusively as our own or declaring them to be nothing but psychology.

Until the nineteenth century, psychology was treated more fully within the field of philosophy and Christian metaphysics and was still entirely beyond the scope of the methods of the natural sciences.

We can probably discern the earliest signs of an empirical, scientific approach to genuinely psychic phenomena in the Swabian doctor and poet Justinus Kerner (1786–1862), and particularly in his observations on his woman patient Friderike Hauffe.[6] It should also not be forgotten that the inkblot test developed by Kerner made him a genuine precursor of Rorschach.

However, the first really systematic attempt to capture the psychic dimension with the measuring techniques of natural science, and in fact of physics, was made by Gustav Theodor Fechner (1801–1887). His biography is of considerable psychological interest in its own right. He began by being a successful physicist who also had pronounced leanings toward the Philosophy of Nature. But when he was practically blinded by an eye complaint, he ceased practicing physics and gave free rein to his philosophical inclinations.

In philosophy, we should have to describe him as an objective idealist, since in his view spirit is the essential nature or "in-itself-ness" of things. Psychic life is not confined to man but is an intrinsic property of all existing things; all whole entities are animated by this principle. Fechner also developed a considerable interest in parapsychological phenomena. The titles of his books (in chronological sequence) are revealing in this respect: *The Little Book of Life after Death* (1836), *The Supreme Good* (1846), *Nanna*[7] *or the Psychic Life of Plants* (1848), *Zend Avesta,*[8] *or the Realities of Heaven and the Hereafter* (1851), *The Problem of the Soul* (1861), and *The Day View in Contrast to the Night View* (1879). But his pioneering achievement in scientific psychology was his *Elements of Psychophysics* (2 vols.), which appeared in 1860 and on the basis of which Fechner is still regarded as the father of experimental psychology.[9] It represents the first heroic attempt to penetrate to the actual reality of the psyche by the use of quantitative scientific measurement. Unfortunately, for us today it is almost unreadable.

Fechner starts from the perceptions of the senses and aims at bringing them into a quantitative relationship with the corresponding stimuli. In this he resembles the French psychology of the period, for example Condillac. In collaboration with the Leipzig anatomist and physiologist Ernst Heinrich Weber,[10] he formulated the "psycho-physical law," also known as the "Weber-Fechner Law," which was designed to provide natural scientists with a key to psychology. Expressed in simple terms, it stated that equal differences in the intensity of sensations correspond to equal relative differences between stimuli, in such a way that the intensity of a stimulus must vary in geometric proportion if the intensity of a sensation is to vary arithmetically. Fechner wrote once again about this subject in Wundt's *Philosophical Studies* (which we shall be discussing shortly) under the title "The Principles of Psychic Measurement and Weber's Law."[11]

Nowadays we understand as a matter of course that an equation of this kind cannot validly be formulated. Although it is true that the intensities of stimuli can easily be measured in terms of physics, the same does not apply to the intensities of sensation which, moreover, exhibit considerable individual variations. We have only to recall the extreme forms which may be assumed by localized hysterical anesthesias and analgesias in order to convince ourselves that these intensities cannot be objectivized. Yet Fechner's "illusion" at least had the merit that it gave other scientists the courage to undertake further experimental investigations into the psyche, which in turn eventually resulted in the replacement of physical by psychic stimuli. Strictly speaking, it is at this point that the real psychological experiment began.

But is it not possible that we have now once again lost that approach to the psyche from the standpoint of natural science which we had at last achieved? This question must probably be answered in the affirmative. From now on we observe a dichotomy. On the one hand, there is the development of a *physiological psychology*[12] in the form of an experimental science which is essentially concerned with reflexes and similar phenomena, but in which the psyche as such is given no opportunity to manifest itself. On the other hand, we see the blossoming of a purely *psychological psychology*, which does not hesitate to allow the psyche to bear witness to its own nature. Of course, there is a hidden danger here that such a science may become tautological; to obviate this danger, it proved necessary to introduce a further dichotomy—the distinction between the conscious and the unconscious psyche. This step was actually taken in the clinical sphere by Freud, and it was emphatically endorsed by Jung, who at the same time, true to his scientific attitude, introduced the experimental approach. Here Jung was able to rely on the following previous studies, which in their turn had been inspired by Fechner's initiative.

The first association experiments were made in the school of the physician, physiologist and psychologist Wundt (of Leipzig, 1832–1900[13]), the founder of the first laboratory for experimental psychology. This research owed its immediate impulse to Sir Francis Galton[14] (1822–1911), who is probably best known for the statistical distribution curve named after him. As early as 1878 he carried out experiments on himself in which he suddenly directed his attention toward a given specific impression and then recorded the idea that entered his consciousness immediately afterward, i.e., whatever involuntarily "occurred" to his mind. He was also already trying to measure the time that elapsed between the "impression" and the associated "idea"—what we call the "reaction-time."

The research of Wundt's school is to be found in the *Philosophical Studies*, twenty volumes of which were published between 1881 and 1902. The first volume contained Martin Trautscholdt's basic paper on "Experimental Researches into the Associations of Ideas." It was hoped that with the aid of this method it would be possible to find out what happened within the psyche between sensory perception and apperception (or comprehension). This was the assumption which ran through all the work produced by this school, right up to G. Cordes' "Experimental Researches on Associations" in Vol. XVII (1901).

Rather later, the psychiatrist Emil Kraepelin (of Munich; 1856–1926), who was a pupil of Wundt, introduced the psychological experiment into psychiatry ("The Psychological Experiment in Psychiatry" in Volume I of *Psychological Papers*, 1896). In Vols. I, II, and IV of the same series (1896, 1899 and 1904) some voluminous papers by his pupil Gustav Aschaffenburg appeared. These were specially concerned with the correlation between the formal factor (the stimulus-word) and the association (i.e., the reaction). It was hoped in this way to gain an insight into the succession of ideas within the psyche. The "Classification of Associations" prepared with this end in view is the most interesting item in the comprehensive, prize-winning paper on L'Association des Idées

(Paris, 1903) by Édouard Claparède[15] (Geneva; 1873–1940). In the same year (1903) Jung began his research at the University Clinic in Zurich (the Burghölzli); these were later collected into two volumes and published under the title of *Diagnostic Studies in Word Association.*[16]

2. The Set-up of the Experiment

When we are carrying out the association experiment as developed by C. G. Jung, we need to keep quite pedantically to the regulations, so that results can be obtained which are comparable with those obtained by other experimenters. All types of experiment, whether psychological or not, in fact demand this kind of discipline. Deviations made necessary by special questions not included in the normal list will be discussed later, for example in the section on the so-called experiment for the psychological diagnosis of evidence.

Since we do not deal with associations in the narrower sense, but with the final link in a complicated aggregate of series of associations, we replace the term "association" by the more accurate term "reaction" from now on. However, we retain *"association* experiment" as a title, since this is a time-honored technical usage.

(a) The Setting

For the purpose of carrying out the experiment we will require a room—not too large—where the experimenter and the subject can remain undisturbed and without fear of interruption for approximately one hour. It should contain two chairs and a table—not too wide—at which the experimenter and the subject can sit comfortably facing each other.

(b) Equipment

The experimenter will equip himself with a list of stimulus-words of the 1908 type, which we reproduce below, a pen or pencil and a 1/5-second stopwatch. He will hold the stopwatch in one hand and his pen or pencil in the other.

(c) The Instruction

The subject is now instructed by the experimenter as follows: "I shall call out to you the one hundred words in this list, separately, one after the other, and it is your job to reply to each word as soon as you can with the first word that comes into your mind. Where possible, you should reply with *one* word only, and I shall measure

List of stimulus words (1908 type)

subject: _____ age: _____ sex: _____

experimenter:_____ age: _____ sex: _____

Date:_____

1. head	35. mountain	69. part
2. green	36. to die	70. old
3. water	37. salt	71. flower
4. to sing	38. new	72. to beat
5. death	39. custom	73. box
6. lung	40. to pray	74. wild
7. ship	41. money	75. family
8. to pay	42. stupid	76. to wash
9. window	43. exercise-book	77. cow
10. friendly	44. to despise	78. strange
11. table	45. finger	79. happiness
12. to ask	46. expensive	80. to lie (tell untruth)
13. village	47. bird	81. deportment
14. cold	48. to fall	82. narrow
15. stem	49. book	83. brother
16. dance	50. unjust	84. to fear
17. lake	51. frog	85. stork
18. sick	52. to part	86. false
19. pride	53. hunger	87. anxiety
20. to cook	54. white	88. to kiss
21. ink	55. child	89. bride
22. angry	56. to pay attention	90. pure
23. needle	57. pencil	91. door
24. to swim	58. sad	92. to choose
25. journey	59. plum	93. hay
26. blue	60. to marry	94. contented
27. lamp	61. house	95. ridicule
28. to sin	62. dear (loved)	96. to sleep
29. bread	63. glass	97. month
30. rich	64. to quarrel	98. pretty
31. tree	65. fur	99. woman
32. prick	66. big	100. to abuse
33. pity	67. carrot	
34. yellow	68. to paint	

the time you take till you pronounce your reply." This completes the instruction, but the experimenter will make sure that it has, in fact, been correctly understood.

(d) The Experiment

The experimenter will now read the stimulus words clearly and distinctly, one after the other, in an audible but not unduly loud voice. As he pronounces the first accented vowel of the stimulus-word, he will simultaneously release his stopwatch. He will stop it again the moment the subject pronounces the first sound of his reaction, i.e., of his reply. We then note down after the stimulus-word the time that has elapsed between the utterance of the first accented vowel of the stimulus-word and the initial utterance of the subject's reply; this time will be measured in fifths of a second. Thus if, for example, the reaction-time is 2 seconds, we write the figure "10" in the space provided. After this reaction-time, we note down the reaction, i.e., the full text of the subject's reply.

After we have taken down 100 reactions in this way, we give the subject a further instruction. We tell him that we are now going to repeat the experiment in order to find out whether the subject still remembers his reactions. It is important that we should make it clear to him that on this occasion there will be no measurement of the time-interval, so that the subject can allow himself as much time as he likes to recall his original reactions.

This part of the experiment is known as the *reproduction experiment*. We record a correct reproduction on the scheme of stimulus-words which we have in front of us by entering a plus sign after the reaction, or a minus sign in case of failure to recollect. Where there is a wrong reproduction, we enter this new wrong reply in the appropriate column. The association experiment in the narrower sense has now been completed. For our purposes, however, it is necessary to add to the more technical part of the experiment another, more psychological part, which we call:

(e) The Discussion

The discussion begins with the experimenter asking the subject if, during the course of the experiment, he has been conscious of any kind of disturbance or difficulty in uttering the desired or immediate reply, or if he knows at what places in the experiment (i.e. at which stimulus-words) he has experienced inhibitions in replying spontaneously and quickly, just as the answer had come into his mind.

In a number of cases, the experimenter will receive the reply that at one point or another in the experiment the subject has in fact been conscious that disturbances or difficulties of this kind have arisen. Where this is the case, the subject should be in a position to describe to us the process which has occurred, and in certain circumstances even to provide explanations for the delay or complication. These explanations should also be recorded in another, adjoining column, after the relevant stimulus-word and the relevant reaction. If there is no room for this, a special sheet should be attached for this purpose to the scheme of stimulus-words, so that explanations of this kind, which are sometimes very circumstantial, can be noted down under the number of the stimulus-word concerned.

We shall in any case find disturbances which did *not* attract the attention of the subject, i.e., which did not enter his conscious mind, and we shall therefore be able to draw a distinction between *conscious* and *unconscious* disturbances. As we shall see, these disturbances can be traced back to the influence of complexes, and in fact there is now a recognized technical term which covers the distinction between these two types of disturbance: we speak of conscious and unconscious complexes.

At this point, the subject can be dismissed. The remaining work is the responsibility of the experimenter.

(f) Evaluating the Results

Experience has taught us that the most important criterion for assessing the results of our experiment is provided by the reaction-time. On the basis of thousands of experiments, Jung and his predecessors came to the conclusion that the average normal reaction time for educated men was 6 to 7 fifths of a second, and for educated women 8 to 9 fifths of a second. If we form an arithmetical mean out of the 100 stimulus-words of our experiment, we shall simply obtain a criterion that will enable us to determine whether the subject falls within this normal average or not. This would not tell us a great deal. On the other hand, our measurement of time does provide us with a very sensitive instrument, and we are therefore bound to try in every case to find a mean that applies to our particular subject.

Our measurement of time, however, is not sensitive enough for this purpose if we simply use the *arithmetical mean* of the reaction-times of a given experiment because in every experiment certain reactions with extremely prolonged reaction-times are obtained. As a result, the arithmetical mean will be appreciably raised, so that it is no longer possible by the use of this method to recognize the true nature of less severely disturbed reactions. Jung therefore decided to replace the arithmetical mean by the so-called *probable mean* introduced by Kraepelin. The probable mean is obtained as follows:

We construct a series consisting of all the reaction-times recorded in the first half of our experiment, i.e., of reaction-times 1 through 50. We obtain this by beginning with the shortest reaction-time and including all subsequent reaction-times up to the 26th, since the mean must lie between the 25th and the 26th reaction-time. We now have the probable mean of the first half of our experiment. We repeat this process with reactions 51 to 100, and so obtain the probable mean for the second half of the experiment.

In this way the extremely prolonged reaction-times are eliminated from the field, since they occur in the second half of the series and this second half is no longer taken into consideration. We thus obtain a decidedly more sensitive criterion for the evaluation of prolonged reaction-times, since extremely prolonged reaction-times would raise the average in an unwarrantable manner. The probable mean for the first and second halves of the experiment were calculated separately for two reasons. (1) An increase in sensitivity occurs in every subject during the experiment (the so-called "complex sensitization"), so that in every experiment the reaction-time tends to increase between reactions 1 and 100. (2) The second half of our list contains a larger number of stimulus-words that are calculated to elicit complex disturbances and so to raise the probable mean. We regard any increase in the reaction-time by 2 fifths of a second or more as symptomatic of a difficulty which must have disturbed the normal course of the process that links stimulus and reaction.

As he grew in experience, Jung became aware of a whole series of other signs which could only be understood as disturbances. Furthermore, research into the nature of these disturbed reactions made it clear that the disturbances themselves could only be understood as the effects of an already existing complex; more about this will be said later on. All the criteria we have mentioned were grouped together under the heading of *complex indicators*. They are:

1. *Prolonged reaction-time.* Any reaction-time that is 2 or more fifths of a second above the probable mean.
2. *Incorrect reproduction.*
3. *Perseveration.* This includes all echoes of the emotion produced by the stimulus-word which continue to manifest

themselves in the next reaction, either because they produce a prolonged reaction-time or because the reaction itself relates to the preceding stimulus-word. Thus perseveration can make itself felt either in the reaction-time or in the reaction or in both.

4. *Failures.* We use this term when the subject is unable to produce any verbal reaction at all to the stimulus-word. What we have in this case is a kind of "micro" effect similar in nature to emotional stupor. We record a "failure" when we have waited for 200 fifths of a second without receiving any verbal reaction. Experience has shown that a longer period of waiting offers no prospect of obtaining a reaction after all; the most that happens is that the situation may become still more unpleasant, in fact positively creepy.

5. *Repetition of the stimulus-word.* Often the subject will repeat the stimulus-word to himself before he is able to formulate a reply. It is now known that this is a way in which the subject gains time when a spontaneous reaction has been inhibited.

6. *Mis-hearing or not understanding the stimulus-word.* This form of disturbance can perfectly well be understood as a "faulty action" (see Chap. III).

7. *Mimic or pantomime gestures as accompaniments of the reaction.* This type of disturbance can also be interpreted in terms of the symptomatic actions which we discussed earlier.

8. *Interjection and exclamation.* These disturbances can be understood along the same lines as (5) and (7) above. They represent a kind of warning signal which the subject gives himself.

9. *Stuttering* and

10. *Slips of the tongue.* Both of these disturbances should be understood along the lines of the mechanisms discussed in Chap. III/1.

11. *Meaningless reactions.* In the vast majority of cases there is a connection between the meaning of the stimulus-word and the reaction. Where this connection is lacking, it can be assumed that we are dealing with a defensive reaction, i.e., that there is some reason which prevents the subject from assimilating the meaning of the stimulus-word.

12. *Sound reactions.* Sound reactions arise in the same kind of way as meaningless reactions (11). The subject does not attempt to consider the meaning of the stimulus-word, but

simply takes in its phonetic content and immediately replies with a similar phonetic reaction. They should therefore be interpreted along the same lines as (11). Reactions that rhyme with or complete the stimulus-word can also be classified under this heading.

13. *"Mediate" reactions.* In these cases we have to assume that the immediate reaction is replaced by a "mediate" reaction. Such suppressions of the immediate reaction should be understood in the same way as the disturbances which we have described above as defensive reactions.

14. *Reactions that take the form of several words or of whole sentences.* Such reactions show clearly that the subject was unable to comply with the instruction given at the beginning. This unnecessary garrulousness and verbosity should be interpreted as a sign of a certain disingenuousness in regard to the reply, i.e., the reaction.

15. *Reactions in foreign languages.* It can be assumed that switching over into a foreign language (i.e., a *translation*) does *not* represent an *immediate answer*, so that we are justified in positing a disturbing factor.

16. *Stereotypies.* By this we understand reactions which take the form of a repetition of the same reply at different places in the course of the experiment. This often means that the subject reacts with a word which lies ready to hand, with a view to covering up the immediate reaction, which might perhaps have appeared suspicious.

17. *Deflections which exceed the probable mean in the psychogalvanic experiment.* More will be said about this shortly.

18. *Sharp contraction in the respiratory excursions of the thorax,* recorded when the pneumograph is employed.

Items (17) and (18) are among the physical accompaniments of complex excitation, which will be dealt with later.

This list of complex indicators provides us with a number of additional criteria for evaluating the experiment. We therefore enter the number of complex indicators per reaction in another column, after Reproduction.

In assessing the results of the experiment, we regard the whole exercise as a kind of dialogue between the experimenter and the subject. The stimulus-words represent questions put by the experimenter to the subject, and the reactions represent the subject's replies. This conversation is carried on in a decidedly telegraphic style, which in many places calls for a certain amount of amplification. However brief the stimulus-words may be, from the psychological point of view they are exceedingly rich in possible meanings. And clearly the same must apply with even greater force to the reactions.

Some insight into the kind of amplification that is needed has already been given to us in the discussion, i.e., in the explanations provided by the subject himself regarding the disturbances he has noticed. However, this only holds good in relation to conscious complexes. Where unconscious complexes or disturbances are concerned, we are obliged to rely on our own capacity for psychological combination and on our own intuition. If we wish to throw light on these disturbances, we should be well advised to group all the disturbed reactions together, including incorrect reproductions, and to try to combine them in such a way that a kind of short story can be constructed out of these isolated words.

This is, in our view, an altogether appropriate procedure, since as experience shows, in the vast majority of cases stimulus-word and reaction stand in a specific relationship to one another, which we may compare, for example, with the relationship between the component parts of a sentence. Thus the stimulus-word may be the subject and the reaction the predicate or object. If we do possess the happy knack of combination, we shall be able, in most cases of disturbed reaction, to detect a relationship between the initial stimulus-word and possible incorrect reproductions of it. This is feasible because, as we shall see, even if quite a number of complexes are provoked by the experiment and give rise to disturbances, we know that even the most diverse complexes still stand in an inner relationship to one another. They form groups which, if we understand them individually, will illuminate *one* aspect of the subject's problems, while in their total impact they bring within our range a far deeper knowledge and a far wider grasp of the subject's situation as a whole.

Another well-tried and practical aid to understanding is the construction of a graph showing the movement of the reaction-time during the 100 reactions recorded in the test; for this purpose the reaction-time is marked out along the ordinate. We then record the probable mean in the form of a horizontal line, and we do this for the first and second halves of the test, (i.e., for the first 50 and the second 50 reactions separately), as we have already explained. This graph enables us to determine without difficulty which reactions were prolonged, while at the same time it gives us a vivid picture of the *emotional state* of the subject.

For example, if the curve is comparatively smooth and close to the probable mean, we may assume that the subject was able to encounter the experimental situation in a calm frame of mind. On the other hand, where there are violent oscillations and wide amplitudes, the curve is very much more disturbed—and this again may be assumed to reflect the emotional situation of the subject.

Another advantage of such a graphic representation of the reaction-time is that it enables us to immediately detect the presence of *serial disturbances*. When a disturbance caused by a reaction with a markedly prolonged reaction-time is carried over to subsequent reactions, i.e., to n plus 1 plus 2 plus 3 and possibly even further, we can easily read this from the graph. Such reactions are of two kinds: (1) ones that exhibit a decreasing reaction-time, i.e., in which the disturbing influence gradually fades away, at least as far as its effect on the reaction-time is concerned, and (2) ones in which the reaction-time starts to increase over the next few reactions, i.e., n plus 1 plus 2 plus 3, etc. From this latter the inference would be that the emotional coloration of the critical reaction grows in intensity during the subsequent course of the experiment until finally stimulus-word 4 or 5 succeeds in breaking through this emotional reverberation and the subject once again becomes capable of reacting in normal reaction-time.

(g) Examples

A few examples may serve as concrete illustrations of what we have been describing in theoretical terms.

Example 1:

We obtain the probable mean of the reaction-times for this series of 10 reactions by Kraepelin's method, as follows. We note down all the reaction-times in arithmetical succession, beginning with the shortest, and we thus obtain the following sequence for our first example: 5,6,6,7,7/ 7,8,8,10,15. The probable mean is to be found in the middle of a series, i.e., in our series of 10 reactions it comes between the 5th and the 6th reaction-time, so that in this case the probable mean = 7(i.e., 7/5 seconds). The probable mean plus 2 (tolerance) = 9, so that all reaction-times of 9 or above in this series are definitely to be regarded as prolonged and can be assumed to be complex indicators.

In reaction 2 a disturbance appears which is marked by repetition of the stimulus-word (1), extremely prolonged reaction-time (15/5 seconds) and failure to reproduce the initial reaction (−), i.e. by 3 complex indicators. An additional fourth complex indicator is provided by the perseveration of this disturbance to cover the ensuing reaction 3, which, though verbally not suspect (read—book), nevertheless exhibits prolonged reaction-time (10/5 seconds) and failure

I	II	III	IV	V	VI	VII	VIII
No.	Stimulus-word	Reaction-time	Reaction	Repro-duction	Complex indicators	Galvanometer deflection[a]	Dis-cussion
1	green	5	grass	+	0		Did not take place in this experiment
2	knife| b	15	sharp	– c	4		
3	read	10	book	–	2		
4	bench	7	chair	+	0		
5	round	6	circle	+	0		
6	window	6	glass	+	0		
7	paint	7	color	+	0		
8	cat	8	miaows	+	0		
9	blue	7	lake	+	0		
10	iron	8	hard	+	0		

aSee pp. 137ff.

bThe vertical line behind the stimulus-word is the conventional sign which denotes that the subject repeated the stimulus-word before reacting (repetition of stimulus-word as defined in complex indicator 5).

c – means that there is no memory of the original reaction at all, and therefore no incorrect memory either. If there is such an incorrect memory, this is entered in words in col. V.

to reproduce the reaction, i.e. 2 complex indicators. At this point the serial disturbance ceases to operate and the experiment continues normally.

The following examples are derived from Jung's early period, but were consistently repeated in his seminars at the Swiss Federal Institute of Technology. I quote them here from the original manuscripts and tables confided to my keeping by Jung himself; they still reveal the author's original delight in his discoveries.

Example 2:

A lawyer, roughly 70 years of age, of a critical frame of mind, could not believe in Jung's results and wanted to put him to the proof. After only 15 reactions he became impatient and told Jung, "You see, you're producing no results—just as I thought!" The experiment was therefore broken off. However, 5 of the 15 reactions were disturbed (though Jung had not mentioned the complex indicators). They were as follows:

(a) Money—little   (d) Heart—to prick
(b) Death—to die   (e) To pay—la semeuse
(c) To kiss—beautiful

Jung felt challenged, so he risked some bold conjectures. "I can already tell you something," he said. "(1) You have financial problems [(a)]. (2) You are thinking about dying of heart failure, because you sometimes feel a stitch in the cardiac region [(b) plus (d)], and (3) with this you associate beautiful memories of a French love affair long ago" [(c) plus (e)]. The lawyer banged his fist on the table and shouted "This is the work of the Devil!" Then he ran into the next room and told his wife, "The experiment is marvelous! You must try it too—or rather, no—better not." Jung's reasoning in (1) and (2) is obvious, but on (3) a word or explanation is required. "La semeuse" ("the sower") was the classical figure of a woman sower which appeared on the reverse side of the French coinage of the period.

Example 3:

This is the case of a subject who was employed by Jung and Riklin for the purpose of computing averages. This means that the result reported was no more than a kind of by-product of the experiment. To begin with, we shall reproduce the series of 21 reactions which reveal disturbances and which led Jung to adopt a certain interpretation. We only know the stimulus-words, the reaction-times and the reproductions (+ or −); we do not know the reactions themselves. However, this is enough to provide us with information in regard to the number of complex indicators per reaction.

Subject: 32 years old   Experimenter: Jung

No.		Stimulus-word	Reaction-time	Complex indicators	Repro-duction
1		water	4	0	+
2		round	4	0	+
3		chair	5	0	+
4		to swim	6	0	+
5		grass	5	0	+
6		blue	7	0	+
7		knife	20	3	−
8	1st	to help	15	3	−
9	serial	weight	10	2	−
10	disturbance	ready	8	0	+
11		mountain	6	1	−
12		to fly	5	0	+
13		lance	12	2	−
14		easy	6	0	+
15		house	5	0	+
16		to hit	9	2	−
17	2nd	tree	10	1	+
18	serial	pointed	15	2	−
19	disturbance	bottle	18	3	−
20		to go	10	1	+
21		town	6	0	+

Probable mean = 7

In this case we can observe the emergence of two serial disturbances, which can be seen very clearly in the graph (Fig. 1). The first
begins with stimulus-word 7 (knife) and does not completely fade
away until stimulus-word 12. The second begins with stimulus-word
16 and does not fade away until stimulus-word 21. The first serial
perseveration belongs to the type described above which has a
decreasing reaction-time, whereas the second is of the type which
has an increasing reaction-time. In other respects this experiment was
quiet and very steady. Jung therefore concluded that the two excep-
tions must relate to something unusual, to disturbances triggered off

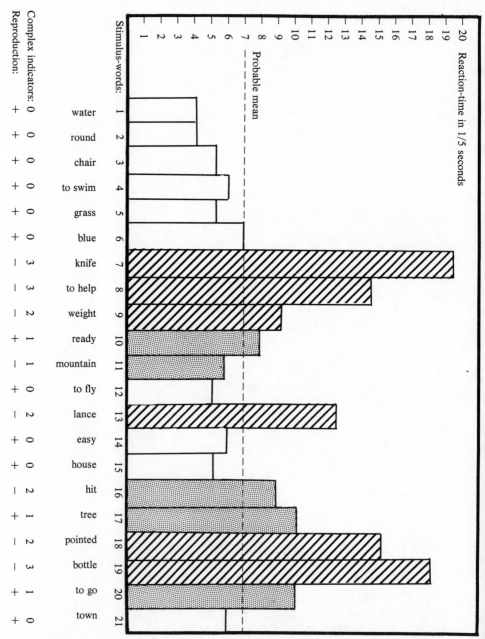

FIGURE 1. *The height of a column represents the reaction-time. The probable mean is 7/5th seconds, i.e. prolonged reaction-time starts at 9 (7 + 2 tolerance) seconds. Dotted columns represent reactions with 1 complex-indicator; striped columns represent reactions with prolonged reaction-time + 1 − 2 further complex indicators.*

by what we know as "critical stimulus-words," and that the persistence of the disturbance over 5 units in each case seemed to point to a very deep-seated and therefore probably unconscious content.

During the discussion it was particularly noticeable that the subject had not been conscious of difficulties at all while the experiment was in progress. Jung therefore adopted the procedure which we described above; he extracted the critical stimulus-words and complex indicators from the list and "built on them a great big house," i.e., he interpreted all these "statements in evidence" as parts of a coherent story and asked the subject "Weren't you once in the past involved in a stabbing incident, with unpleasant consequences?" The man immediately admitted that about 10 years before, when he was abroad, he had severely wounded another man in a quarrel and as a result had been sentenced to prison with hard labor. He had succeeded in repressing the affair completely, and it was this suggestion of Jung's which had recalled it to his mind for the first time. Nothing had been further from his thoughts during the experiment, in fact, and this confirmed Jung's view that it was a case of disturbance caused by an unconscious complex.

Example 4:

This was one of Jung's clinical cases, which I demonstrated, with his consent, at the German Psychiatric Congress at Munich in 1937, so that this time I can follow my own description of the case.[17]

The patient was a woman (32) who had been admitted to the hospital suffering from schizophrenic depression. The case history was meager and only revealed that the depression had started after the death of her 4-year-old daughter. The clinical diagnosis already given appeared to Jung to be questionable, and as no other information was available he had recourse to the association experiment. The graph in Fig. 2 reproduces the first 50 reactions and a group of 5 reactions from the second half of the experiment which followed consecutively after the first group. The probable mean was 12/5 seconds, which in itself is high; as was already known at the time, however, this is characteristic of depressive states.[18]

The scheme of stimulus-words is the one normally used at that time; it has now been discontinued. Stimulus-words are only given where there are critical reactions; the reactions themselves are not listed. Along the ordinate, reaction-times are marked out in fifths of a second; in the columns showing the lengths of the reactions a number of other complex indicators are represented by shading and hatching (see the key). The critical stimulus-words (i.e. those that touched off the disturbances) were as follows: 5 (angel), 14 (defiant), 22 (bad), 26 (blue) (persevering until 28), 30 (rich) (persevering till

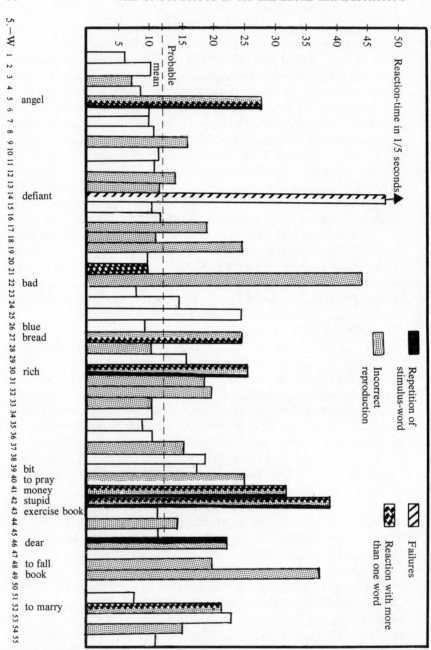

FIGURE 2: *See Example 4 (pp. 85, 87–88).*

33), 39 (habit) (persevering till 42), 41 (money), 46 (dear), 48 (to fall), 49 (book) and 52 (to marry) (persevering till 54).

The discussion revealed that the patient had not noticed any disturbances. However, the *interrogation* relating to the *critical* stimulus-words gradually yielded the following vital additional information. The subject had been in love with a very rich man (stimulus-word 30). She had finally given him up owing to the great difference in social class and had then systematically dismissed him from her mind (stimulus-word 14). Shortly afterward she had married another man, equally well-endowed with worldly goods but not so dearly loved (stimulus-word 52). She lived with him abroad and already had two children by him when she was visited by an acquaintance who told her that her first love had been badly hit when she broke with him.

Two weeks later she was bathing her children. In the town where she lived there was *eau potable* for drinking and *eau non potable* for bathing etc. She had always taken great care to see that the children did not drink any bathwater. But this time she allowed her favorite child to suck the sponge (stimulus-word 22). When her younger child also appeared in the bathroom, she gave him too some *eau non potable* to drink. The result was that her favorite child caught typhoid fever and died (stimulus-word 5). She had beautiful blue eyes, like the patient's former lover. The interrogation had also brought to light the following explanatory remarks. The patient's reaction to stimulus-word "habit" (39) had been "bad habit." She had really wanted to say "immoral," but now she was thinking of "bad" in this connection. Stimulus-word 41 (money) reminds her of her former lover, and stimulus-word 46 (dear) of the favorite child she had lost. Stimulus-word 48 (to fall) was related in her mind to her erotic fantasies about her first lover.

Yet she was still unaware of any kind of inner connection between these elements. Jung, on the other hand, understood this information to mean that after the patient had learned from her visitor about her first man friend's great love for her, she had unconsciously attempted to get rid of the children as a way of negating her present marriage. It was clear, then, that this was a case of unconscious attempted murder. Jung found himself confronted with a terrible conflict. He knew that the patient would only recover if she were made conscious of the connection between her reactions and the death of her child, and if she could then in reality accept this guilt and take it upon her own conscience.

On the other hand, it was of course necessary to calculate the possibilities of the shock which might be caused by such a revelation. Since apart from this cathartic trauma the prognosis remained extremely poor, Jung decided to undertake the critical intervention. So he told the patient the conclusions he had drawn from the experiment. She immediately collapsed, but in less than three weeks she had recovered completely and could be discharged from the clinic. Jung was able to follow her subsequent history for over 25 years, and it is a fact that she remained healthy throughout this period and never suffered a relapse.

It should be clear from Examples 1 through 4 that the association experiment is what the pharmacologists would call a highly unpredictable remedy. It can elicit unsuspected specific effects, the danger of which should not be underestimated. In fact, no one should make use of this instrument who does not have a thorough knowledge of the dynamics of the psyche, preferably acquired through experience in medical psychiatry. Any use of it by people who lack these qualifications can only be irresponsible.

It should also be apparent from Examples 2, 3 and 4 that the experiment can be used to bring to light either repressed—i.e., willfully forgotten—contents of the psyche, or carefully guarded secrets. As a result of experiences of this kind, Jung, in conjunction with Wertheimer and Klein, and Hanns and A. Gross, conceived the idea of modifying the experiment so that it could be used to provide a basis for conclusions about the guilt or innocence of people accused of offenses against the law. We describe this modified version of the association experiment below.

3. The Evidence-Experiment

Lucian tells us about a psychological experiment which the physician Erasistratos made 22 centuries ago:[19]

I believe this was the same Stratonice whose stepson fell in love with her; this was brought to light by the sagacity of a physician. When her stepson was smitten by this unlucky passion, which he himself regarded as shameful, he was inconsolable and fell a victim to a protracted disease. He suffered no pain, but his color changed completely and his body visibly wasted away. The doctor could not find in him any symptoms of a physical complaint, but recognized that his illness was love. There were in fact several indications of a secret passion—the wan eyes, the weak voice, the pallor and the surreptitious tears. He noted these signs and set to work accordingly. He placed his right hand over the young man's heart and then asked everyone in the house to come and pass through the room in turn. So one after the other they entered the bed-chamber, and the sick man remained entirely unmoved. But when his stepmother appeared, he changed color, broke out into a sweat, and trembled all over; at the same time, his heart pounded like mad. When he saw these symptoms, the doctor knew beyond all doubt that it was love; and he healed his patient as follows . . .

We return to this story later when we consider the physical accompaniments of the effects of complexes. The point we wish to stress here is simply that Erasistratos was able, by devising an "association experiment" in which the role of the list of stimulus-words was played by the line of persons parading through the room, to discover the object of his patient's love-complex and so to reveal his most carefully guarded secret. The therapy was then equally clearly indicated.[20]

There is a suggestion here that in the association experiment we are no longer looking for unknown complexes but assume that they are known, use them as stimuli, and then find out how the subject reacts to them. In this way, the original formulation of the question in the association experiment is simply inverted. An ancient but ever popular prototype for this phenomenon is provided by the Cranes of Ibycus (the βύχου γερανοι of Suidas), a legend which is familiar to us from Schiller's ballad of that name (1797).[21] Whereas in the association experiment we aim at results not premeditated by ourselves, in the evidence-experiment the experimenter *postulates* a real set of circumstances, and then extracts the essence of this in the form of individual stimulus-words, which are taken from and specific to it. He aims in fact at a particular topic which will only be known to the person who is intimately familiar with the real set of circumstances.

It is true that when this method is applied forensically to legal cases certain difficulties will be encountered. This is because as a rule the accused will have been accurately informed about these details at the preliminary investigation, so that stimulus-words which relate to the particular set of circumstances involved will have complex-like effects on the suspect as well as on the guilty party. On the other hand, the following example, once again derived from Jung's early period, should make it clear that in certain circumstances it may be possible to identify the most suspicious person among a number of suspects. This case has previously been published only in English,[22] and it is reported here because it contains some new criteria which are of general interest from a theoretical standpoint.

There had been a minor case of theft at the Burghölzli, and suspicion had fallen on three nurses, A, B and C. In view of her general behavior, it seemed to Jung that B was the most likely of the three suspects to be the guilty party. He proceeded to put each of the three nurses through the evidence-experiment, which he arranged as follows. He inserted into the normal list of stimulus-words 24 words taken from the particular circumstances of the case. In addition, he inserted 12 stimulus-words which, though not specific to the circumstances of this particular case, would be calculated to produce emotional reactions in a person suspected of any offense (e.g., theft, police, to arrest, court, suspicion, etc.).

Both groups were described as "critical stimulus-words," but in the case of the second it can be assumed that these words would have a complex-like effect even on an innocent person. Jung maintained, however, that the disturbances aroused by them would be quantitatively less severe in a person who was falsely suspected than in the guilty party—a statement which, it is true, still really requires verification on the basis of a larger sample of cases. The "critical stimulus-words" were distributed over the list in such a way that each one was followed by at least two "neutral stimulus-words."

An evaluation in purely qualitative terms yielded no indications that would have made it possible to reach a decision in regard to the question of guilt. Jung expressly emphasized the point that a most careful calculation of the results of the experiment must be carried out in every case. The importance of this requirement emerges with unusual clarity from the case which Jung described in "The Psychological Diagnosis of Evidence."[23] I shall now summarize in tabular form the results of the computations relating to the three suspects we have just been considering (see the table on p. 91).

The first result which strikes us is that in contrast to B and C, A exhibits a series of maxima (A 3,5,6,8,9 (min.), 14,15,16,17,19, and 21) which suggest a specific psychological interpretation.

The critical stimulus-words produce the strongest effect on A; this also comes out in the great difference between A2 and A3 (A5). The effect is very rapidly reduced, as is apparent from the maximum in A6. Moreover, this subject has a maximum of disturbances in reproduction (A7), another effect which is speedily and thoroughly reduced to a minimum (at A11). On the other hand, the disturbance reaches a maximum in serial reactions (A8), which makes this result particularly significant. Again, among the disturbances in reproduction themselves, the maximum is to be found in A's reactions to critical stimulus-words (A10) and is also quite appreciably higher than the expected number (A16). In the post-critical reactions,

		Subjects		
Reaction-time	No.	A	B	C
Probable mean of all reactions	1	10	12	13
Probable mean of reactions to neutral stimulus-words	2	10	11	12
Probable mean of reactions to critical stimulus-words	3	*16*	13	15
Probable mean of reactions to post-critical stimulus-words	4	10	11	13
Difference in probable mean between reaction-times for neutral and critical stimulus-words	5	*6*	2	3
Difference in probable mean between reaction-times for critical and post-critical stimulus-words	6	*6*	2	2
Reproduction				
Incorrect reproductions (total)	7	*34*	28	30
Incorrect reproductions in series ('%)	8	*65*	55	30
Incorrect reproductions (neutral stimulus-words)	9	10	12	11
Incorrect reproductions (critical stimulus-words)	10	*19*	9	12
Incorrect reproductions (post-critical stimulus-words)	11	*5*	7	7
Incorrect reproductions to be expected[a] (neutral stimulus-words)	12	11.2	9.2	9.9
Incorrect reproductions to be expected[a]	13	12.5	10.3	11.1
Incorrect reproductions to be expected[a] (post-critical stimulus-words)	14	10.2	8.4	9.0
Difference between expected and actual no. of incorrect reproductions				
(1) for neutral stimulus-words	15	−1.2	+2.8	+1.1
(2) for critical stimulus-words	16	+6.5	−1.3	+0.9
(3) for post-critical stimulus-words	17	−5.2	−1.4	−2.0

continued

Complex-indicators				
Complex indicators/reactions to neutral stimulus-words	18	0.6	0.9	0.8
Complex indicators/reactions to critical stimulus-words	19	*1.3*	0.9	1.2
Complex indicators/reactions to post-critical stimulus-words	20	*0.6*	1.0	0.8
Difference in complex indicators/ reactions between neutral and critical stimulus-words	21	*0.7*	0	0.4

[a]Theoretically, this figure is calculated on the supposition that disturbed reproductions are distributed evenly over *all* reactions. Its purpose is to make it possible to establish in quantitative terms the preponderance of disturbances in reproduction in any one of the groups (neutral, critical or post-critical), independently of the size of the groups.

however, there is another very rapid return to normal and in fact to a figure *above* the norm (-5.2 at A17). Here too, then, there is a masterly recovery of control after the shock of the critical stimulus-words, an effect which we have already observed at A6 and A11. We find the same phenomenon in the figure expressing the proportion of complex-indicators per reaction, which, after recording a maximum for the initial stimulus-words (A19), falls to a minimum in relation to the post-critical stimulus-words (A20); this points in the same direction as the maximum attained by the difference between A18 and A19 (A21).

To sum up, the results indicate that A has the longest reaction-time to critical stimulus-words, but shows surprisingly few perseverations; i.e., she is able to "pull herself together," which she probably only succeeds in doing because she realizes that everything depends on it. However, this conscious tendency is frustrated by the unconscious, since perseveration seeps through from a deeper level, in the form of *serial disturbances in reproduction*. In other words, the subject becomes increasingly forgetful. Forgetfulness is a sign of heightened emotion; that is why emotional people "tell lies" so easily. In this case, the emotional excitement, coupled with the other indications, make A, not B, the most likely subject, contrary to Jung's original expectation. On the same evening A actually made a full confession. Of course the methods used here for the calculation of averages are by no means adequate to satisfy the requirements of modern mathematical statistics; yet as the result of the case confirms, the psychological conclusions derived from them retain their validity.

In light of these examples it may readily be appreciated that the association experiment, both in its original form and in modified versions such as the evidence-experiment, can help us to clarify situations in which, whether as a result of conscious concealment or through gaps in memory caused by amnesia, we are deprived of vital information.

It was with this in mind that Freud, in his lecture on "Psychoanalysis and the Diagnosis of Evidence" (1906) dealt primarily with Jung's results (see No. 17 in the Chronological Review of the Literature on the Evidence-Experiment on p. 197). This review of the literature should enable the student to extend his knowledge of the history and criticism of the procedure we have described. In the interests of historical justice we would like to recall that in 1907 Max Wertheimer claimed precedence over Jung as the discoverer of this method. The question was amicably settled by a statement from Jung.[24] In recognition of his unquestionably great achievement, the honorary degree of LLD was conferred on Jung in 1907 by Clark University, Worcester, Massachusetts, on the occasion of its twentieth anniversary.

Our review does not claim to be complete for the period after 1911, at which time the main emphasis in research shifted to the psychophysiological accompaniments of the effects of complexes and at the same time moved overseas to the United States, where it produced an enormous literature. In the same year Otto Lipmann published a careful classification and summary of all the assured results regarding the diagnosis of evidence which were available at that period.[25] That paper also contains a reliable compendium of the literature. Later work on this subject is all very secondary and tertiary (i.e., Jung and the questions which he raised are forgotten); further discussion of them would therefore be superfluous from the point of view of the present volume. Subsequently, as we explain later, the "lie-detector" was developed in the United States, and questions connected with this development dominated the field for a considerable period. However, the methods employed deviated so widely from the strictly psychological point of view that they can no longer detain us here. We would only recall once again that this whole line of research and the "psychosomatic medicine" associated with it owe their initial impulse to the work of Otto Veraguth and to its continuation in the research carried out by Ludwig Binswanger and H. Nunberg under the direction of Jung at the Burghölzli (see Sec. 5 below).

Even into the late thirties Jung still occasionally gave expert opinions for courts of law and private firms on questions of guilt in cases of suspected murder or theft, basing his conclusions on evidence-experiments. This is an excellent illustration of the great care which was taken throughout his career by the originator of the method; and it shows, too, how conscientious his work was in purely quantitative terms. It also becomes very clear indeed that the successful application of this method—though it does give such an impression of objectivity—in fact presupposes great experience and demands considerable psychological sensitivity.

4. Results of the Association Experiment (Literature)

When in 1903, at the suggestion of Eugen Bleuler, Jung began his research at the Burghölzli, "association psychology" had already been fully developed by the schools of Wundt and Kraepelin and was regarded as the rising hope of psychology. Claparède's exemplary classification of the results provided the basis on which Jung's work was planned. Excellent contemporary reviews of the ever-increasing literature on this subject are to be found in the literature section of the *Archiv für Psychologie*, VII (1906) ff.[26] On the model of the existing prototypes, a number of original *lists of stimulus-words* were produced, of which the "1908 type" still in use today proved to be the most generally applicable. In this list the stimulus-words are distributed as follows: noun, adjective, noun, verb—which corresponds to the average frequency of words in these categories in German colloquial usage. The careful statistical inquiries of F. W. Kaeding provided a basis for this arrangement; in fact, it was possible to organize the scheme in such a way that the experiment corresponded to the average vocabulary of practically all subjects.[27] Thus the experiment was given a "harmless" character, and the subject was not confronted by unpredictable difficulties. It was generally easy to follow the instructions. And the atmosphere of the experiment was something like an informal conversation in telegraphese, on the lines of an interview, in which each stimulus-word represents a question, so that, for example, stimulus-word 21 would mean something like "What do you think about ink?" or stimulus-word 55 "What would you say about a child?"

Seen in this context, it is perfectly understandable that the association psychologists should have tried in the first place to use research into the "syntactical" relationships between stimulus-word and reaction as a means of gaining an insight into the nature of the concatenations linking inner conceptions or "ideas" (= associations).

In fact, they interpreted stimulus-word and reaction as component parts of a dialogue. Of course it was subsequently realized that this involved short-circuiting; yet here too the method yielded valuable insights in directions quite other than those originally intended. Of these I will mention only three. The calculation of averages from many thousands of reactions confirmed that (1) our vocabulary is very much more restricted than we are inclined to imagine (Kaeding had already shown that the 66 most common words actually make up 50.66% of our ordinary language!) and (2) that the individual is by no means free in his choice of expressions, as we like to flatter ourselves that we are, but is in fact nothing less than compulsively bound. Our individual "style" is thus a very elementary linguistic phenomenon. How far this holds good when it is applied to questions of literary criticism is an interesting question. We shall have to return later to the problem of the origin of this striking "imprint" in the style of the individual.[28] (3) In the case of critical reactions, the sounded vowel has a tendency to reappear in the first post-critical reaction (n plus 1) and in some cases to persevere in reactions n plus 2 and 3, with the result that something like an "agglutinate language" is formed (cf. Hungarian and Turkish). The average extent of such "phonetic sequences" is as long as 2.38 reactions.[29]

It was also established that "phonetic sequences" of this nature contain more complex indicators than the average run of non-phonetic reactions and that stimulus-words which trigger off phonetic sequences on an average trigger off three times as many complex indicators as other stimulus-words. The inference may be drawn that agglutinate languages are associated with a higher degree of emotionality than others. Jung also thought that alliteration such as is found in certain epic poems may suggest similar conclusions.

(a) The Classification of Reactions

In the first great series of experiments, which he undertook in collaboration with Riklin,[30] Jung elaborated a scheme of classification for the grammatical and syntactical relationships stimulus-words and reactions which with minor modifications followed the lines laid down by his predecessor. We reproduce it here in a slightly modified form.

The criterion for *internal associations* is similarity of content between stimulus-word and reaction. There is an association based on *affinity* between them. They are linked together by a common conceptual element.

External associations are associations of a kind which in ordinary usage often occur simultaneously with the stimulus-word. There is

Classification of reactions

subject	Name	Sex
experimenter	Name	Sex
	Date	

Internal associations
1. *Coordination*
   (cat – animal)
   (father – worry, lake – depth)
   (to give in – peace-loving)
   1a. simple contrasts
   (good – vicious)
2. *Predicates*
   2a. value judgments
   (mother – dear)
   2b. other predicates
   (snake – poisonous
   to cook – mother)
   2c. definitions
   (ink – fluid for writing with)
3. *Causal relationship*
   (pain – tears)

External associations
4. *Coexistence*
   (ink – pen)
5. *Identity*
   (squabble – quarrel)
6. *Linguistic-motor forms*
   (needle – holder,
   hunger – suffer)
   (war – peace)
   6a. linguistic-motor contrast
   (sweet – sour,
   light – dark,
   good – evil)

Sound reactions
7. *Word completion*
   (wonder – ful)
8. *Sound*
   (humility – humidity)
9. *Rhyme*
   (king – ring)
Miscellaneous
10. failures
    (bride . . . .)
11. *Indirect associations*
    (repentance – black, via
           mourning)
12. *Meaningless reactions*
    (to sin – exercise-book)
13. *Simple repetition of the
     stimulus-words*
     (lake – lake)
14. *Perseveration*
    (sick – hospital) n
    (proud – Burghölzli) n − 1
15. *Egocentric reaction*
    15a. *direct ideas of reference*
    (to love – I)
    15b. *subjective value
         judgments*
    (to be lazy – pleasant)

Total   Total

an association based on *practice* between them. They are linked together by our habit of seeing or hearing these concepts together.

On the basis of this classification, the two authors were able to identify certain *typical forms of reaction*:

I. A case is described as being of an *evaluating type* if the subject produces more than 50 percent internal reactions (1-3).

II. The *superficial type* denotes a subject more than 50 percent of whose reactions are external or shallow (4-6a).

III. The *simple predicate type* produces at last 33 percent of his reactions in the form of predicates (2a-c). In psychological terms, this means that the subject evaluates the stimulus-words from a personal point of view and consequently reacts by naming an attribute which is appropriate for this purpose.

IV. The *mixed reaction type* produces more than 10 percent and less than 33 percent predicates among his reactions.

V. The *objective type* of subject understands the stimulus-word in terms of its objective significance or of its function as an objective linguistic stimulus.

VI. The *egocentric type* of subject understands the stimulus-word subjectively. There are two subgroups of this category: the *constellation type*[31] and the *predicate type* (see above). The constellation type in turn is subdivided into (α) the *simple constellation type*, whose reactions are essentially conditioned by an actual subjective experience from everyday life which has been lived through egocentrically and which dominates the situation in the form of an unusually vivid memory, and (β) the *complex constellation type*, in whose case the situation is dominated by a complex with a strong feeling-tone (see Sec. 5 below).

Of course there are always particular cases in which a single class of reactions is strikingly predominant, so that, for example, we might sometimes speak of a *definition type* (2c). At this stage, however, it becomes quite clear that a *typology* based on the association experiment alone would be a questionable undertaking. It is unlikely that the association experiment will be used again on a scale involving large numbers of subjects; the wise course would therefore seem to be not to base more on the rudimentary typology outlined above than the few conclusions which arose out of practical experience and have stood the test of time. Even these should be adopted subject to the criticism recommended by the authors themselves; the number of subjects was in fact too small to make valid generalizations based on them.

I. The *evaluating reaction-type* is to be found mainly among uneducated subjects.

II. The *shallow type* is characteristic of educated subjects. The explanation for this finding is that uneducated people regard the experiment as an examination and therefore take the meaning of the stimulus-word seriously. As a result, their reactions are more deeply concerned with the essential meaning of the word. Educated people, on the other hand, tend to feel superior to the situation and to make use of their acquired facility in verbal expression to react linguistically; thus instead of considering the meaning of the stimulus-word, they are much more inclined to produce external associations such as linguistic-motor forms or contrasts. The *general* conclusion which may be drawn from this phenomenon is that the "merit" of the reactions does not depend in any way on the intelligence of the subject, but is clearly a function of the emotional effect of the experiment upon the subject.

III. The *predicate type* comes into being because the subject evaluates the stimulus-word primarily in terms of its emotional significance, and in the second place because he (or she) wishes to impress the experimenter by showing him the "depth of his (or her) feelings." A familiar accompaniment of this approach is that the subject may react with a *higher tone of voice*, which is intended to express tenderness and fineness of feeling. This type occurs more frequently among feminine subjects. Yet we must never forget that the result of the experiment must always be interpreted *in relation to the experimenter*. Feminine subjects tend to react with predicates in relation to a masculine experimenter, whereas if they are confronted with a feminine experimenter they will wish to demonstrate their intelligence, and may well react, e.g., as a definition type. In general terms we can formulate this insight by saying that the *attitude* of the subject to the experimenter will have a considerable influence on the result. It has also been established that the frequency of the predicate type increases with age. This may be due to the fact that emotionality declines physiologically with age. The phenomenon would then be explicable as an *attempt at compensation*.

IV. The *definition type* is closely related to the predicate type, since this type, also, understands the stimulus-word as a question, which might be formulated roughly as "What bright ideas do *you* have about it?" Strictly speaking, then, this, too, is an emotional reaction. Thus while the predicate type shows signs of an *inferiority complex* in relation to feeling, the definition type probably suffers from a similar complex in relation to intelligence. But the plus or minus sign, as it were, would vary according to the relationship between the experimenter and the subject.

V. The *objective type* seems to represent the opposite of the predicate and definition types; it reveals the subject as emotionally uninvolved in the experiment. Here, however, as with the two previous types, the question of *compensation* would arise once again, this time in a special form. The presence of an intelligence complex does not necessarily mean that the possessor of it is intellectually inferior. In fact, if this feeling of inferiority is rather too overtly demonstrated, it would be pertinent to inquire whether it is not actually an alibi. An unusually intelligent person can afford to appear comparatively stupid, while at the same time he may be laboring under a compulsion to preserve at all cost the secret of his corresponding weakness in the feeling realm. *Mutatis mutandis*, the same may hold good of a feeling complex. Complexes are often displaced or interposed to deceive the public or—if the mechanism is completely unconscious—the possessor of the complex himself. It is easy to see that we are already in the midst of the contradictoriness, or rather complexity, of psychic phenomena. This is to be found everywhere, as soon as we introduce the dimension of the unconscious.

VIa. The *simple constellation type* requires no deeper psychological discussion, whereas

  b. The *complex constellation type* will be dealt with in greater detail later on.

(b) Familial Agreement in Reaction Type

At the suggestion of Eugen Bleuler and C.G. Jung, Emma Fürst[32] carried out experiments into the distribution of the reaction types which we have just discussed above among members of the same family. Here, too, we must bear in mind the fact that the statistical resources deployed by the author would no longer be adequate to contemporary requirements.

For purposes of classification, Fürst adopted the 15 groups of kinds of reaction which we listed above and investigated the average differences in distribution among these groups as between unrelated and related male and female subjects, husbands and wives, fathers and sons, fathers and daughters, mothers and sons, and mothers and daughters. I have summarized her results in a tabular form below.

Subject to the necessary reservation (the calculations are not defensible in mathematical terms!), the following conclusions may be derived from this material:

		Mean Difference Between
1.	unrelated males	5.9
2.	related males	4.1
3.	unrelated females	6.0
4.	related females	3.8
5.	fathers and children	4.2
6.	mothers and children	3.5
7.	fathers and sons	*3.1*
8.	fathers and daughters	4.9
9.	mothers and sons	4.7
10.	mothers and daughters	*3.0*
11.	brothers among themselves	4.7
12.	sisters among themselves	5.1
13.	unmarried brothers	4.8
14.	unmarried sisters	3.8
15.	brothers and sisters	4.4
16.	husbands and wives	4.7

1. Both in males and females, relationship is correlated with a higher degree of similarity in reaction type (see 2 and 4 as contrasted with 1 and 3), and this is truer of females than it is of males.

2. Children tend to display a greater similarity with the reaction type of their mothers (see 6 as compared with 5). This fact is already expressed in common usage; we speak of our *mother* tongue, not of our father tongue.

3. Daughters obey this "law" more strictly than sons (see 10 as compared with 9), yet it would appear that the formative influence of the father is appreciable on the latter (see 7).

4. It follows that there is a very high degree of agreement between parents and children of the same sex (see 7 and 10).

5. Sisters show little difference from each other; if they marry, however, the difference is accentuated. The question as to whether marriage in itself exerts an influence in the direction of individuality or whether these cases are accounted for by assimilation to the possibly different type of the husband remains unsettled. The latter hypothesis seems on the whole less probable, since husband and wife display little agreement (see 16). If a comparison between 11 and 13 permits any conclusion, it is that marriage exercises no perceptible influence on the reaction type of husbands.

Jung made an additional special evaluation of some of Emma Fürst's cases, and from this purely experimental material he was able to draw a number of conclusions which were interesting from a psychological point of view and which have stood the test of practical experience. As the graphs constructed by Jung demonstrate these cases in a very vivid way, I am reproducing them in Figs. 3–6.[33] Along the abscissa are to the found the 15 classes of reaction shown on p. 96; the ordinate gives the percentage of reactions actually occurring in a given class.

While the two sisters who *live together* show a high degree of agreement, although one of them is married (Fig. 5), a third sister, who is also married, displays a diametrically opposite type, which however is practically identical with that of her husband (Fig. 6). So far as it is admissible to draw conclusions from a single case, the psychological question arises here as to whether the wife has to such a large extent become assimilated to her husband that she has departed from her family type, or whether she chose this particular man because he to such a large extent corresponded with her own type. The third possibility—which, however, is less likely—is that the husband became assimilated to his wife's type.

Jung subjoins to these graphs several additional observations.

1. He points out that mother and daughter often share an unexpectedly large number of verbally identical reactions to the same stimulus-word. This is in fact an astonishing contrast to our customary naive assumption that we possess a large measure of individual freedom in the choice of the words we use.

2. In connection with Fig. 3 he inquired in greater detail into the reasons for the high degree of agreement in reaction type between mother and daughter. It then emerged that the father was a drunkard. The marriage was naturally very unhappy for the mother, and as a wife she was bitterly disappointed. She was a most pronounced predicate type, with a plethora of personal value judgments, and this should probably be interpreted as a compensatory expression of her emotional frustration. In the nature of things, however, these conditions cannot have applied to the daughter, who nevertheless agreed with her mother in type. The reason for this, we can only assume, was that the daughter imitated her mother. However, when a young woman mimics emotional disappointment to such an extent, there is a real danger that she, too, in due course, will choose a husband who will fulfill this condition and who will, in fact, emotionally disappoint her—and, if possible, will also be an alcoholic.

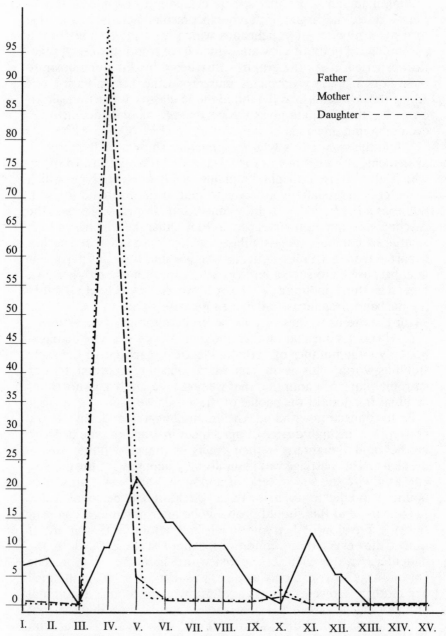

FIGURE 3: *The father reveals a purely objective type; the mother and daughter belong to a subjective pure predicate type which is practically identical. This exemplifies conclusion 3 and No. 16 in the table.*

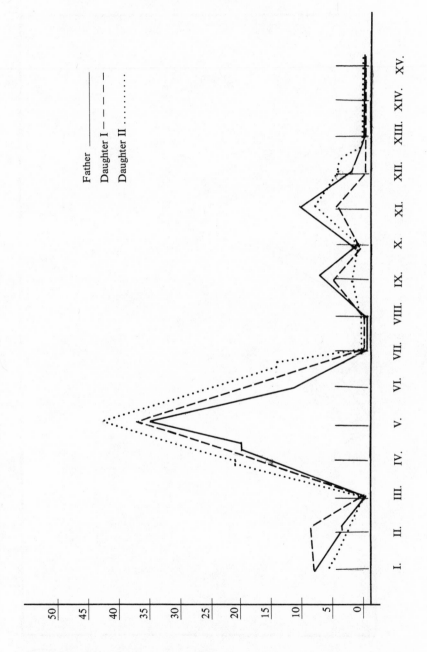

FIGURE 4: *This shows an unusually high degree of agreement in reaction type between the two daughters (aged 12 and 15) and the father (an objective predicate type).*

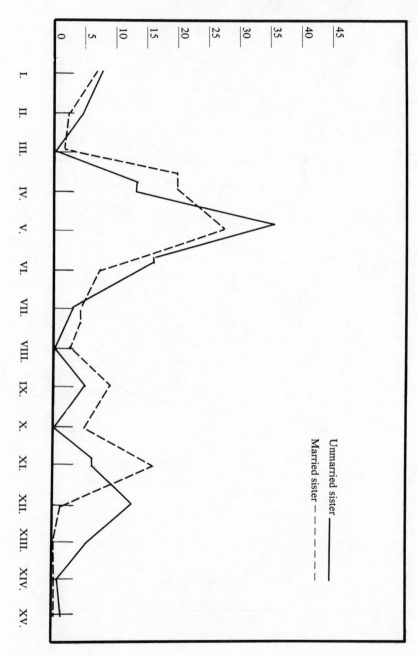

FIGURE 5

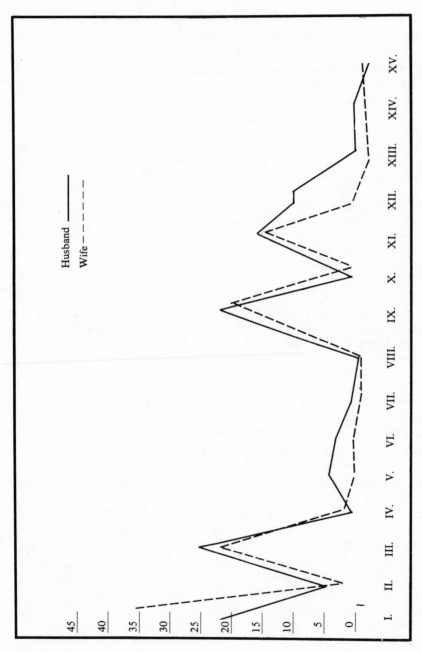

FIGURE 6

3. Jung drew the inference that emotion, whether positive or negative, is infectious, and that this applies with particular force in a family setting.

4. Analytical experience has largely confirmed this finding; in neurotic entanglements especially, the neurosis, in every case, *"contains the negative aspect of* the patient's *relationship with the person closest to him,"*[34] whether this person is the mother, husband, wife or a brother or sister.

Josef B. Lang applied the same line of reasoning to psychotic cases, and he was able to confirm its applicability to patients of this kind. Here is his summary statement of his findings:

> Of all members of the family, the sufferer from dementia praecox has the smallest average deviation. If he falls a victim to ideas of persecution, those members of the family will be selected as persecutors with whom he shows the highest measure of agreement in reaction type.[35]

Lang's researches also confirm a finding of Pfenninger's that

> . . . sufferers from dementia praecox show the highest measure of agreement (in reaction type) with normal people of the opposite sex, and that in our special case, male sufferers exhibited the same resistance to the experimenter as normal women, and women sufferers the same as normal men.[36]

We have now summarized the more interesting results of the research carried out at this period on the basis of classification of reactions, i.e., on the reaction type. The authors were circumspect enough to describe their findings as contributions to the discussion, and if we regard them as early attempts, they are still interesting to us today, all the more so as most of them are constantly being confirmed by practical experience.

However, all this work is no more than a by-product from the point of view of our main purpose, which is to give an account of the effects of the unconscious. The same applies to a considerable number of papers which attempted to use the association experiment for *purposes of psychiatric diagnosis.* Their results did not lead to any refinement in diagnostic technique, and unfortunately they were not subjected to a more detailed psychological elaboration later on, though this would certainly be well worthwhile. They are, however, briefly reviewed in Chap. V, since they give the reader an insight into some of the developments which were inspired by Jung's initial impulse at this period.

Within the framework of the considerable literature on this subject produced by the Zurich School, we first encounter the experiment in 1903, when it was, in fact, first applied clinically in a study "On Simulated Insanity" which was carried out by C.G. Jung at the Burghölzli, the psychiatric clinic of Zurich University.[37] The setup of the experiment was still primitive; there was no fixed scheme of stimulus-words, no time-measurement and no reproduction. The classification of the reactions, which follows Aschaffenburg, was still clumsy, though it served as the only criterion. Yet the author was already in a position to emphasize that *emotional* disturbances can be clearly demonstrated (in quantitative terms!) by the use of this simple experimental setup.

The experiment was carried out when patients were admitted to the clinic, and again when they were discharged; in the latter case, the experiment represented the criterion of normality. The differences between Experiment I and Experiment II were regarded as characteristic pathological effects, and in the special cases which concern us here as the results of "emotional stupidity." Attention was drawn to analogies with Ganser's syndrome, which in Jung's view was to be explained as the result of the repression of an *affect*, in Freud's sense of that term. In support of this hypothesis, Jung and Riklin carried out for the purposes of this study an identical association experiment on two normal subjects, twice in each case, the first time under normal conditions and the second time under the conditions of so-called "inner distraction" (the "A-phenomenon" of Cordes[38]). In the second experiment in each case striking analogies became apparent with the abnormalities observed in the so-called "malingerers" of Experiment I. This seemed to support the hypothesis.

We now propose to deal in rather greater detail with the subsequent work of the "Zurich School," i.e., with the research inspired by Bleuler and Jung and carried out by Jung and his pupils which related to the conditions of the association experiment itself.

1. The basic work of Jung and Riklin (Diagnostic Studies I) appeared in 5 parts in the *Journal für Psychologie und Neurologie*.[39] Its aim was to create as broad a basis of comparison as possible from the reactions of normal subjects, so that subsequent inquiries could evaluate the deviations that psychiatric patients might be expected to show against the background of this "normal" average. For this purpose the authors used the classification scheme prepared by the school of Kraepelin and Aschaffenburg, which they modified to some extent in the interests of simplicity. The school of Wundt, in

their work on the association experiment, had concentrated on *attention*, believing that the quality of the subject's reaction was essentially dependent on this factor. With most of their subjects therefore, Jung and Riklin carried out three distinct versions of the experiment. The first of these was conducted under normal conditions, the second under conditions of *external distraction*[40] and the third under conditions of *internal distraction*[41]; under this last heading, such factors as exhaustion, sleepiness, etc. would also, of course, have to be included.

Certain changes in reaction type did in fact emerge under the second and third conditions; this was particularly true of educated subjects, whose reactions tended to become more shallow, i.e., there was an increase in external and sound reactions and hence a shift in the direction of common usage. This was interpreted by Aschaffenburg as a shift toward the manic dimension. However, the opposite conclusion is also possible, i.e., that the shallow type of reaction occurs when there is an internal distraction which disturbs attention. On the other hand, predicate types remain unchanged even when their attention is divided. Their attention is in fact held captive by their vivid primary inner images.

Apart from this distinction, the authors also inquired whether there were regular differences between the average reactions of *educated and uneducated subjects*. They found that on an average, educated subjects react in a noticeably superficial way; by comparison, the reactions of uneducated subjects were decidedly superior. On the face of it, this seemed paradoxical. Educated subjects produced almost 7 times as many sound reactions as their uneducated counterparts, and this probably reveals the reason for the phenomenon. Educated people take the experiment far more casually than the uneducated. Thus it would appear to be primarily rather a question of attitude than of attention in the strict sense, since uneducated subjects are more impressed by the *meaning* of the stimulus-word than the educated subjects are.

We have already noted that different groups of subjects habitually prefer one or the other class of reactions. However, with the exception of the predicate type, membership of these types is by no means rigid, but in part at least is a function of a number of objective conditions.

The existence of clearly marked psychosexual differences could not be established; on an average, however, women tended to react more subjectively and with greater feeling than men did. In the case of educated men, however, this distinction tends to become effaced, since they display as much subjectivity and as many value judgments in their reactions as women do. On the other hand uneducated men react more objectively than women. Yet the distraction experiments showed unequivocally that women experience greater difficulties than men in dividing their attention.

It was already clear to the authors in this initial inquiry that although the reactions provided a fine test for the detection of individual variations among the subjects, they were in fact an even more specific instrument for the measurement of *affective processes*, even when these processes were actually unconscious.

As we have already remarked, affective processes make themselves felt in the association experiment in the form of disturbances, or, in other words, because the subject, when confronted with a stimulus-word that has an emotional effect, may no longer be capable of reacting in accordance with the instructions. It became apparent that a large number of the disturbed reactions Jung and Riklin recorded were attributable to the presence of a "feeling-toned complex of representations." In such cases they spoke of a *complex constellation type*.

The definition of a complex was still by no means clear at this time. It was provisionally stated that a complex must consist of a group of representations (i.e., memories) which are firmly held together and that the binding agent must be the feeling-tone or affect which was common to them all. In most cases of this kind in which it was possible to explain the underlying psychological content, this seemed to be of an erotic, sexual nature. The authors were interested to find that uneducated subjects showed appreciably fewer complex constellations and indeed fewer reactions disturbed by complexes in general than educated subjects.

The problem now was to obtain stricter definitions of the indicators of disturbance. With this aim in view, Jung first turned his attention to the *reaction-time*. He published the results of these measurements in Contribution No. IV to the *Diagnostic Studies*.[42] The complicated process—at once physical, physiological and psychological—which has to take place between the utterance of the stimulus-word by the experimenter and the formulation and utterance of the reaction by the subject is left on one side at this stage, since whether we consider it from the point of view of physics and physiology as an approximately constant factor, or in terms of psychology as conditioned by the nature of the experiment, it is not susceptible to further analysis. Claparède provides a diagram which justifies this procedure.[43] Measurement by hand with the 5th second stopwatch proved accurate enough, for the same reasons. In particular, it is possible to assume that the reaction-time of the experimenter when he starts and stops the watch is equal in each case and can therefore be ignored as an individual factor which remains constant.

Moreover, experimental conditions which require time measurements up to a precision of σ (= 1/1000 second) and involve, e.g., electric labial keys, Hipp's chronoscope, etc., are altogether too disturbing for our purpose, and in fact the order of magnitude of reaction-times is 100 to 1000 times greater than this (ranging from seconds to tenths of a second). Here too the aim was to obtain averages derived from large numbers and to look for correlations between known variables such as sex, age, education, reaction type, nature of stimulus-word on the one hand and the subject's average reaction-time on the other.

It soon became obvious that the *arithmetical mean* was unsuitable as a device for computing the average reaction-time. It proved in fact to be an insufficiently sensitive instrument, for since it embraced all reaction-times, including those which were extremely prolonged, it was too great to allow less violently disturbed reactions to stand out clearly in contrast to it. Jung therefore decided to employ the *probable mean* recommended by Kraepelin in *all* evaluations of his material (see p. 80 above). This is always *below* the arithmetical mean. In the table below we reproduce the average reaction-times obtained in this way for the classes of reactions and subjects mentioned. The times are indicated in *seconds*.

The following results are immediately evident from the table:
1. Educated subjects and men have a shorter reaction-time than uneducated subjects and women (1F and 2B in contrast to 1D and 3B).
2. Concrete nouns as stimulus-words elicit shorter reaction-times than general concepts and verbs (4B in contrast to 5 and 7B).
3. The reaction-time to abstract nouns is longer than the reaction-time to adjectives and verbs (9B in contrast to 10 and 11B).
4. Internal associations have a longer reaction-time than external associations (12C to F in contrast to 13C to F).
5. Sound reactions have the longest reaction-time of all, which establishes that on an average these reactions are disturbed; this is completely corroborated by practical experience (in any case, sound reactions exhibit a maximum of complex indicators).

A	B		D	F	
			Uneducated subjects	Educated subjects	
Total average:	1.8		1.9	1.5	1
Men	1.6		1.8	1.3	2
Women	2.0		2.2	1.7	3

A	B	C	D	E	F	
		Uneducated subjects		Educated subjects		
Stimulus-words:		Women	Men	Women	Men	
Concrete nouns	1.67	2.0	1.7	1.6	1.4	4
Abstract nouns	1.95	2.8	1.9	1.8	1.3	5
Adjectives	1.70	2.2	1.7	1.7	1.2	6
Verbs	1.90	2.4	2.0	1.9	1.3	7
Reaction:						
Concrete nouns	1.81	2.2	1.85	1.7	1.5	8
Abstract nouns	1.98	2.7	2.0	2.0	1.4	9
Adjectives	1.65	2.0	1.7	1.7	1.2	10
Verbs	1.66	1.9	1.7	1.8	1.3	11
Kind of association:						
Internal associations		2.8	1.9	2.1	1.6	12
External associations		1.9	1.7	1.8	1.3	13
Sound reactions		2.6	2.4	2.0	1.8	14
Probable mean		2.2	1.8	1.7	1.3	15
Arithmetical mean		2.9	2.4	2.2	1.7	16
Difference		0.7	0.6	0.5	0.4	17
% of prolonged reaction-times		49.2	40.9	42.4	41.8	18

Jung reached two further conclusions, which were of basic importance for the whole future development of research into complexes:

1. Reaction-times longer than the probable mean are to a large extent caused by the emergence of intense feeling-tones which are attached to vital complexes of representations. At the moment it occurs, the subject is generally unconscious of the reason for the prolongation of the reaction-time. Prolonged reaction-times can in fact be utilized as a means of discovering affect-toned complexes of representations, both conscious and unconscious.[44]

2. Often the disturbance only dies away *after the subsequent reaction*, which thus also contains indications of disturbance, although these cannot be brought into relationship with the stimulus-word which belongs to this reaction. This phenomenon is interpreted as the perseveration of the feeling-tone.

By closely questioning the subjects, Jung was able to illuminate in a very striking way quite a number of unusually prolonged reactions, which he explained along the lines of the mechanisms demonstrated by Freud in *Psychopathology of Everyday Life* (1904) and *The Interpretation of Dreams* (1900). So we have really now reached the authentic birthplace of the famous theory of complexes.

The strikingly high level of disturbance among sound reactions (14C to F) was the occasion for another study, by R. Hahn.[45] He starts from the position that sound reactions ("verbigeration") are a well-known phenomenon in cases of psychopathological excitation such as mania or excited catatonia, and he shows that psychomotor excitation encourages the emergence of sound reactions. He is, however, lacking in analytic insights.

The next criterion which was selected by Jung for closer investigation was disturbances of reproduction.[46] In principle, it is clear enough that failures or mistakes in reproduction are caused by a disturbance of memory. It is also well-known that our memory is strongly affected by emotional factors. Thus G. Ch. Lichtenberg (cf. p. 43) had already observed that "Past pain is agreeable to remember; so too is past pleasure, future pleasure and present pleasure. It is only future and present pain that torments us. In fact, there is a remarkable preponderance of pleasure in the world."[47] This reminds us of Kowalewski's "Optimism of Memory"[48] and of Wilhelm Busch's "Pains I have had I quite enjoy."[49] The psychologist W. Peters found striking experimental confirmation of this fact in an extended series of experiments.[50] One special point which might be highlighted is his finding that the tendency to forget memories charged with unpleasure was characteristic of adult subjects; young people do not display this tendency in such a pronounced form. In fact, during adolescence memories charged with unpleasure may actually be preferred.

Of an author's report on this line of research,[51] Jung writes:

> The writer here describes the procedure introduced by him for the "reproduction" of the association experiment. At the end of the experiment, the subject is questioned as to whether he correctly recalls the reaction he gave previously to each single stimulus-word; it then

becomes apparent that forgetting normally takes place at or immediately after disturbances caused by a complex. We are in fact dealing with a kind of "Freudian forgetting." This procedure provides us with complex indicators which have proved to be of practical value.[52]

On an average, faultily reproduced reactions have a reaction-time which is higher than the probable mean and are subject to twice as many complex indicators as correctly reproduced reactions. Thus disturbances of reproduction are established as an additional source of evidence for the part played by complexes in the genesis of these phenomena.

Some further hypotheses can be ventured in the context of these results. In essence, a disturbance of reproduction is an amnesia. But unpleasant contents of the conscious mind are not always forgotten. On the contrary, they may possess the force of an obsession and obtrude themselves on our memory in a peculiarly obstinate way—in fact, we can actually be persecuted by them. Evidence for this phenomenon may be found in the association experiment when obsessive reactions make their appearance in the most inappropriate places and insist on repeating themselves there. The frequent occurrence of the same reaction in the same experiment, which is known as "stereotypy," can therefore also be interpreted as a complex indicator.

It is still true, however, that the most frequent effect of emotion is failure to remember, a fact which is particularly important in the evaluation of the evidence-experiment. The real point of the reproduction experiment is that the subject is asked "What did you think and say at that *critical* moment?" The "lie" which the subject told the experimenter on each occasion is disturbed in memory by emotion and is therefore liable to be reproduced incorrectly. The fact whose existence is here demonstrated experimentally has long been known and exploited forensically in the form of crossexamination, which makes use of the mechanism that we have just described to reveal contradictions in legal testimony.

In certain cases, the phenomena of disturbance of reproduction even make it possible to detect a *retroactive amnesia* in the process of formation. This happens when in a reproduction experiment it is not only the reaction to an obviously critical stimulus-word that is forgotten, but also the reaction to its predecessor (i.e. stimulus-word n − 1). In such cases the shock occasioned by the critical stimulus-word actually extends its influence backward in time. The fact that it extends its influence forward (i.e., that it perseverates) is of course readily intelligible; this effect comes through in the form of serial disturbances of reproduction which start from the critical stimulus-word and then move forward (n + 1, 2,3, etc.).

Further experimental confirmation of this finding was obtained by Pfenninger.[53] He carried out the experiment repeatedly with the same subject at considerable intervals of time and established that in a series of this kind, a change in the reaction to a given stimulus-word was most likely to occur in cases where the reaction had been disturbed by a complex. This phenomenon can be understood to mean that the contents of complexes tend to be talkative and to "enjoy a good chat."

We have already pointed out that if the unconscious background of the disturbances in the association experiment is to be elucidated, the stimulus-words and reactions which exhibit complex indicators must be construed together and that an attempt should be made to create a "short story" out of these "fragments." But if the experiment is repeated several times, we should obtain an even more copious vocabulary for this literary enterprise. The credibility of this approach will be appreciably enhanced if we bear in mind that *on an average* there is a very striking constancy or identity of reactions in repetitive experiments of this kind, and moreover that this is not, as we might expect on rational grounds, simply the result of practice.

Pfenninger regards changes in the subject's reactions as an essentially emotional phenomenon which is primarily attributable to complexes, and he even goes so far as to say that "a complex brings with it a need (sic!) for a changed mode of expression." This supposition was checked by Hoffmann in Kraepelin's clinic at Munich in 1915 and was substantially validated.[54] But his paper includes the additional insight that disturbances brought about by complexes have an individual significance of their own. In other words, the "choice" of a particular complex-indicator has its own evidential value; the term "complex representative" was coined later on to express this fact. It is important, then, not only to pay attention to prolonged reaction-time or to explain that it is invariably conditioned by a complex, but also to scrutinize each single reaction for any perceptible signs of complex indicators, and especially for disturbances of reproduction.

A paper by Eberschweiler on the linguistic component of association, which was undertaken at Jung's suggestion, falls within the same period.[55] This very careful inquiry arrived at the following interesting conclusions. It established that so-called *vowel sequences* occur in the association experiment, i.e., that several consecutive reactions have the same accented vowel. If these "perseverations" are examined for possible coincidences with complex indicators, it is found that, whereas the overall average content of complex indicators per reaction is 0.36, 0.65 complex indicators occur to each word which forms part of a vowel sequence. If we take the two associations without sound affinity which precede the vowel sequences, the following succession is obtained:

l. association without vowel sequence: 0.10 complex indicators

m. association without vowel sequence: 0.58 complex indicators

n. beginning of the vowel sequence (association the accented vowel of which perseveres in the sequence given below): 0.91 complex indicators

n + 1st member of vowel sequence: 0.68 complex indicators

n + 2nd member of vowel sequence: 0.10 complex indicators

n + 3rd member of vowel sequence: 0.05 complex indicators

o. association *with new accented vowel*: 0.42 complex indicators.

It will be seen that after complex disturbances there is a definite tendency to sound perseveration; this finding is important for our understanding of the mechanism underlying rhyme and forms of witticism such as puns which depend for their effect on similarity of sound.

One final paper from the Zurich school on the basic elements of the association experiment remains to be mentioned in this context. This is a dissertation by H. Huber.[56] However, apart from the discovery that the acoustic transmission of the stimulus-word (where the experimenter calls it out) is more effective than optical transmission (where the stimulus-word is printed on a card and exhibited to the subject in the tachistoscope), this study contributed no new insights. From the psychological point of view it can be appreciated that confrontation with the stimulus-word pronounced viva-voce by the experimenter makes a decidedly more vital impact on the emotionality of the subject than the impersonal process of reading it in print. The subject in fact assimilates the experimental situation in a quite specific way, as we have already pointed out. One particular aspect of this phenomenon had attracted the attention of the writers on this subject at a very early stage. They found that the outcome of the experiment varied according to whether the test is administered, say, to a female subject, by a male or by a female experimenter. This means that for purposes of evaluating the experiment, sufficient account must always be taken of the psychosexual conditions under which it is administered.

(c) Consequences for Psychiatry

The association experiment was developed in the context of experimental psychology, which was flourishing at that time under the leadership of Wundt. We owe its introduction into psychiatry to the initiative of Kraepelin and Aschaffenburg, together with R. Sommer.[57] Their work, however, never progressed beyond questions of methodology. At this juncture, Eugen Bleuler became convinced that he had discovered in the person of Jung the right man to adapt these methods and make them serviceable for purposes of psychiatric diagnosis, and it was at his suggestion that the twelve *Diagnostic Studies in Word Association* by Jung, Bleuler and their associates were produced in the period between 1904 and 1910.[58] Thus the idea proved extremely fruitful. It is true that, as so often happens, the results did not fulfill the original expectations of Jung and Bleuler, since no new insights were obtained at this stage from the point of view of diagnosis, though the method was adopted with great enthusiasm both in Europe and America.

As early as 1905, we find a paper by S. I. Franz of the United States,[59] which confirmed the fact, well-known from clinical practice, that reaction-times are prolonged among manic-depressive patients in the melancholic phase.

Also in the United States, Kent and Rosanoff[60] collected material from 1000 normal subjects with a view to the preparation of frequency tables per stimulus-word for all recorded reactions. They had hoped on this basis to establish criteria for the abnormalities in verbal expression which were known to occur in various mental illnesses (247 cases). However, the differences they discovered were matters of degree only, not of kind. What is memorable about this result is that it confirmed that in this respect at any rate there is no difference in principle between insanity and what we call normality.

In 1911 another work of considerable scope appeared. This was a study by Ley and Menzerath which covers almost all types of psychiatric disorder.[61] The authors are enthusiastic in their assessment of the diagnostic possibilities of the association experiment and to a large extent they confirm the findings reported by Jung and his school. In particular, they stress the fact that the experiment supplies us with a first-class tool for analyzing the conditions governing the affectivity of the subject; they actually wished to interpret the experiment as providing the materials for a differential diagnosis.

However, the experiment was never extensively used for this purpose. Under Jung's guidance it was developed in an entirely different direction. But before we enter on this theme, we should like, as a matter of historical interest, to consider briefly all the papers on the subject of the association experiment which arose out of the work of the Burghölzli Psychiatric Clinic of Zurich under the leadership of Eugen Bleuler, C.G. Jung and H.W. Maier.

The first paper was written by Bleuler himself and is entitled "Upon the Significance of Association Experiments."[62] It was originally intended as a foreword to the *Diagnostic Studies* and the author takes a very optimistic view of the diagnostic significance of the experiment; already at that period the diagnosis in certain cases of dementia praecox (i.e., schizophrenia), epilepsy, various types of imbecility, hysteria, mania etc. at the Burghölzli was based on "associations." Bleuler hoped that many new insights would be acquired in this way not only for purposes of the differential diagnosis of this and other mental diseases but also for our deeper understanding of the interrelationships between the different classes of disorder in psychiatry. And he is also already making the point that with the aid of the association experiment it was possible to identify "certain psychological types" among normal subjects. But he was also very much concerned to stress the fact that the use of the experiment had made the *unconscious mechanisms of our psyche* to a large extent accessible to our consciousness.

This introduction was immediately followed by Jung and Riklin's paper on "The Associations of Normal Subjects" (*Diagnostic Studies I*), which we have already discussed in detail.[63]

The second contribution (*Diagnostic Studies II*) was a paper by K. Wehrlin on "The Associations of Imbeciles and Idiots."[64] The writer established that patients suffering from a severe degree of imbecility display a marked tendency to definition and are unable to confine their reaction to "a single word," as instructed. They almost invariably give their answer in long, unwieldy sentences with a subjective reference to the stimulus-word and concentrate upon its *meaning*, like Jung and Riklin's uneducated subjects. The tendency to reply in sentences had already been explained by Cordes as an echo of the schoolteacher's injunction to "answer in complete sentences."[65] Wehrlin had already introduced time-measurement into psychiatry; at that period, Jung had not yet published any work on this subject. Wehrlin found that his imbecile patients had an average reaction-time of 3.5 seconds as compared with an average of 2.5 seconds among normal uneducated subjects (we should now express this by saying "17–18 as compared with 12–13 fifths of a second").

The third contribution to *Diagnostic Studies* comes once again from Jung himself and relates to "An Analysis of the Associations of the Epileptic."[66] This paper describes a single case, complicated by a fracture of the skull; the whole subject was, moreover, dealt with more exhaustively in a subsequent paper by Eitingon. We therefore do not discuss the results here, but simply note that the average reaction-time was more than twice as long as that recorded for normal subjects, that the links between the stimulus-word and the reaction were primarily emotional, and that where there was a complex reaction the corresponding feeling-tone emerged later and lasted longer than in a normal subject. These peculiarities are in fact well known to us from our clinical observation of epileptics.

The fourth contribution to *Diagnostic Studies*, which appeared in the same year, was Jung's paper on "The Reaction-time Ratio in the Association Experiment,"[67] which we have already considered in detail. At this stage, we should like to make the additional point that a number of complexes were subjected to an exhaustive analysis in this study, for example the "sexual complex," the "family complex," the "money complex," and "ambition." In a footnote, Jung also discussed when, in contradistinction to Freud's usage, we should speak of conscious "repression," and when of unconscious "repression."

In the fifth contribution, entitled "Consciousness and Association," Bleuler shivers a lance in the most courageous fashion on behalf of the unconscious. We reproduce his summary verbatim:

> There are effective and numerous processes in us which comport themselves in all respects like conscious processes with the exception that consciousness is absent.
>
> Psychology cannot ignore them because the processes influence the conscious mind just as well as conscious sensations, thoughts and wishes.
>
> The study of these unconscious (mental) functions is quite indispensable in psychopathology for they often control its symptoms.
>
> We can best represent such processes to ourselves by imagining that physical processes in the brain, which form the foundation of all psychical happenings, only become conscious when they become functionally linked—associated—with the ego complex.[68]

Bleuler is also amazingly farsighted in his discussion of the phenomena of split personalities and of what we nowadays would call parapsychology. Both these areas represent fascinating quarries of source material for the phenomenology of the unconscious, as Jung's doctoral dissertation had already shown.[69] But Bleuler's stimulating ideas—like those in Jung's own dissertation—were not destined to fall on fruitful ground. Only quite recently, since Rhine provided us with quantitative techniques,[70] has the world begun to take a serious interest in parapsychological questions. Even in the USSR there are already several state institutes devoted to parapsychological research. Bleuler's definition of conscious awareness in this essay as the association of a representation with the ego is a formulation which we can scarcely improve upon, even today.

In the sixth contribution to *Diagnostic Studies*, Jung returns to the subject of *Psychoanalysis and Association Experiments*[71] (he had meanwhile qualified as a lecturer in psychiatry in the medical faculty of the University of Zurich by submitting Contribution IV to *Diagnostic Studies* (see p. 118)). This sixth contribution marks the turning-point mentioned on p. 116 above. Jung had already read Breuer and Freud's *Studies in Hysteria* (1895) and Freud's *Interpretation of Dreams* (1900) at an earlier stage in his career. Now Freud's "Fragment of an Analysis of a Case of Hysteria" was available.[72] This convinced Jung that the association experiment actually contained experimental evidence confirming the correctness of the conclusions which Freud had drawn from his method of "unconstrained association." The "free associations" of Freud's patients had consistently resulted in the discovery of complexes which could only be regarded as pathogenic (i.e., as disease-producing agents). In this paper Jung took the view that the intensity of the emotions with which the pathogenic complexes were charged was much greater than in the case of normal subjects. Moreover—and partly as a consequence of this—the pathogenic complexes remained in the unconscious, i.e., they became repressed, probably owing to their incompatibility with the conscious attitude. This made them particularly difficult to detect. But now, Jung believed, the association experiment had provided a most reliable instrument for aiming directly at these complexes. He concludes his paper with the following summary:

1. The complex that is brought to light through the associations offered by patients with psychogenic neuroses constitutes the causa morbi, apart from any predispositon.

2. The associations may therefore be a valuable aid in finding the pathogenic complex, and may thus be useful for facilitating and shortening Freud's psychoanalysis.

3. The associations supply us with an experimental insight into the psychological foundations of neurotic symptoms: hysteria and obsessive phenomena stem from a complex. The physical and psychic

symptoms are nothing but symbolic manifestations of the pathogenic complexes.

This publication of Jung's was actually the means whereby Freud's psychoanalytical ideas were really and truly confirmed by academic psychology and consequently found acceptance for the first time in those previously so "exalted circles"; this is a fact which has often been stressed. The paper represented a bold advance, and Jung himself was well aware of its possible dangers, as we can see from his concluding sentence:

It appears, from some recent publications, that Freud's theory of obsessional neurosis is still consistently ignored. It therefore gives me great satisfaction to draw attention to Freud's theories—at the risk of also becoming a victim of persistent amnesia.

Contribution VII to *Diagnostic Studies* was a paper by Franz Riklin entitled "Cases Illustrating the Phenomena of Association in Hysteria."[73] The writer had already on a previous occasion applied the association experiment to what we know as hysteria.[74] On the basis of eight further cases, he now confirmed previous findings, which had indicated that particularly vehement complex effects can be detected in this type of neurotic disturbance. These take the form of "failures," lapses of memory reminiscent of the well-known phenomenon of "persistent amnesia," prolonged reaction-times, reactions in the form of sentences accompanied by intense feeling-tones, etc. In cases where a sexual complex is involved, what are known as screen-reactions tend to appear—i.e., contents are produced which are calculated to distract the experimenter from the complex. This phenomenon, like the equally common "distraction by the environment," is interpreted in terms of Freud's mechanisms of repression and displacement. "The complex," again, is seen as the common denominator of all hysterical symptoms. The patients were treated mainly by hypnosis, as was still customary at that time owing to the influence of Auguste Forel.[75] At the same time, Freud's discoveries were taken into account and in fact confirmed, since "free association" was employed to elucidate the complex reactions.

In the eighth contribution to *Diagnostic Studies*, Jung dealt with a case of hysteria by comparing and contrasting "Association, Dream and Hysterical Symptoms."[76] In the association experiment he confirmed Riklin's findings, and in addition established that (a) the subject did not concern herself with the meaning of the stimulus-word, (b) there was a most marked predominance of external reactions and (c) a strong tendency toward fatigue emerged during the experiment. He concluded that all these manifestations could be interpreted as symptoms of a pathologically heightened emotionality.

In the meantime, it had been established that the differences in the results of the experiment recorded for the same subject but under different degrees of "distraction" (*Diagnostic Studies*, Contribution I) were also attributable to the variations in "affectivity" produced by these distractions. Distraction and attention are in fact reciprocal magnitudes, and, as Bleuler had shown, attention itself is nothing but "a special case of the results of affect," i.e., an emotional phenomenon.[77] This direct connection with the subject's emotional participation in the experiment also holds good for the various "types" of reaction distinguished by Jung and Riklin (in *Diagnostic Studies*, Contribution I), although there, in the "type," it appears simply as a habitual attitude.

At the time when Jung was administering the various association tests to the woman patient we mentioned above,[78] a form of treatment similar to that adopted in Riklin's cases (*Diagnostic Studies*, Contribution VII) was carried out. The main emphasis here was on the numerous physical symptoms (e.g., hysterical chorea, dull sensations in the head, sensations of heat, etc.) and the psychotic symptoms (e.g., sensitiveness to caterwauling, fear of mice, compulsive cleanliness, compulsive performance of gymnastic exercises, etc.). At the same time, dreams that coincided with the association tests were analyzed. However, in view of the fact that we deal with dreams in Volume II of this Textbook, we confine ourselves here to providing a schematic summary of the way in which Jung found correspondences between the three phenomena of (1) association, (2) dream, and (3) hysterical symptom.[79]

1. *Association Experiment*:

erotic ideas	relationship to doctor	illness complex	mother complex

2. *Dream*:

sexual complex	transference	brother-incest complex	regression to mother

3. *Hysterical symptom*:

marriage complex		illness complex	mother complex

So far as the physical symptoms (Freud's "conversion symptoms") were concerned, Jung established that this case was an example of what Freud had called "displacement from below upward" (from the genital sphere to the head), and he summarizes his findings as follows:

> The complex revealed in the associations is the root of the dreams and of the hysterical symptoms.
>
> The interferences that the complex causes in the association experiment are none other than resistances in psychoanalysis, as described by Freud.
>
> The mechanisms of repression are the same in the association experiment as in the dream and in the hysterical symptom.
>
> The complex has an abnormal autonomy in hysteria and a tendency to an active separate existence, which reduces and replaces the constellating power of the ego-complex. In this way a new morbid personality is gradually created, the inclinations, judgments, and resolutions of which move only in the direction of the will to be ill. This second personality devours what is left of the normal ego and forces it into the role of a secondary (oppressed) complex.[80]

We have already considered Contribution IX to *Diagnostic Studies*, which relates to disturbances of reproduction in Jung's association experiment (pp. 112 ff. above); and we have also dealt with Contribution X by Emma Fürst[81] on familial types of reactions (pp. 99 ff. above).

Contributions XI (Binswanger) and XII (Nunberg) will receive a detailed evaluation in Chapter V.

To supplement the foregoing reports on the *Diagnostic Studies* a further selection of studies on *psychiatric* topics which were directly inspired by the *Diagnostic Studies* and which were based on work with the association experiment appears at the end of this volume.

At the same time, it should not be forgotten that as late as 1916 a dissertation was submitted to the Philosophic Faculty at Zurich (at that time under the direction of G.F. Lipps) by H. Hintermann, entitled *Experimental Investigation of the Processes of Consciousness with the Aid of Reactions to Stimulus-words (including a Consideration of the most important pathological Manifestations)*, the author of which did not consider it necessary to take the slightest notice of Jung's findings. And the intellectual gulf which separated the medical from the philosophical faculty at this period can scarcely be interpreted in this instance as a function of the geographical distance between them! In conclusion, it is on the whole true to say that since the time when Jung made his original contribution, the considerable literature on the association experiment has not advanced beyond the initial stages recorded.

(d) The "Zurich School"

If we now recapitulate and ask ourselves what causes were responsible for the rise of the "Zurich School" (i.e., a group of psychiatrists with a psychoanalytical orientation), then, apart from the fascinating personalities of Bleuler and Jung themselves, our answer would have to include the following factors.

Very soon after the introduction of the association experiment, Jung, with the intuition of genius, grasped the point that it was precisely the disturbances which emerged during the tests and which had hitherto been "rejected by the builders" that were in fact most relevant from the psychological standpoint; and he subjected these disturbances to a thoroughgoing quantitative analysis. As a result of this research, the idea of complexes was originally formulated. The disturbing stimulus-word and the disturbed reactions were collated and summarized and by this means it was often possible to extract a résumé which represented the common denominator of the disturbances.

In most of these cases the experimenter had asked the subject to react to the critical stimulus-word along the lines of Freud's technique of "free association," and the successful elucidation of the cause of the disturbance was in fact due to the adoption of this method. Thus the association experiment actually provided an objective confirmation of the validity of Freud's technique.

At the same time it was established that the complexes themselves were highly charged with emotionality, and that where this component was unusually strong it could cause not only disturbances of memory but actual psychogenic symptoms; in hysterical patients the latter could also develop into physical symptoms (Freud's "conversion symptoms"). The "kernel of the poodle,"[82] however, was always a carefully guarded secret; in fact, it was often completely unconscious, i.e., in Freud's terminology, "repressed." In cases where the emotional charge of a complex was extremely intense, this inner core could actually be regarded as pathogenic, or in other words as the causal factor in a mental illness.

The first subjects who were examined on the strength of this hypothesis were women patients suffering from hysteria. But Bleuler and Jung did not stop at this point. They soon came to believe that complexes might also be the pathogenic villains of the piece in cases of schizophrenia (or dementia praecox, as it was called at that time). The impulse for this development came primarily from Freud's analysis of the case of Dr. Daniel Paul Schreber,[83] a former Chief Justice of the Kingdom of Saxony, a schizophrenic, who had published an extended account of his own case history as a kind of *apologia pro vita sua*.[84] Jung expressed these views on schizophrenia at this time:[85]

With reference to the foregoing discussion by Bleuler, with which I am essentially in agreement, I should like, if I may, to add a few remarks which may serve as a kind of résumé of the argument. I agree with Bleuler on the following points:

1. The content of the symptomatology in dementia praecox is *to a large extent* determined by complexes.

2. Acute attacks, exacerbations, deteriorations, remissions etc. *very frequently* have psychological causes, the effects of which develop on the basis of the peculiar predisposition of the brain which is characteristic of dementia praecox.

In the following points my views differ from those of Bleuler:

1. The nature of the peculiar predisposition of the brain in dementia praecox does not seem to me in the present state of our knowledge to have been adequately elucidated. Does it, for example, already constitute a "latent illness"? I should therefore prefer to leave this question open.

2. I also do not know whether—and if so what—primary psychic symptoms occur in dementia praecox which are, in Bleuler's terms, entirely devoid of any tendency to engender ideas.

3. It seems to me, as it does to Bleuler, an incontestable fact that the predisposition of the brain which is peculiar to dementia praecox can result in an organic pathological process for certain other than psychological reasons; however, in contrast to Bleuler's opinion, I doubt whether this necessarily holds good of all cases (or forms?) of dementia praecox.

In my view there is an organic process at the bottom of every case of dementia praecox, but I take the view that this process (provided the necessary predisposition is present) can also on occasion be triggered off by affects. It was for this reason that I formulated the following suggestion in my book as an additional hypothesis:

The influence of an affect can trigger off the organic process in dementia praecox just like any physical cause (possibly, for example, by producing a toxin). It would be analogous, in fact, to the manifestation of tuberculosis in a contused joint. The disease develops at the place of least resistance; this means that in the case of dementia praecox the entire pathological process of the illness, both physical and psychic, can develop from a feeling-toned complex, exactly as, in other circumstances, it may develop from a physical trauma, an infection, etc. If in such a case the complex did not exist, the actual illness would not develop at that moment, in that place or in that manner. Thus in such cases the complex does not simply play its accustomed role by determining the content of the symptoms; it also plays a significant part in the genesis of the organic pathological process of the illness.

We can now see how purely experimental inquiries actually provided confirmation in quantative terms for some of Freud's purely clinical insights about the importance of the unconscious in the genesis of mental trouble. The convergences were unmistakable. Jung's hopes for the future were regarded by the majority of skeptics as daring in the extreme. He actually believed that schizophrenia could be influenced by psychotherapeutic treatment, since he regarded the pathogenic complex, which was now known to be responsible for the existence of neurosis, as providing a "tertium quid" or third element, by means of which healing might be effected. And owing to the experiences of Breuer and Freud, the stage had now been reached when the neuroses themselves were susceptible to treatment by psychoanalysis.

However, so far as schizophrenia was concerned, Freud himself was for a long time unwilling to agree with Jung's opinion; the publication—now long overdue—of the correspondence, comprising hundreds of letters, between the two pioneers, will one day make this quite plain. In any case it is already possible to state definitely that subsequent developments have entirely justified Jung's standpoint on this question.

The Zurich research, then, had established the following propositions:

1. The associative reaction, an elementary and apparently most subjective psychic process, is not in the slightest degree arbitrary.
2. The attitude of the subject is one of the most potent determinants of the associative reaction, although on the whole it tends to remain unconscious. This finding provides the starting point for a psychological typology (later described by Jung as the extraverted and introverted attitudes).[86]
3. The unconscious manifests itself in the form of disturbances, and the character of these disturbances provides us with indicators which enable us to determine the contents of a complex.
4. It is possible to provide scientific confirmation for the method of "free association" which was developed by Freud for the

purpose of discovering the most deeply "repressed" contents of complexes.

5. Emotion, as the dynamic component of the complex, is responsible both for the effects of the complex in the association experiment (the complex indicators) and also for the symptoms thrown up by complexes in psychiatric disorders.[87] It is for this reason that "feeling-toned complexes" are so constantly mentioned in the literature of the period.

6. The contributions made by Breuer and Freud,[88] Freud,[89] Janet[90] and Flournoy[91] to psychological and psychiatric biography must have had an exceedingly stimulating effect on these new points of view in psychology.

The new discoveries strongly attracted a considerable number of young doctors, to whom they were like a breath of fresh air which brought promise of a new depth in psychiatry. As a result, during these years a group of colleagues gathered round Bleuler and Jung who were committed to Freud's insights and who set out to tackle the problems involved in research into psychiatric disorders with the aid of the experimental approach developed by Jung. The team formed a unit under Jung's aegis, and was closely attached to Freud's "Vienna School."

In 1909 the *Jahrbuch für Psychoanalytische und Psychopathologische Forschungen* (Yearbook of Psychoanalytical and Psychopathological Research) was founded as the organ of this "movement." It was published by Bleuler and Freud and edited by C.G. Jung. In 1910, the foundation of a second organ, the *Zentralblatt für Psychoanalyse* (The Central Review of Psychoanalysis) had become necessary; this was published by Freud with the cooperation of the "Zurich group" of C.G. Jung, Alphonse Maeder, Oskar Pfister, Franz Riklin, and others. From 1913 the *Internationale Zeitschrift für ärztliche Psychoanalyse* (International Journal of Medical Psychoanalysis) was published by Freud, with regular contributions from the "Zurich group" of Ludwig Binswanger, Alphonse Maeder, Oskar Pfister and Franz Riklin. Among other "regular contributors" were A.A. Brill (from New York) and Max Eitingon and Karl Abraham (both from Berlin). All these had worked for a considerable period at the Burghölzli.

The year 1913 also witnessed the inauguration, in Lancaster and New York, of *The Psychoanalytic Review*, which in Nos. I/1 (1913), I/2 (1914) and II/1 (1915) published Jung's comprehensive survey "The Theory of Psychoanalysis,"[92] as well as translations of papers from the "Jahrbuch," such as Riklin's "Wishfulfillment and Symbolism in Fairy Tales" (II/1, 1915). As Ernest Jones writes,[93] Jung's works were at that time better known and accepted in America than those of Freud himself.

The life of the "Zurich School"—which we cannot pursue further in this context—is excellently conveyed in a review of the literature written by Jung for the "Jahrbuch."[94] Other papers are recorded in the special List of the Literature of the Zurich School at the end of this volume.

(e) The Problem of Schizophrenia

Jung became increasingly fascinated by the *contents* of the psychotic ideas of mentally ill people, and particularly of schizophrenics, and it was in fact his interest in this material which culminated in his discovery of the collective unconscious. He outlined this development quite briefly as follows in a speech on the occasion of the foundation of the C.G. Jung Institute at Zurich on April 24, 1948:

> Without the hypothesis of the unconscious, it is not possible to give an adequate account of such realities as complexes and the typical habitual attitudes. From the outset, therefore, research into unconscious processes ran parallel with the experiments and enquiries I have described. The former culminated in the actual discovery of the *collective unconscious* around the year 1912. The term itself is of subsequent origin. The theory of complexes and the formulation of a psychological typology had already transcended the limits of the psychiatric speciality, but with the advent of the hypothesis of the collective unconscious the scope of the object of our research was really quite immeasurably widened. Normal psychology, ethnopsychology, folklore and mythology in the widest sense became part of the subject matter of Complex Psychology.

Let us now consider how this development in Jung's specialist researches appears in relation to the problem of schizophrenia. We treat this subject as a connected whole, from its beginning right up to the very recent past.[95] In the first place, however, we recall that in his standard work on schizophrenia, Bleuler explicitly states that so far as the psychopathology of schizophrenia is concerned, his work is based on the discoveries of Freud and his school, and in this context he specifically singles out for emphasis the work of Riklin, Abraham and Jung.

(f) The Association Experiment and the Problem of Schizophrenia

Jung was always interested in the problem of schizophrenia; his early publications in 1907[96] and 1908[97] make this clear. Subsequently, at intervals over the years, he read four short papers on this subject before various medical societies.[98] Those who now had the privilege of working with Jung know how vital this problem always remained for him and what pleasure it gave him to talk about his famous cases—for example, Babette Staub[99] or "Dr." Schwyzer.[100]

When the correspondence between Freud and Jung is published, it will be seen how keenly interested Jung already was at this time in applying the psychoanalytical point of view to dementia praecox. And it will be abundantly clear that he was not only concerned to acquire a theoretical understanding of this illness, but that he also went to very great pains to persuade Freud that it was possible to help these poor patients by means of psychoanalysis. And all this was more than 50 years ago!

Jung's short book on *The Psychology of Dementia Praecox* starts with the proposition that psychotic ideas can be treated in the same way as dreams. This would imply that ideas of this kind are to be regarded as normal material—the only difference being that they are not produced during sleep but in the waking condition. However, the waking condition in schizophrenia differs from the corresponding state in normality owing to the fact that it is marked by a severe reduction in the *fonction du réel* and that we find in it all the characteristics of what Janet has described as *abaissement du niveau mental.*

For the first time in the history of psychiatry, psychotic ideas were treated as something more than unintelligible nonsense and in fact were regarded as a kind of language, the interpretation of which might yield valuable results. In this task of interpretation, Jung was assisted by the technique of word association analysis on a Freudian basis, and also by his own clinical studies in word association. With these aids he was able not only to understand the meaning of these exceedingly bizarre and grotesque schizophrenic neologisms, but also to fit many of these fragments together like a jigsaw puzzle. And so, in certain cases, he succeeded in recovering the entire history of the development of this very peculiar language. The meaning of many other symptoms was also elucidated in the same way.

With regard to psychogenesis, Jung came to the conclusion that in almost every case there is a psychological problem which is present in the first instance, and that for one reason or another this problem gains momentum; it then depends on the original disposition of the personality of the patient whether he goes on to develop hysteria or schizophrenia. The toxic factor—which is often very pronounced—in Jung's view only operates in the second instance, though the process may of course work the other way around.

To Jung's great pleasure, Bleuler accepted most of his conclusions about schizophrenia and published them in his monograph on dementia praecox in 1911. For the next ten years the "Zurich School," under the leadership of Bleuler and Jung, concentrated on the interpretation of schizophrenic material. Among the publications to which reference may be made in this context are the numerous essays by Nelken, Spielrein, Riklin, Maeder, Abraham, etc., which are also included in the special list of literature at the end of this volume.

In 1908 Jung's lecture on "The Content of the Psychoses" was published.[101] In a supplement to the second edition of 1914, Jung formulated a number of general conclusions which had emerged from his practical work with schizophrenics. He states that in his analysis of Schreber's autobiography, Freud had succeeded in reducing the delusional system of this patient to a few simple and universally valid ideas. But Jung then poses a different question. What in fact were the unconscious *intentions* of the patient, on the basis of which he erected his system? To answer this question, Jung also reduced the pathological material, but he reduced it not to infantile wishes (Freud) or to demands for power (Adler), but to *typical motifs*.

Here we encounter one of the most fundamental differences between Freud's views and those of Jung. This difference has been formulated too often in the past, and invariably in the same terms. For a change, let us now try to see it in a new perspective.

From the very beginning, Jung was passionately interested in the question of a possible healing aspect of the pathological material. He therefore concentrated his efforts on an attempt to bring home to the patient the possibility that his delusory ideas might have a positive meaning. He did this with the aid of what he was later to describe as amplification. In fact he assumed that schizophrenic patients actually experience a need or drive to create a new *Weltanschauung* for themselves—a *Weltanschauung* which would enable them to assimilate hitherto unknown psychological phenomena by which they have been overwhelmed.

In *The Psychology of the Unconscious* (current title *Symbols of Transformation*), the book which he published in 1911, and which also marks his inner breach with Freud, Jung gave a classic example of his method.[102]

In a paper read before the British Medical Association in 1914 (see note 98(a)), Jung once again expressed his point of view quite explicitly. He said, "Primitives may have visions and hear strange voices without their mental processes being at all disturbed."[103] We could maintain with equal justice that phenomena of this type are essential to the normal functioning of primitive man in society. Why then should we not regard the symptoms of our schizophrenics in the same light? Jung did so, and he came to the conclusion that if the individual is to remain healthy, he needs a healthy balance; in other words, a more comprehensive personality has to be created. Sooner or later, onesidedness of any kind will inevitably be compensated by a reaction from the unconscious which will take the form of resistance against the onesidedness.

This process of compensation may remain within the bounds of normality; but a person who is mentally unbalanced will try to defend himself against his unconscious and will therefore refuse to accept its compensatory significance. By so doing, he will fatally reinforce his onesidedness; in other words, he will miss the opportunity offered him by the healing intention behind the manifestations of his unconscious. As a result, the pressure from the unconscious will be intensified; its contents will appear even more distorted, and the forms in which they become audible and visible will become increasingly bizarre. Since the material we are dealing with is derived from the unconscious, its language will be peculiar in any case; however, owing to the resistance of the conscious mind, it will become even weirder than before.

Posidonius of Apamea drew attention to this problem and came to the conclusion that normal stimuli may be intensified and turned into affects (a Stoic term connoting extremely undesirable if not actually pathological passions), either as a result of something unusually impressive in the nature of the object or because of some special weakness in the perceiving subject. The discussion of this basic problem was taken up again by Jung in his last writings on schizophrenia.[104] He was still of the opinion that the psychological complications which may be involved in a process of this kind could easily culminate in paranoid reactions.

In the paper which he read before the Royal Society of Medicine in 1919, Jung attacked scientific materialism and causalism which in his view overestimated physical causes and lost sight of the purely psychological factors in mental illness. He maintained that doctors were hypnotized by their belief in physical causation, since they only saw the worst cases in the mental hospitals—cases that could be accounted for largely as the terminal states of prolonged hospitalization. Doctors and psychiatrists have practically no opportunities for following the gradual process of the development of the pre-psychotic state in such patients.

Jung describes an acute catatonic state and demonstrates how this can be regarded as no more than an exaggerated condition of excitability, compounded by "an instinctive reaction against being deprived of freedom." "Wild animals," as he says, "often show similarly violent reactions when they are caged."[105] He also points out that modern medicine never speaks of a disease as having only *one* cause and that causation has in fact been replaced by conditionalism. Jung takes the view that owing to a certain inborn susceptibility on the part of the patient a particular psychological conflict takes on a higher degree of intensity than would occur in a normal person, and that as a result the patient falls a victim to panic fear. However, this phase only belongs to the incubation period of the present psychosis, and is therefore scarcely ever observed by the doctor.

Jung mentions a case in which he actually witnessed the solution of the critical conflict, and he is convinced that it was owing to this development that the patient was saved from the outbreak of a psychosis. Conclusive proof is of course never possible in such cases. And it also has to be conceded that the careful analysis of a psychosis demands almost unlimited time and is therefore not a practical possibility in mental hospitals.

On the basis of the results of his research and practical work, Jung summarizes his position by stating that "considered from the psychological standpoint, psychosis is a mental condition in which formerly unconscious elements" are given the value of a real factor to such an extent that they "take the place of reality."[106] During the subsequent development of the illness the patient's innate disposition will determine the clinical nature of the resulting split. In the case of dementia praecox the split takes the form of the destruction of the patient's feeling relationship with other people.

In conclusion, Jung repeats what he had already said in 1907 and 1909, namely that many cases of dementia praecox are primarily psychogenic in origin, and that the toxic factor is most often secondary. He admits, however, that this whole field is extremely wide, and that it still remains largely unexplored.

Exactly twenty years later Jung wrote a paper on the psychogenesis of schizophrenia (cf. note 98(c)). In it he complains that what he had said twenty years before had left no visible traces in medical circles. In spite of the fact that the *consensus doctorum* was agreed on the psychogenesis of hysteria and the neuroses, the dogma of the organic etiology of schizophrenia still seemed to claim universal validity. Bleuler had admitted that the secondary symptoms were of psychic origin, but he did not agree that the same was true of the primary symptoms.

Nevertheless, Jung continued, Bleuler pointed to a peculiar disturbance of the association-process as *the* primary symptom. And this disturbance closely resembles Pierre Janet's *abaissement du niveau mental* and is accompanied by a *faiblesse de la volonté*—two phenomena which regularly occur in cases of schizophrenia and hysteria. The difference between them is simply that in hysteria the potential unity of the personality is maintained, as can be shown under hypnosis, whereas in schizophrenia the split between the ego and the complexes is almost absolute.

In the course of time the complexes become disconnected and develop such a degree of autonomy that the dissociation is no longer fluid and changeable but fixated and frozen. If there is a drama at all, in the sense of a compensatory process, it is far beyond the understanding of the patient. In most cases it transcends even the physician's comprehension, so much so that he is inclined to suspect the mental sanity of anybody who sees more than plain madness in the ravings of a lunatic.[107]

Interestingly enough, Jung's insights into schizophrenia persuaded an American colleague to classify Jung himself as a schizophrenic. Of course, such an affect-laden verdict contravenes the spirit of the legal stipulation which lays down that a doctor should never issue a certificate relating to a patient, or in other words should never confer upon him the benediction of his diagnosis, without having seen him personally at least once!

Jung states, then, that in schizophrenia the very foundations of the personality are impaired and that the cleavage between the dissociated psychic elements amounts to a real destruction of the indispensable connections between them. In any case, psychological causes produce secondary symptoms exclusively on the basis of the extreme *abaissement*, which Jung regarded as the root of the schizophrenic disorder. Such an *abaissement* means in fact that there is a weakening of the supreme control and is equivalent to a loss of the connection with the psychic totality, i.e., a depotentiation of the conscious personality. It is the curse of the schizophrenic that he no longer fights for this unity, but prefers to identify himself with the unconscious contents. But as soon as the patient gives up the struggle, the danger line between neurosis and schizophrenia has already been crossed.[108]

In the same paper, Jung emphasizes that the unconscious material found in the so-called normal personality is the same as that found in schizophrenics, a fact which is confirmed by the frequent occurrence of latent psychoses. The real trouble begins with the disintegration of the personality and the divestment of the ego-complex of its habitual supremacy. We find the same analogy existing between the primary symptoms of schizophrenics and the dreams of normal people. You can even say that "the dreamer is normally insane." Both personal and collective dream material is reflected in the symptomatology of schizophrenia, though collective material seems to predominate. But it also prevails among normal people in decisive periods of life and in particularly difficult psychological situations, just as schizophrenia also tends to develop at critical moments of this kind.

Jung takes the view that the question of whether the outbreak of a psychosis is a matter of a primary weakness of the ego or of a primary inordinate strength of the unconscious is still open (cf. Posidonius). Primitive man takes the latter view, and Jung wonders whether an inordinate strength on the part of the unconscious may not represent a form of atavism in the human species, or correspond to a kind of "arrested development." He allows for the existence of two groups of schizophrenia: one with a weak consciousness and the other with a strong unconscious. In either case, the pathogenic conflict will become manifest at a time when a special effort at adaptation is required of the organism.

Jung concluded his paper by confessing that he was not optimistic either about the theory or the therapy of schizophrenia. But he insists that the psychic side of this perplexing disorder must be given a fair deal; and—as he himself pointed out—this position had certainly not been reached by 1939.

So far as the theory of schizophrenia is concerned, Jung had little to add to his previous statements in the lecture he wrote for the Second International Congress for Psychiatry at Zurich in 1957.[109] He did, however, emphasize in stronger terms the occurrence of archaic motifs in schizophrenia and he equated these with archetypal patterns. Since archetypal patterns coincide with the "patterns of behavior" of the ethologists, he took the view that the biological foundations of the psyche are affected to a far greater extent in schizophrenia than in the neuroses. He therefore regarded the schizophrenic process as an archetypal, instinctive reaction which is distorted by grotesque, absurd and chaotic associations.

In this state the normally unconscious perceptual variants are experienced as vividly as any of the normal components of stimulation, and the patients are naturally fascinated by the extraordinary richness and profusion of the material, which in fact bears a distinct resemblance to the experiences reported by subjects under the influence of mescaline and other psychotomimetic drugs. This naturally reminds us of Jung's hypothesis of a toxic factor, which he had advanced as early as 1907. However, in this paper Jung remains convinced that psychogenesis is a more plausible hypothesis than the theory of a toxic causation.

In this final paper on schizophrenia, Jung also laid greater stress on psychotherapy. He specifically mentioned the value of drawing and painting, though at the same time he issued a warning against the danger of subscribing exclusively to any particular method or of preaching any kind of dogma. Whatever success the therapist may achieve will be due to his personal strength and devotion; this alone can reestablish psychic rapport with the patient. However, work in this field presupposes a strong constitution and good general health on the part of the therapist; it is, in fact, wearisome, demanding and exhausting. The therapist would be well-advised to avoid undue concentration upon the personal complexes of the patient; he should rather stress their universal, impersonal meaning.

The patient should be given as much psychological knowledge and understanding as he can stand.[110] This procedure naturally implies that the doctor should be well versed in mythology, the history of religion and primitive psychology. Just as there is an objective human body whose functions can only be understood by those who possess a thorough knowledge of *comparative* anatomy, physiology and pathology, so too there is an objective human psyche which can only be understood from both sides. We should like to add that if Cicero quite rightly says "quod di cum dormientibus conloquantur" ("the gods speak to those that are asleep"), it follows that the gods must also speak to schizophrenics, who pass their lives in a dreamlike condition. This reminds us of an experience which Jung once had with an American black woman in a psychiatric institution in the United States. She said to him, quite confidentially, "You know, Doc, God talks to me all the time, funny and serious."

Later, Jung expressed the view that psychosis is a gigantic process of compensation. He based this conviction on his finding that in all those cases which he was able to investigate, analyze and follow up in detail, it was possible to demonstrate a logical development.

At the end of his paper, Jung makes it clear that the chaotic nature of the schizophrenic disturbance must have been precipitated by a toxic factor. But what was responsible for producing this toxin or toxins? Was it "physis" or psyche? Jung held that the answer to this question remained an enigma. Certain phenomena of a symbolic nature seem to point to the paleencephalon as the place of origin of the pathogenic affect—i.e., to the neighborhood of the fourth ventricle in the brain. But the question as to which came first—the hen or the egg—remained open. Jung concluded with a statement of his personal conviction that a solution to the problem of the relationship between psyche and soma might one day be found, as a result of unremitting effort.

(g) Further Results of the Zurich School

Two other essays complete the series of clinical studies dating from the period of Jung's professional activity at the Burghölzli: "The Significance of the Father in the Destiny of the Individual"[111] and "Psychic Conflicts in a Child.[112]

In the first of these, Jung cites four case histories as examples to illustrate the significance which the father-image may have for the destiny of the daughter. He bases his argument on the experimental results produced by Emma Fürst,[113] which showed that within families by far the largest measure of agreement in reaction-type was to be found between parents and children, and he considers this kind of identification with the parent's type to be responsible for the daemonic role of the father.

In the second paper, Jung contributes a case history which supports Freud's findings in regard to infantile sexuality; at the same time, however, he underlines the decidedly independent part played by the *fantasies* connected with infantile sexuality in the development of *thinking*. There is a clear parallel here with Jung's interest in the mythological germs contained in the delusional ideas of schizophrenics.

After the separation from Freud in 1913, Jung felt obliged to establish an organ of his own for the publications of his school. For this purpose he created the *Psychologische Abhandlungen* (Psychological Treatises), the first volume of which appeared in 1914.[114] The later volumes (II–XII, 1928–1957) contain almost exclusively the results of Jung's own research.

In the course of time, when the differences between the approaches of the "Zurich School" and the "Vienna School" of Freud became apparent, Alphonse Maeder, in an attempt at mediation, advanced the suggestion that it would in all probability do no harm if Zurich did in fact tend to lay greater stress than Vienna on the "reality principle" as a relevant factor in therapy (see No. 61 of Chronological Review of the Literature Published by the Zurich School, at the end of this volume). Herbert Silberer, too, in his remarkable opus on the problems of mysticism and its symbolism,[115] took great pains to reconcile the two points of view and hoped, as he confessed in an author's note, to bring Freud and Jung closer to one another again by means of this book. Unfortunately, however, these efforts proved fruitless.

After this period, the term "Zurich School" passed out of use, and, as is well-known, Jung's approach to "psychoanalysis" grew more and more far removed from that of Freud and was ultimately renamed "Analytical Psychology."

5. Psychophysical Relations

For some years now, medical literature has been full of articles and books on the subject of psychophysical relations. A great number of specialist journals and associations are entirely devoted to what is known as psychosomatic medicine. To what extent these efforts actually get through to the general practitioner, which is where their knowledge and discoveries are most urgently needed, remains an open question. However, the real *doctor* has always known about these interconnections, since they must have been present at the cradle of medicine itself. I have given examples of what I mean elsewhere.[116] In practice, the doctor can best acquire a knowledge of these aspects of his patient's case by taking the trouble to record a detailed anamnesis. This has always been the practice in psychiatry, where a personal and a familial case history have been prominent features since the earliest days.

However, after the experimental discovery of complexes, the next step in psychiatry took the form of a scientific investigation of those complex indicators which manifest themselves in the *physical* sphere. As we have seen, when a complex is touched, an emotional reaction invariably follows. The emotion seems here to represent the *tertium* or third reality between psyche and soma, since it is a psychic factor which automatically changes the state of the body. That is why we like to speak of "being moved": in emotion, dynamic effects actually appear in the soma (= the body), and this is no doubt the idea that underlies the word *e-motion* itself (L. *motio* = motion).

In actual practice, what first struck the experimenters in the association experiment was the way in which critical reactions might be accompanied by psychomotor phenomena, such as, for example:

1. sweeping movements with limbs or parts of limbs or tic-like movements with the head
2. trembling
3. sweating
4. blushing and turning pale
5. tears
6. sighing or panting
7. inhibition or acceleration of respiration
8. stammering
9. palpitation of the heart, irregularities in the pulse, etc.

Once a quantitative element had been introduced into the investigation of emotion, e.g. by the measurement of the reaction-time in the association experiment (to take only one obvious factor), it was a natural step to seek and to introduce objective methods of registration for some of the other concomitant phenomena which we have mentioned. So far as the activity of the heart and the circulation of the blood are concerned, appropriate techniques were already available (the sphygmograph and the plethysmograph etc. for 9 above); and the same was true in the case of the respiratory movements of the thorax (the pneumograph for 6 and 7). Sommer[117] had already constructed an apparatus (the tremograph) for the quantitative, three-dimensional analysis of trembling.

(a)   The Psycho-Galvanic Phenomenon

Empirical results had also recently become available on electromotive processes in the skin which exhibited measurable fluctuations when subjected to various sensory stimuli that are closely bound up with emotion.[118] As it happened, experts on these phenomena such as E. K. Müller,[119] an electrical engineer, and Otto Veraguth, a neurologist,[120] were already at work in Zurich, and owing to its high degree of sensitivity this technique seemed likely to provide interesting information on the detailed interconnections between complexes and their physical effects. Encouraged by Veraguth, Jung had begun to observe the "psychogalvanic phenomenon" in subjects with whom he was conducting an association experiment. The first report on this research appeared in 1907.[121] On Jung's suggestion, Ludwig Binswanger then concentrated entirely on this type of experiment; the result was the eleventh contribution to the Diagnostic Studies.[122] The essential aim of these experiments was to measure the fluctuation in the electrical resistance of the body, and especially of the skin, with the aid of a galvanometer.

Set-up of the experiment

A galvanic circuit of about two volts is conducted through the body of the subject, who places his palms on two electrodes. The hands are weighted down with sandbags to keep the contact between the skin and the electrodes beneath it as constant as possible. A highly sensitive mirror galvanometer is connected up to the circuit; it is damped by an adjustable shunt. The reticle of the galvanometer mirror is projected by a ray of light onto a scale (cf. the diagram in Fig. 7).

The subject is seated in such a way that his forearm rests comfortably on a table-top and he can place his hands on the electrodes. The current is then switched on. After some minutes during which the usual fluctuations caused by expectation die away, the reticle can

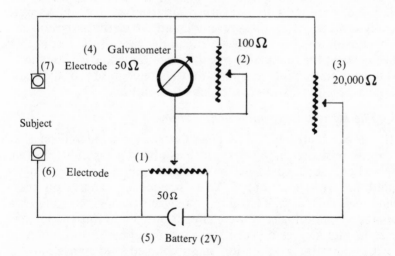

FIGURE 7: *Diagram for the psychogalvanic experiment. The circuit is conducted through the body of the subject, whose left hand rests on one electrode (7) and whose right hand rests on the other electrode (6). Resistance (1) and resistance (3)) form with the galvanometer (4) a Wheatstone bridge. (2) is the shunt, parallel with the galvanometer.*

be adjusted to zero on the scale with the aid of the resistances ((1) and (3) on the diagram); the experiment can then begin. This takes the form of an orthodox word association experiment, in which, after a characteristic latent period, each stimulus-word produces a deflection in the galvanometer. This deflection will exhibit a certain amplitude in mm or cm, which is then noted down in another column (VII) after the reaction (see p. 81).

When the deflection has died away, the next stimulus-word can follow. The ray never again returns to zero during the experiment, but describes an ascending curve. This means that each new deflection must be measured from the relative zero point left behind by the deflection of stimulus-word n − 1, which has just died away (cf. Fig. 8). To obtain a differentiated evaluation of the "prolonged galvanometer deflections" (= larger amplitudes), it proved necessary—exactly as in the case of the prolonged reaction-times—to obtain a *mean* amplitude; here too the so-called "probable mean" was selected for this purpose; it was calculated by Kraepelin's method, which was described on p. 80.

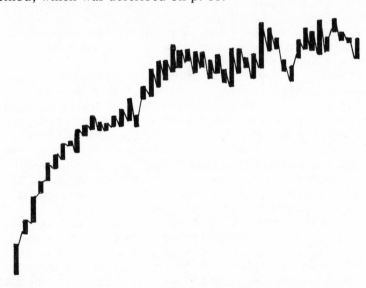

FIGURE 8.

The results of Ludwig Binswanger's very careful research (Diagnostic Studies XI) are summarized below in the author's own words.[123]

The basis of this paper, which is a product of the psychological laboratory of the Burghölzli, was provided by 30 association experiments on 23 normal subjects, both educated and uneducated, who were connected during the experiment to a very low tension electric circuit. Part I begins with a historical review of the literature on the psychogalvanic phenomenon up to 1906; it then gives a detailed account of the set-up, the technical arrangements and the method used for recording the results in the present series of experiments. The writer only deals briefly with the conditions governing the occurrence of the psychogalvanic phenomenon. He ascribes a leading role to the perspiratory gland system, but is very reserved in his comments on the detailed physiological and physical processes which may be involved. However, it seems clear to him as a result of his experiments that we are in fact dealing here with extremely subtle physical processes—processes "whose development can be constantly controlled, stimulated or inhibited by a central organ". The only psychic processes whose impact on the psychogalvanic phenomenon was observed by the writer were *affects*. The value of the phenomenon from the point of view of the association experiment is in fact based on this finding.

In Part II, four experiments are reproduced in extenso. The explanatory graphs relating to these experiments, in which the galvanometer deflections are shown in the form of little rods, and the reaction-times are recorded beneath on a horizontal line, are contained in the Appendix (cf. Fig. 8). Analysis of particular reactions is undertaken with the aid of Freud's technique. The principal result of these experiments is the evidence which they provide that complex reactions are in most cases represented by deflections which are "too long", i.e. above the probable mean for the experiment as a whole. *Thus deflections which are too long constitute a valuable new link in the chain of complex-indicators.* Another important finding is the distinction between Veraguth's "association curve" and *complex curves*. The latter are sections of the association curve which stand out from the general line of the group in the form of secondary waves. An examination of these complex curves proved a valuable aid in determining the affective type of the subjects. The writer discusses in detail the declining slope of the complex curve and its relationship to the declining curve which is obtained where there is a strong affect independent of the experiment or where there is internal or external distraction from the experiment (the attached tables illustrate these different cases). Owing to considerations which cannot be reproduced in detail here, he comes to the following conclusion: "An existing complex (for example, a long-lasting affect or a continuous state of concentration on something other than the stimuli of the experiment) will inhibit the psychological digestion of the stimulus. The result will be a deficiency of associations and feelings, and this lack of new affects will in turn give rise to a lack of new innervations and hence to the disappearance of deflections. The gradual falling away of the curve is explained by the fact that the acute affect gradually dies away, whereas the inhibiting attitude created by the affect still lingers on for a time". Since the falling away of the galvanometer curve is the result of an increase in the electrical resistivity of the subject (and of his skin, in particular), the situation can also be expressed as follows. The electrical resistivity of the subject always decreases when there is an increase in the number of innervations. On the other hand, resistivity increases whenever there is an inhibition or a falling-off in the number of innervations (for example, when the subject is resting or asleep, when he is engaged in purely intellectual activity or when his attention is continuously distracted).

In Part III, the relations between deflection and reaction-time are evaluated in detail and an explanation is given of the causes which may result in a marked discrepancy between the behaviour of these two complex-indicators. Intellectual and linguistic factors may be involved here, but the principal cause is perseveration, which plays a major role in the association experiment as a whole, as emerges very clearly from these experiments. Particular attention is paid by the writer to the very interesting behaviour of the deflections during the occurrence of sound distractions. He comes to the conclusion that the coincidence of an unduly prolonged deflection with a sound reaction points to a linkage in content at a deeper level between the two sound associations; this however is often located in the unconscious and can only be uncovered by psychoanalysis. An attempt is made to prove by examples that repressed complexes may have an effect on the psychogalvanic phenomenon.

Part IV contains five tables giving detailed calculations on the deflections and reaction-times recorded for the four groups of educated and uneducated men and women. The principal results are as follows. "The difference between the probable and the arithmetical means of the deflections is a more reliable criterion of the emotivity of the subjects than the difference between the same two means in respect of the reaction-times. *In all four groups of subjects, unduly prolonged deflections in fact correspond to unduly prolonged reaction-times. In all four groups, the size of the deflection increases with the number of complex indicators. We owe our understanding of this observation entirely to the theory of complexes, which infers the existence of a feeling-toned mass of representations.*"

In relation to what we said earlier about complex indicators, Binswanger's paper confirms that sound reactions should in all probability be interpreted as the result of disturbance by complexes (see (12) on pg. 77). He also confirms that galvanometer deflections above the probable mean should be regarded as complex indicators. Another finding which emerges from his observations is that if the psychological situation of the subject at the time of the experiment is powerfully charged with affect, the occurrence of the psychogalvanic phenomenon may be inhibited; an alternative formulation would be that *conscious complexes* may in certain circumstances suppress the psychogalvanic effect. On the other hand, Binswanger's results clearly demonstrate that *unconscious complexes* are unmasked by this electrical phenomenon. We must, however, note in this context that the author keeps strictly to the Freudian definition current at that period, which equates unconscious complexes with repressed complexes, i.e., complexes that have never been conscious and that can only be detected by means of analysis. There is a contradiction here, and we shall be returning to this question in our final chapter.

On the technical side of the experiment, a word of explanation should be added here in regard to the way in which Jung and Binswanger recorded the deflections. The transparent horizontal scale was fitted with an indicator on a little slide; this enabled the experimenter to follow the light-beam along the scale. Attached to the slide was a cord, which ran over two pulleys and converted the horizontal into a vertical movement. This in turn moved the ergograph writer of a kymograph, which inscribed the curve on a drum (see Fig. 9).

The figure is derived from Jung and it reproduces the apparatus with which he and Binswanger actually worked. The original apparatus is kept in my Laboratory for Experimental Sleep and Dream Research. Nowadays the experiment is carried out with modern technical equipment; this makes it all the more interesting to observe with what simple aids these basic results were originally achieved.

As early as 1907 Jung had also published some experiments of his own.[124] We reproduce one of these here, since it became, incidentally, a kind of "evidence-experiment" on a small scale. The subject was a young man of whom Jung knew nothing, except that he was a total abstainer.

The experiment lasted 120 seconds and consisted of 13 reactions. The graph (see Fig. 10) represents such a severe damping-down of the galvanometer that for practical purposes only "prolonged"

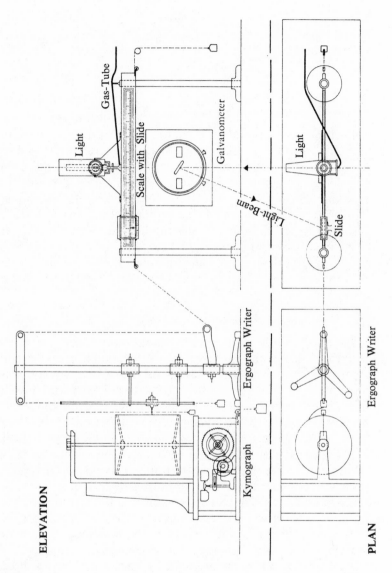

FIGURE 9.

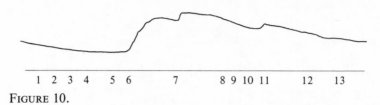

1 2 3 4   5 6   7   8 9 10 11   12   13

FIGURE 10.

deflections are observable. Reactions 1–5 are normal, but after the stimulus-word "restaurant" (no. 6) a sudden and prolonged rise sets in, followed by the reaction "non-alcoholic." Stimulus-word 7 ("polished") again precipitates a rise, with the reaction "glass." Reactions 8–10 present no special features, but the stimulus-word "full" (no. 11)[125] produces another deflection and elicits the response "man." On being questioned, the subject confessed that once, in a fit of drunkenness, he had assaulted and seriously injured someone, and that as a result he had been sentenced to a long term of imprisonment. That was why he had resolved to become a total abstainer.

(b) The Pneumograph

As early as 1907, the clinical observation that affects modify respiration led to the employment of the pneumograph in conjunction with the association experiment. The pneumograph was then a simple instrument in the form of a rubber tube which was fitted like a belt round the subject's chest and transmitted the respiratory movements of the thorax by means of a rubber tube to a Marey tambour, which in turn inscribed them directly on a kymograph.

Professor Peterson, of Columbia University in New York, in collaboration with Jung at the Burghölzli, carried out association experiments on a number of normal subjects and a number of schizophrenics, in which the pneumograph and the galvanometer were used together, simultaneously with the verbal tests.[126] The results only served to confirm the previous findings that prolonged reaction-times and disturbed reproductions are in fact affective phenomena and are therefore rightly regarded as complex indicators. On an average these manifestations occurred more frequently and in an intenser form among schizophrenics; this seems to corroborate Jung's hypothesis that there is a correlation between schizophrenic symptoms and complex effects. Inhibition of respiration and changes in amplitude and frequency show up very clearly on the 19 graphs reproduced in this study. One example should suffice to demonstrate this point (see Fig. 11).

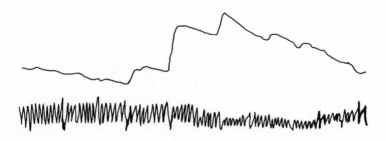

FIGURE 11.

The work of Charles Ricksher and C. G. Jung, which was also carried out at the Psychiatric Clinic of Zurich University, was much more meticulous in its approach.[127] It was established that the amplitude of respiration decreases on an average during the rise of the galvanic curve. The findings in the case of a large number of psychiatric patients with the most diverse diagnoses did not in fact possess any specific diagnostic significance (the example reproduced in Fig. 11 corresponds to Fig. 2 in the paper by Ricksher and Jung).

In the final, twelfth contribution to the *Diagnostic Studies*, Hermann Nunberg attempted to introduce a third instrument for recording the physical accompaniments of complexes, in addition to the pneumograph and the galvanometer.[128] This was

1. *Sommer's tremograph*. His success in this was not very impressive, but he did make it clear that the movements precipitated by complex effects possess a considerable measure of autonomy; alternatively, it could equally well be said that they behave like uncoordinated or split-off fragments. When a complex was stimulated, the trembling movements recorded in this study showed a frequency which was higher or lower than the norm, depending on the personality of the subject in question, so that I personally take the view that a difference in *typology* was involved in these cases. So far as his findings with the galvanometer and the pneumograph were concerned, Nunberg confirmed the conclusions reached by other investigators.

2. *The pneumograph*. Nunberg discovered that as a rule the stimulation of complexes was accompanied by a shallowing of the respiratory process, i.e. by an inhibition of respiration. He then succeeded in demonstrating quite convincingly by an analysis of the respiratory curves that there is a characteristic difference between the effects of conscious and of unconscious complexes.[129] Unconscious complexes simply inhibit respiration; conscious com-

plexes, though they, too, have this effect, may also be accompanied by an excitation of respiratory activity. Here again Nunberg directs our attention to *two types* of "complex respiration":

> There are two types of complex respiration. The one shows itself by laboured breathing. The inspiration is more difficult, there is a kind of dyspnoea, and a feeling of oppression which is probably a partial manifestation of the feeling of anxious dread. The causes of this oppression are not known. Such respiration almost corresponds to the respiration type of unconscious complex associations. In the other type the respiration is irregular, alternately deep and superficial, quasi-sighing. The sighs either occur spontaneously or when a complex is aroused during conversation. When asked the reason for the sighing one is often told that an emotional-toned event has been stirred up. This second kind of breathing corresponds to our respiratory type with conscious complexes. Further investigation must be made to decide the question whether these two types can be separated in practice.[130]

3. *The galvanometer.* The deflections are most marked where there are *conscious* complexes and rather less so in the case of unconscious complexes. Nunberg also confirms the finding of Ricksher and Jung that the amplitude of respiration decreases during the rise of the galvanometer curve and increases as it falls.[131]

I should like now to refer to some secondary literature which was produced at this time under the impulse of the work done by Jung and Veraguth. For the sake of completeness, I should like to mention that on 11th November 1907 Peterson gave a demonstration of the apparatus before the New York Neurological Society.[132] On this occasion he also used the psychogalvanic technique, in collaboration with Morton Prince,[133] to examine one of the latter's well-known cases of multiple personality.[134] I reproduce the two writers' summary below.

1. Under certain pathological conditions, active unconscious processes in the form of memories may exist which do not enter into the conscious life of the personality.
2. Conscious experiences which the patient cannot recall, and which are therefore subject to amnesia, remain alive and can produce the same psychogalvanic reaction as conscious emotional contents.
3. These reactions confirm the thesis that unconscious processes of this kind are psychic (the writers use the term "co-conscious").
4. A physiological explanation of these reactions is unsatisfactory.

Morton Prince returned to these results and dealt with them at length in his book *The Unconscious.*

Sidis and Kalmus then subjected the galvanometer curves to a very careful examination and in particular succeeded in removing the obscurity which existed regarding the contact between the skin and the electrodes in an ingenious manner.[135] Their results provided the first unimpeachable confirmation of the results obtained by Jung and others and demonstrated in terms of physical science that the psychogalvanic phenomenon was the effect of an electromotive force and was not, as was commonly supposed, directly related to the secretion of the sweat glands.

Hugo Müller,[136] who made a special study of the so-called "rest curve" and who also used fluid electrodes, came to the same conclusion. He found that the application of the current from the battery induced in the subject an extremely labile condition of polarization, which was sensitive to psychophysical influences. Another study, by J. Aebly,[137] on the physical problems involved in the experiment attracted the interest of the great Albert Einstein, who was at this time working at the Physical Institute of Zurich University. The only findings which we need to mention in our present context are (1) that the resistance of the body to alternating current proved invariable in the face of psychic influences and (2) that the results obtained by E. K. Müller were confirmed.[138] In 1910 Sidis once again investigated the nature of the psychogalvanic phenomenon, this time in collaboration with L. Nelson.[139] On the whole, he was able to confirm his earlier findings, i.e. he reached the position that what was involved was essentially the production of an electromotive force—though admittedly, in the recent past he had taken the view that it was necessary to postulate muscular activity as the causative agent.

Sidis subsequently corroborated these conclusions once again.[140]

A paper by Coriat confirmed that prolonged reaction-time is a complex-indicator, and that this is particularly true of schizophrenic patients.[141] On the other hand, the psychogalvanic phenomenon did not always react to the so-called "complex-disturbed" stimulus-words in the case of patients of this type, and the same observation was also made by other writers. This finding was ascribed to the well-known emotional "stupidity" of schizophrenic patients. However, the writer found that the pulse rate was always higher after complex stimuli of this kind.

In 1912, Bleuler commissioned two more dissertations on the psychogalvanic phenomenon. The first, by Esther Aptekmann, confirmed Pfenninger's rules related to changes in reaction.[142] She also found that with the utmost consistency the psychogalvanic phenomenon runs parallel with psychological (i.e., emotional) processes that are conditioned by a complex. On the other hand, when the experimental situation is dominated by a violent conscious affect, the galvanometric deflection ceases. This study demonstrates very elegantly that the *personality* of the experimenter may in certain circumstances entirely overshadow the familiar psychosexual effects of the experiment, although normally an experimenter of the same sex as the subject will tend to constellate the "social" complex, while an experimenter of the opposite sex is more likely to stimulate the erotic complex.

The second thesis, by J. Klaesi, once again tackles the question of the behavior of the psychogalvanic reflex when the experiment is repeated several times with the same subject.[143] He found that with 72% to 76% of all deflections above the probable mean the effect is reproducible. When the experiment is repeated several times, the effect at first dies away—but only to reappear later on! The galvanic deflection increases in size with the number of other complex-indicators displayed by the reaction. On repetition, the stimulus is interpreted more and more in terms of the complex; i.e., the complex assimilates more and more elements. On the other hand, a complex inhibits the association of ideas which do not fit in with its contents.

Abramowski, the Director of the Polish Psychological Institute at Warsaw, also adopted Veraguth's method, and we obtained the following information about his findings from V. Kuhne of Geneva:[144] (1) The psychogalvanic phenomenon is a first-class instrument for diagnosing the emotional qualities of the subject. (2) Nonemotional psychic processes produce no psychogalvanic effect. (3) The latency period fluctuates between 5 and 14 seconds. (4) Unconscious impressions (noises, etc. which are not perceived consciously and which therefore remain subliminal) produce an appreciably more powerful galvanometric reaction than the same stimuli when conscious. This points to the conclusion that those unconscious contents which play a real part in the life of the psyche are essentially of an emotional nature. The writers believe that they have established that, both in cases of amnesia caused by repression and in cases of simple forgetting the place of the gaps is taken by a vigorous "vie psychique," which becomes accessible to the investigator through the medium of the experiment.

A final Zurich dissertation on the psychogalvanic phenomenon was the work of V. J. Müller.[145] Experiments were carried out on

Macacus Cynomolgus, now known technically as Macaca fascicularis (crab-eating macaque or Java monkey), with a view to discovering the nerve paths of the psychogalvanic "reflex." The nerves which supply the palms of the hands and the soles of the feet (to which the electrodes were attached) were anaesthetized or severed, whereupon the phenomenon ceased. However, in both cases the backs of the hands and feet stepped into the breach, as it were, although in normal circumstances they do not transmit any reactions! (In this experiment with animals, the stimuli applied were, of course, sensory, not verbal.)

After this date, the investigation and the practical use of the psychophysical accompaniments of complexes passed almost entirely to the United States, where the literature reaches enormous proportions. However, the interested student will find convenient summaries in Wittkower[146] or Flanders Dunbar.[147] Note 148 contains no more than a brief selection of shorter studies, the writers of which still had some personal connection with Jung.

Reference should, however, be made to a work which, in view of the misgivings repeatedly expressed about the statistical methods previously employed in this field, does represent a considerable step forward. This is the remarkable book published by Whately Smith. Under the name of Whately Carington, the writer subsequently devoted himself almost exclusively to research in parapsychology, and he must be regarded as one of the most reliable investigators in this field.[149] His book is still very much worth reading and deserves to be ranked with the classic William McDougall[150] or the more modern "reader" *Emotions: Bodily Change. An Enduring Problem in Psychology.*[151]

CHAPTER V

SOUL AND BODY

In the preceding chapter we have tried to present, in summary form, an account of the literature of "The Zurich School" and of some of the secondary literature to which it gave rise. Anyone who has taken the trouble to read this brief survey will have been impressed more than anything else by two things. (1) Though a considerable mass of evidence has been unearthed and accumulated, this research has not produced anything remotely resembling a final conclusion and has in fact not advanced beyond the initial stages. (2) Here, in the first years of the present century, we find the unmistakable origins of that branch of science which was later to reemerge in our own day and to attract widespread publicity under its new title of "psychosomatic medicine."

To pursue the influence of the Zurich School on psychiatry beyond this point is not part of our program in the present volume. Yet the point should be made that there is a kind of hiatus between 1910 and the present time, and the literature leaves us quite uncertain what in fact the fate of the ideas of the Zurich School has been; they seem as it were to have vanished in the bush.

It is no longer remembered today, either on the psychic or on the somatic side of the literature of psychomatic medicine, what decisive stimulation this whole movement received at the very outset from the Zurich School; I hope in fact that the previous chapter will go some way toward filling this gap and rectifying a historical injustice.

In the present chapter we shall try to throw light on another problem which affects the very basis of Complex Psychology and still im-

150

pedes our understanding of this discipline. This is the problem of the interrelationships between psychic and physical phenomena.

We have seen that all manifestations of the effects of complexes have a common denominator in *emotion*. This factor must be regarded as responsible not only for the existence but also for the constancy of psychological complexes. Its name—like the name of its synonym, *affect*—already implies that it sets something in motion, i.e., that it has a dynamic side. As is well-known, the Latin *e-motio* means precisely "movement out of something." The phenomenon is also known as affect, because it "affects" the body, or, as we also say, "irradiates" the physical sphere. Involuntary innervations appear, which we can regard (depending on our point of view) as the results or the accompaniments of an affect, or even as its cause.

We have seen how respiration or the electrical resistance of the skin may change under the impact of complex stimulation. The same holds good of the pulse or heartbeat, which undergoes all kinds of variations *pari passu* with the emotional condition of the subject. The normal unconscious trembling movements of the fingers, when measured by Sommer's tremograph, exhibit parallel fluctuations, as does the volume of blood in the extremities when measured by the plethysmograph. These are only examples that were already known in the early period of psychosomatic medicine which we have been discussing. In the course of time such phenomena were examined with ever-increasing accuracy by the new research techniques of physics, chemistry and physiology. At the same time, practically all the bodily functions known to physiology, together with their organs and organic systems, were scrutinized for possible changes in function under variable emotional conditions; the results of these tests can be summarized by saying that every organ in the body, with the possible exception of bones and teeth, reacts to psychic stimuli in a more or less specific way. These changes in function can generally be described as plus or minus, depending on whether the effect of the change is to stimulate or to inhibit the function. There are, however, differences which initially at any rate give the impression of being qualitative in nature.

These experimental findings make it slightly less difficult to understand how, as a result either of emotional lability or the presence of extremely intense, persistent and rigid complexes, physical changes may occur and may actually cause real organic diseases. Although these exact, measurable findings are new, the approach they embody is as old as medicine itself. Yet modern scientific medicine did not believe in it until the research of the Zurich School began to make this point of view acceptable in academic circles.

And here I should like to place on record an observation which is not without interest from the point of view of the history of medicine, and which is certainly relevant in this context. It is probable that in primitive times human beings experienced illness as something that belonged to the realm of religion. Remnants of this attitude are still to be found among so-called civilized people (for example, in the idea that sickness is a punishment, particularly in the case of psychic disturbances). Originally, then, the treatment of sickness belonged to the domain of the priests, and this is in fact the origin of the concept of the priest doctor which is known to us from the history of civilization.

Religious cults were actually established whose function was the therapy of sick people and whose priests described themselves as θεραπευταὶ τῶν θεῶν ("therapists" were originally attendants of the god). As we know, similar places of pilgrimage still enjoy a high reputation today. We have only to think of Lourdes, and also of the thousands of chapels where there are images of saints, and particularly of the Blessed Virgin Mary, which possess healing powers. Often they contain a holy well, and this is especially common in Greece, where the Panhagia or All-Holy One is revered as ζωοφόρος πηγή or life-giving spring.

For the ancient prototypes I would refer the reader to my monograph on *Ancient Incubation and Modern Psychotherapy*. The cures occurred—and still occur today—through the agency of a psychic experience, which in antiquity generally took the form of a dream, the so-called "healing dream." This theurgic medicine had entered so deeply into the bloodstream of the ancient physicians that they never forgot the psychic factor in the healing process. A writer as late as Constantinus Africanus, the monk and prolific translator to whom we owe our knowledge of Hippocrates and Galen, comes out clearly on the side of psychogenesis in the antithesis of the following statement: *Corpus enim anima sequitur in suis actionibus. Animam corpus in suis accidentibus.* (The soul follows the body in its activities, the body the soul in its symptoms.[1])

However, the only truly medical attitude, which is to consider psyche and soma always together as inseparable elements with equal rights, can be traced right back to the early days of antiquity. One of the most impressive examples is reproduced below, in the translation by Edward Eyth. We owe this version of the story to Plutarch, but a number of other versions are also extant.[2]

. . . he also learned from his daughter (Stratonice) who was married to Seleucus, that she had now become the wife of Seleucus' son and had been proclaimed Queen of the Upper Provinces. This had come about as follows. Antiochus had fallen in love with Stratonice, who was still young, but who already had a child by Seleucus. This put him in a very agonizing situation, and he did his utmost to fight and conquer his passion. Finally, however, he was forced to realize the culpability of his attachment and the incurability of his feelings, which rational arguments were powerless to mitigate. All he now sought was some friendly stratagem, by means of which he could take leave of this life and do away with his body without attracting attention, simply by depriving it of care and nourishment. So he decided to feign sickness.

But the doctor, Erasistratos (304 to 240 B.C.), recognized without difficulty that he was in love, though the object of this passion was a mystery to him. To solve the enigma he stayed in the sickroom throughout the day, and whenever an attractive young man or woman came in, he watched Antiochus' face and observed all those parts and movements of the body which act in sympathy with the tender feelings of the soul. When anybody else entered the room, Antiochus remained quite unmoved; it was only when Stratonice visited him, as she often did, either alone or in the company of Seleucus, that all those signs which were described so unerringly by Sappho made their appearance in him: the sudden speechlessness, the crimson blushes, the twitching eyes, the profuse perspiration, the agitated pulse—and finally, when the psyche succumbs to the storm, embarrassment, dismay and deathly pallor.

From all these symptoms Erasistratos drew the obvious conclusion, i.e., that it was scarcely likely that the prince would remain silent unto death on account of any other person. Of course he knew how difficult it would be to break the news of his discovery. But he had sufficient faith in Seleucus' friendly feelings towards his son to brave this danger, and so he told the king, "The young man's complaint is love, but it is a hopeless love, for which there is no remedy."

The king was horrified; "Why is there no remedy?" he asked. To this Erasistratos replied, "I am afraid it is true; he loves my wife!" Then the king said, "And are you not willing to play the noble friend, and to sacrifice your marriage to my son, since as you see, this is our only hope of salvation?" "Yes," replied Erasistratos, "but you as a father would not do that either, if Antiochus yearned to possess Stratonice!" "O my dear friend," replied Seleucus, I would surrender my kingdom to save Antiochus!" He said these words with passionate sincerity, weeping as he spoke. Then the doctor gave the king his hand, and told him, "You have no more need of Erasistratos. As father, husband and king, you are the best possible physician for your royal house!"

Then Seleucus summoned a general assembly of his people, at which he declared that he was willing and resolved to appoint Antiochus king and Stratonice queen over all the Upper Provinces; this would be made possible by the marriage of these two. He was convinced that his son, accustomed as he was to showing the obedience of a subject in all things, would raise no objections to this marriage. But if his consort was dissatisfied with this unusual proceeding, he begged his friends to instruct her and to persuade her that it was her duty to accept as right and good all decisions made by the king for the common welfare.

In our context this story is also noteworthy as an example of an "evidence experiment." Erasistratos arranges for the stimulus-words to parade before the subject, Antiochus, in the form of the dramatis personae of the plot, and he prepares his "diagnosis" in light of the physical accompaniments of the complex, which is constellated by the appearance of Stratonice. This dramatic effect of the association experiment leads up to an equally dramatic lysis or solution, and the experienced doctor also knows the ideal therapy, which has the power to convince even the king, badly hit by it though he was himself. Antiochus' sickness, his forbidden love, is a passion engendered by the *telum passionis* or dart of passion of Eros, and it can only be healed by a supreme act of renunciation on the part of the king.[3] The climax of this most impressive psychosomatic drama was portrayed by Ingres in a painting which we are able to reproduce here by the courtesy of Prince De Broglie[4] (see Plate 1).

It is true that, as we have already pointed out, there have always been doctors who have paid attention to the psychic background of their patients. Others, again, who belong to the "somatic" school, will have nothing to do with this "superstition." No doubt these two attitudes should be interpreted in terms of typological differences— in fact, they can already be clearly discerned in the medical schools of antiquity. But differences of this kind have secular effects in the pendulum swings between dominant movements; these are invariably heralded and followed by the outbreak of the most violent polemics.

One of these reversals coincided in time with the turn of the present century, and was ushered in by Charcot and Bernheim, Breuer and Freud, who espoused the unfashionable cause of psychogenesis and whose striking therapeutic successes agitated the medical world of the time, characterized as it still was to a large extent by a mechanistic and materialistic attitude. Superficially, it is true, this agitation had a "moralistic" coloring, since the findings of these pioneers constituted a violent affront to Puritanism.

PLATE 1—*STRATONICE, BY INGRES*   *Chantilly. Musée Condé. No. 432.*

However, the influence of this particular motive has probably been exaggerated by those who were themselves still affected by Victorian ideas. It had been forgotten that whenever the psychic realm begins to manifest itself after an age in which it has been exiled and held in contempt, it makes its presence disturbingly felt (cf. Chap. III) and represents "unto the Jews a stumbling-block, and unto the Greeks, foolishness." At this point, Freud appeared and claimed that at any rate in one small sector of medicine (the neuroses) he had introduced the psychic element and even a so-called unconscious psychic element as a factor into the etiology (or cause) and therapy (or treatment) of these disorders. The doctors of the period, who had only recently qualified as medical men, would hear nothing of this, until Bleuler and Jung boldly took up the cudgels on Freud's behalf. These authorities were in the advantageous position of being able to contribute results which had been obtained in the laboratory and could be verified in the world outside.

Today, however, a whole "new" branch of medicine had arisen which claims to be able to restore the psyche to its rights in practically *every type* of physical disease. It has now become a task worthy of "the sweat of the brow of noble minds" to set to work with the whole armoury of experimental science in the attempt to demonstrate once and for all the existence of the soul of man in the test tube. It is to be feared, however, that such an enterprise will never succeed. Today scientists have justifiably become very skeptical; the soul is αἰόλος (iridescent) and "hard to understand, and you cannot capture it."[5] And yet she is never tired of making her presence felt in the form of measurable effects, for this aspect, too, is by no means foreign to her nature, since so long as she lives in the body, she continually produces in it measurable variations.

Perhaps people—or at any rate responsible medical scientists— still shake their heads today at the thought that there are other responsible investigators who have actually founded an International Psychosomatic Cancer Research Association, and who seriously believe that a significant correlation can be shown to exist between the growth rate of a tumor and the habitual psychic attitude of the patient.[6] Here again, we find the starting point for a psychological *typology*, and we shall have more to say about this subject in Volume III. It seems clear, at all events, that this development is another instance of a pendulum swing, and it would even be possible to calculate that in this case the secular process which we mentioned above had a duration of approximately fifty years.

On closer examination from a historical viewpoint, this modern trend turns out to be an ancient form of wisdom in a new disguise, since as we have said there have always been good doctors who possessed a total overall conception of the nature of a sick or healthy human person. I will only mention here the Dutchman, H. Boerhaave (1668–1738), who was celebrated as the finest physician of his day, and who was also an outstanding scientist (a chemist). His psychosomatic convictions are best illustrated by the following quotation:

> Violent or long-lasting affects in the soul—with all their diversities in type and duration—change, paralyze and corrupt the brain, the nerves, the general condition of the body and the muscles and imprint themselves on these organs in such a remarkable and highly effective way that they are capable of producing and fomenting practically every kind of illness.[7]

Detailed clinical examples of this approach are to be found in the two volumes entitled *Praelectiones Academicae de Morbis Nervorum* by Boerhaave, which can perfectly well be recommended as a psychomatic textbook for our time.[8] With regard to the new work on this subject which has been produced in our own century, we append a brief summary of those parts of it that are relevant to our present theme.

Alfred Adler, who was at that period still a member of the "Vienna School" and who subsequently developed, under the title of Individual Psychology, an orientation of his own which—in contrast to the primacy of the sexual complex in Freud's system—assigns a decisive role in character formation and the etiology of psychic disturbances to the "power complex" and its correlate, the "inferiority complex," made a detailed study of physical disorders which follow in the wake of these disturbances. It is still not sufficiently recognized that his comprehensive treatise entitled *Study of Organic Psychical Compensation*[9] marks the real beginning of modern psychomatic research; it is, moreover, a model work in its theoretical restraint. If a physical symptom has a psychic component, such a symptom clearly provides the doctor with a source of *evidence* about the nature of the disturbance, just as "purely" physical symptoms do. And the localization of the symptom is a particularly revealing piece of evidence in this context; for example, if we know nothing else except the name of the organ which is affected, this already tells us something about the nature of the psychic problem concealed behind it—provided, of course, that we are able to "read" or understand this "organic language." Adler was convinced that he had demonstrated that in every human being certain organs or organic systems are "stronger" and others "weaker" than other organs, i.e., that specific "organic inferiorities" exist. The extent to which the subject is successful in "coping with" his weakness will determine whether or not he will develop a corresponding neurosis. In certain circumstances, he may actually derive an advantage from his organic inferiority—the so-called "illness benefit." This whole approach has been criticized, over-rationalistically, as "organ mythology." Yet it is in fact an intelligent approach, since it does ascribe a definite function to the somatic factor, without being causalistic. As we shall see, this restraint is entirely justified, since it allows for the fact that in case of need the psyche does possess a crucial capacity for making something meaningful out of somatic disorder.

The major comprehensive surveys in this field which now follow are all based on a strictly Freudian foundation. Freud had coined the concept of conversion, according to which—especially in cases of hysteria—the psyche (i.e., the complexes) is capable of producing physical equivalents in the form of symptoms (e.g., hysterical anesthesias and paralyses). Thus *psychogenesis* was now postulated, and this meant that the psyche was regarded as the *cause* and the physical symptom as the *effect*. This conception fitted in with the picture of the world projected by the natural sciences much better than Adler's standpoint, which could be described as occasionalistic.[10] That is why Freud's view was so much more popular.

At this point we encounter Oswald Schwarz's basic treatise on *The Psychogenesis and Psychotherapy of Physical Symptoms*.[11] This provided evidence that the important schools of internal medicine associated with the names of von Krehl and von Bergmann were now favorably disposed toward the psychological point of view. The most exhaustive summary of the innumerable results published in this field is to be found in the book by Erich Wittkower on *The Influence of Emotion on the Body* which we have already quoted.

America then took the lead in psychosomatic research and an immense literature began to appear. Fortunately for us, Flanders Dunbar undertook the tremendous task of reviewing this literature. Her book has in fact become an indispensable standard work.[12] Among the major representatives of this tradition in the United States were Ed. Weiss and O. S. English,[13] R. Grinker and F. P. Robbins[14] and Franz Alexander.[15] In Germany today, A. Jores of Hamburg has espoused the cause of the recognition of the psychic factor in internal medicine and has brought about something like a direct confrontation between psychosomatics and "academic medicine." So the struggle is still being carried on.

It seems to me that what is happening here is no longer covered by the ancient antithesis between "psyche or soma," considered as a pair of alternatives. Nowadays it is simply a question of the preference felt by different investigators for this or that way of looking at things or of approaching the problem of the relationship between body and soul within the phenomenon we know as man. It is true that the work has to be carried forward onesidedly by each of the two parties; yet the aim remains always to achieve a breakthrough somewhere in the middle of the tunnel. A predilection for one aspect of the question or another will always be a matter of temperament, or as we could say with Jung, a typological problem. If this interpretation is correct, it would be necessary to infer the existence of an objective third component of the situation which would dissolve the original dichotomy between psyche and soma and make room for a synthetic trichotomy. To explain this more clearly we shall have to retrace our steps and start a little nearer the beginning of the story.

For a long time the world of Western civilization was much more deeply impressed by the dynamics of the psyche than by the contents or images within it. And our experience of emotion is in fact one of an extremely direct and immediate manifestation of energy, and this energy, although of psychic origin, is experienced by us essentially in or on the body. Emotions have a tendency to appear in situations with which we cannot cope at the moment, situations which are in some way beyond our control. As a result, if we think about them at all, we are liable to evaluate them in negative terms—an attitude in which, incidentally, Western and Eastern ideas essentially concur. The Samkhya philosophy, for example, considers it highly desirable for the same reason that the soul should be entirely disengaged from the body, since contamination between these two dimensions can only lead to suffering. Greek antiquity was of the same opinion. Thus Aristotle represents the union of soul and body as an unnatural and embarrassing state for the soul, and it is this connection between an immaterial psyche and the material soma which is responsible for the affects.

This doctrine about the affects then found its way via St. Thomas Aquinas into the ethical teaching of the medieval Schoolmen. In their moral theology the affects were given a quite onesidedly negative evaluation, which resulted in the formulation of a "catalogue of the vices" and a corresponding doctrine about the virtues (the so-called "aretalogy"). According to the teaching of the Peripatetic School, the affects are derived from the body; the Stoics, on the other hand, held that they originate in the soul, and laid the blame for the evil they cause on wrong education and in particular on a false orientation toward the "seductive attractions of things." Philo was the first to inquire after the possibility of a metaphysical origin of the affects, and later they degenerated into demons. They were also compared to wild beasts or to fire, for they tear us, burn us or make us hot.

Violent quarrels (affects!) also broke out between the various schools of philosophy over the nature of the desirable goal of therapy—whether it was *symmetria* (due proportion) or *harmonia* (harmony) of the affects, or *ataraxia* (insusceptibility to suffering), *euthymia* (contentment), *apatheia* (insusceptibility) or *metriopatheia* (control of the passions). "Apathy" in the form of impassibility was however finally ascribed only to God the Father, since it was recognized that it would be nothing short of inhuman to have no affects whatever. Even in relation to God himself, impassibility of this kind was open to question, and in fact it is probably for this reason that God had to concede to us a Son of Man who is "passible" by way of compensation.

On the whole, then, it was considered expedient that man should rest content with metriopathy or restraint of the passions. Normally, the prescription for control of the passions was that they should be subjected to the authority of *ratio* or reason; as a result there was only one passion, Christian Love in St. Augustine's sense of the term, which could be allowed to prevail without restraint.[16] Many thick and well-meaning volumes have been written on this question of the government of the emotions; some of them appeared as recently as the seventeenth century. Of these I will only recall *'De l'Usage des Passions*, by the Oratorian P.J.F. Senault, with its delightful allegorical title page, in which all the passions, including love, are held in chains by "Reason" and a little spaniel, called "Judgement," is on the watch (this final item probably represents a recourse to the "dogged" instincts, as contrasted with Reason, which is always a gift of divine grace).[17]

We have already observed, in our study of the associated experiment, that when an emotion appears, i.e., when a complex has been activated, the reactions of the subject become inadequate and unwelcome effects are produced. This in itself is enough to make the ancient classical contempt for the affects intelligible. Pierre Janet shared this basic attitude when he drew the causalistic conclusion that emotions are excessively powerful excitations, which arise *as a result of* our inability to react adequately to a given situation. Janet

The VSE of PASSIONS *Written in French by* J.F. Senault. *And put into English by* Henry Earle of Monmouth 1649.

Divine Grace

Reason

Joy

Feare

Sorrow

Choller

Despaire

Hope

Boldnesse

Eschewing

Love

Hatred

Desire

Passions araing'd by Reason here you see,
As shee's Advis'd therein by Grace Divine:
But this, (yow'll say)'s but in Effigie !
Peruse this Booke, and you in ev'ry line
  Thereof will finde this truth so prov'd, that yow
W·M·Sculp: Must Reason contradict, or grant it True .

Tafel 2: Stich von WILLIAM MARSHALL zur englischen Ausgabe
von SENAULT's Buch.

observed a striking synchronism between the well-known physical symptoms caused by affects and such familiar *psychic* concomitants as the classical *belle indifférence* of hysteria. Janet brings together these psychic symptoms in his concept of the *abaissement du niveau mental*; Jung, following him, explains that when a complex is excited, it will make its presence felt by causing this kind of drop in psychic potential, in whose wake all possible types of regression into archaic mechanisms can be observed. In such a state of mind we become primitive and react with *projections*. We become subjective and "personal" because an objective attitude would demand a form of mental superiority which the excitation of the complex has made impossible for us.

Seen in this light, the complex is precisely an area of inadequate adaptation to reality, and in psychological terms this is simply equivalent to a specific unawareness of embarrassing weakness. And at this point the "trouble-maker" who has touched us on the "sore spot" (in the association experiment this is of course the experimenter), becomes an antagonist and is made responsible for our failure. This primitive, automatic procedure is what we call *projection*, which means literally the throwing outward of a content of the unconscious onto the first fellow creature we meet who offers himself as a potential carrier. The apparent advantage which we gain from the automatic operation of this "method" is that we no longer find it necessary to become conscious of our weakness, although if we looked at it from a reasonable standpoint this would actually be a unique opportunity. But it is of course precisely reason which is dethroned by the domination of emotion, and this makes Father Senault's admonitions a pious hope every time.

It is not until we undergo the discipline of analysis that we learn from our experience, as analyst and as analysand, with what *emotional* resistances we have to reckon, since it is these which oppose our realization of our weakness. Becoming conscious in this way amounts to paying a big bill—something which none of us particularly likes doing! This also brings it home to us that in these cases emotion is confronted by emotion, so that the problem here involves a clash between opposites—a point, incidentally, which Senault did take into account. Once again, then, the situation calls for intervention by a third party.

The physical changes which occur simultaneously with these psychological manifestations in the "environment" of the complex give rise to some interesting reflections on the subject of the cause and effect of emotion. Speaking naively, we would say that the affect which appears when we suddenly find ourselves in a situation with which we are unable to cope imposes itself on us as a result of our psychological recognition of our inadequacy. For example, if we are really frightened, we very soon recognize this feeling of fear, and it is probably only in the second instance that we become aware of the physical manifestations connected with it, such as trembling, bated breath, sweating, gooseflesh, hair standing on end, etc. So we naturally assume that the emotion which is the psychic equivalent of these manifestations is actually the primary factor.

On the other hand, there is of course the alternative possibility that the physical phenomena were there in the first place and that we only became conscious of our fear through our perception of these physical effects. It would probably be a fruitless undertaking to attempt to settle this question, either way. The most that can be established by empirical means is that the two kinds of manifestations appear to be simultaneous. It is, however, possible to produce one argument which can be convincingly demonstrated with the aid of the psychogalvanic phenomenon. If the subject deliberately takes a deep breath, this is followed by a deflection of the galvanometer which is in no way different from those produced by the complex stimuli; in other words, a high respiratory amplitude which is produced at will for purely experimental purposes has exactly the same relationship to the effect as one which follows involuntarily (like sighing) as a result of the stimulation of a complex and reduces the resistance of the skin in the same way.

This inversion of the causal nexus as compared with the naive view does provide us with food for thought; for example, it tends to support the theory of emotions held by James[18] and Lange,[19] which states that we do not cry because we are sorry, but are sorry because we cry, angry because we strike, fearful because we tremble; i.e., that "the bodily changes follow *directly* the perception of the exciting fact, and that our feeling of the same changes as they occur IS the emotion." James's thesis is that the states of mind that appear in "the *coarser* emotions, grief, fear, rage, love" are the results of their bodily expression, and that "Without the bodily states following on the perception, the latter would be purely cognitive in form."

This is a point of view which undoubtedly merits serious consideration.[20] An attempt has actually been made to isolate from tears a substance which, when administered, would produce depression. But obviously this makes the whole problem ridiculous, and we can only ask ourselves, "In that case, what are we to make of tears of joy?'' At all events, the relationships between body and psyche are extremely subtle and multifarious, and the time is by no means ripe yet for anything approaching an analysis in terms of strict causality. Reference should be made here to one further complication, which has its experimental basis in the association experiment, especially when the test is combined with the psychogalvanic phenomenon. The research of Pfenninger, Aptekmann and Klaesi has established that complex stimuli have a periodic function and that their physical accompaniments also wax and wane in intensity and in fact exhibit a wave-like appearance on the graphs. It looks as if an exponential function is involved here. Similar behavior has been observed in certain allergic phenomena such as, for example, insect bites, which tend to swell and itch in phases. This is a vagary of the time factor and we are still completely in the dark as to its workings.

It was naturally a matter of considerable satisfaction to investigators concerned with any of the known physical concomitants of emotion when it became possible to obtain measurable physical quantities which could be correlated with purely psychic events. This raised the question of a possible causal relationship between them. As we have seen, this question was answered in two directly opposite ways, each of which was conditioned by temperament. According to one view, emotion (i.e., the psyche) was understood to be the cause of the physical effects. We shall call this approach (2). According to the other view, the relationship is inverted. We shall call this approach (1). In the following diagram φ = physis and ψ = psyche

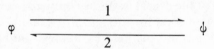

Plausible arguments can be adduced in support of both these approaches, and we find ourselves compelled to accept an unsatisfactory "both . . . and" situation. Both orientations have considerable achievements to their credit. We need only recall, in the case of (1), the development which led from Darwin[21] via James to Watson and behaviorism. This has a striking Russian parallel in Pavlov and Bechterev. The inevitable result of this position is a form of psychological materialism, in which the psyche dissolves into a delusion. But the question "*Who* is deluded?" is *not* asked in this context. In philosophical terms this position would be called epiphenomenalism; it denotes the view that the psyche, and consciousness in particular, is a by-product or epiphenomenon of the chain of physical causation. In itself, the psychic element that is conditioned in this way and arises ad hoc, so to speak, can exert no influence at all on the processes of the cerebral and neural systems. That this model does not work we already know from experience; we have only to recall the simple fact that a physical action—a voluntary movement, for example—does not necessarily proceed from an external stimulus along the lines of the classical stimulus-and-response pattern; on the contrary, an identical effect can be produced by unaided conscious psychic intention (as in (2)).

It is true that we cannot conceive how these relationships operate; this, however, does not prevent any one of us from continuing to execute voluntary movements of the utmost precision and skill; but it does show us how fundamental the difficulties in the way of our understanding must be. Kant expressed the following opinion on this problem: "It is no more intelligible to me that my will is able to move my arm than it would be if someone were to say that the same arm could arrest the moon in its orbit. The difference is simply that I have experience of the former, whereas the latter has never come within the purview of my senses."[22]

It is probably wrong in principle to ascribe priority either to the psychic or to the physical dimension. The *way in which* both (1) and (2) operate is equally incomprehensible, and would remain so even if we knew much more about physis or psyche than we do. It is precisely this that makes so-called psychophysics such an enthralling subject. But it must be recognized for what it is if we wish to pose questions that are meaningful from a scientific point of view. In the field of psychosomatic medicine there are writers today who certainly do just that. For example, H.G. Wolff has this to say: "The emotions which are precipitated by a threatening situation are not the cause of the bodily reactions. The two processes occur simultaneously and belong together, though the way in which this happens remains an open question."[23] V. von Weizsäcker puts it as follows: "The introduction of the psyche into pathogenesis signifies a change which relegates the causal approach to a subordinate position."[24]

The question as to whether the cause of an illness is psychological or physical is nowhere more keenly debated than in *psychiatry*. There are obvious reasons for this, but more specifically it is due to the apparent failure of psychotherapy to deal effectively with severe psychoses, which has hitherto placed a powerful argument at the disposal of the advocates of somatogenesis. More recently, this problem has entered on a new phase owing to the discovery and synthesis of substances which create conditions in normal subjects similar in many respects to authentic psychoses. The scientists working in this field seem to be on the track of the "toxic factor" postulated by Jung as early as 1907 as responsible for the onset of schizophrenia.[25, 26] Even at that early date, however, Jung was cautious enough not to identify the possible discovery of such a factor with the concept of the somatogenesis of this psychosis; he left open the question as to whether in certain circumstances the schizophrenic illness might not itself produce a toxin of this kind.

It seems probable that this aporia cannot be eliminated, since body and soul represent an authentic pair of opposites. Jung's psychology has taught us that in such cases a so-called "unifying symbol" may appear in the psychological realm by means of which the problem of the opposites may be transcended. A little historical reflection may remind us that the ancient world was already aware of the insolubility of this dilemma, and that on this subject ancient writers have suggestions to offer that are decidedly reminiscent of *symbols*. In every case, the problem of the dichotomy is dealt with by reference to a trichotomy. Thus Posidonius proposes that *phantasy* should be regarded as a mediating *tertium* or third component.[27] This suggestion certainly appealed to Synesius, who coined the term *phantastikon pneuma* or imaginative spirit for it.

In Plotinus we read that the *pathē* or affects do not belong either to the soul or to the inanimate body but to a *synamphóteron* made up of body and soul. συναμφότερον means "both at the same time" and is a term which denotes a "complex magnitude."[28] Proclus describes the same entity, but he defines it not as consisting of the four elements, but as constituting a fifth. Thus we have the two stages 2 → 3 (in Posidonius, Synesius and Plotinus) and 4 → 5 (in Proclus), a point which should be of interest to connoisseurs of numerological symbolism. The fifth body of which Proclus speaks is spherical, or to be more precise its *eidos* or image is spherical. This recalls Plotinus IV, 3, 9, 15, where there is a discussion of circulation as the most perfect form of movement, which he says can also be observed in the motions of the stars.

Plotinus also tells us that something of the nature of circulation is also to be found in the human body, and as a *tertium* it is also in some way related to the *soma pneumatikon* or spiritual body. Aristotle had already laid down the proposition that the natural movement of the ordinary elements or bodies leads from a place that is contrary, to one that is conformable, to nature.[29] A circular body, however, could never leave its natural place and yet remained in perpetual motion—a teaching which reminds us of the *opus circulare* (circular work) or the *rota* (wheel) of the alchemists, and also of the "circulation of the light" in Taoism.[30] In Plotinus the *soma pneumatikon* has many names. Examples of these are *pneuma somatikon* (bodily spirit), *astroeides soma* (starlike body) or *augoeides soma* (raylike body). Proclus speaks of an *augoeides* or *astroeides ochema* or vehicle. At death all these *somata* pass over into the *eidolon*, the *imago* or the *simulacrum* (phantom, spectre or shade)—or, in a word, into the *skia* (Gk.) or *umbra* (Lat.), both of which mean literally "shadow" and correspond roughly to our concept of the soul which leaves the body at death.

Clearly, there was a considerable measure of agreement in antiquity about this *tertium* or third party between body and soul, and so recent an authority as Paracelsus is still referring to this concept when he speaks of "a second, invisible body, which forges the bodily symptoms."[31] It is in fact quite a useful exercise to ask ourselves what the Greek word *symptoma* actually means. In the first place it is a synonym for *coincidentia* and *accidens* and denotes a chance occurrence either in a good or a bad sense. Moreover, it can signify a specific geometric property of a curve. *Symptosis*, again, is the confluence of two streams or the point of intersection of two curves.[32]

In addition to these older connotations, there is of course the modern meaning of a sign of disease which is familiar to us all. Common to all these conceptions, however, is the notion of a meeting of *two* things out of which a *third* arises; this fits in perfectly well with Paracelsus' formula. Perhaps the disturbances produced by complexes which we encounter in the association experiment can also be understood from this angle; the entity which interferes with the conscious intention of the subject would in that case be the "invisible body" of which Paracelsus speaks. The "probe" represented by the stimulus-word would then play the part of an accidental and not of a causal factor—which is probably still the only reasonable approach to the subject. At all events, we can see that when we are considering the problem of the relationship between body and soul a third party seems to put in an appearance now and then, and this third component has many of the marks of a symbol. In our own time, on the other hand, it scarcely seems to be around any more.

Yet the conception of the "subtle body," originally an importation from the East, still continues to play a certain part, although perhaps no longer in serious and responsible scientific circles. Today, thanks to an important book by Henry Corbin, we are able to study the magnificent amplifications of the speculation on the "subtle body" which is to be found in Iranian Shiism.[33] He too makes liberal use of the parallels from Proclus.[34] The connections between the Alexandrian-Neoplatonic *corpus subtile* tradition and the early Fathers of the Christian Church have been examined in detail by G.R.S. Mead, but a great deal of additional material still remains to be evaluated.[35]

From the point of view of exact science, we can of course make no progress with this theory, since it affords us no opportunities for experimental verification. Perhaps, however, verification of this kind is no longer as unthinkable as it used to be; the following example may serve to illustrate this point. At any rate, it seems clear to me that in this case the *tertium* simply must be *postulated*, if, that is, we are disposed to accept the findings as reliable.

A young Czech physiologist, Stepan Figar, used the plethysmograph to examine simultaneously the forearms of two subjects who were unaware of each other's presence.[36, 37] Subject (1) alone was exposed to certain psychic stimuli, and this was done at previously scheduled random (i.e., irregular) intervals of time. These stimuli could be detected by the characteristic fluctuations in the volume of the forearm which they produced on the plethysmograph. Yet the volume curve of subject (2) who had played no part in this side of the experiment and had not been exposed to any of the stimuli displayed a significant congruence with that of subject (1). Since that time, the experiments have been repeated and confirmed on numerous occasions. Recently, they have also been repeated in various parts of the United States, where comparable results have been obtained. The statistical basis also proved capable of withstanding criticism.

The situation in this type of set-up is even more complicated than it was in the experiments with only one subject which we described earlier. We said then that the occurrence of these phenomena involved almost insuperable difficulties for any explanation in purely causal terms, since no one had yet succeeded in showing us how the psyche produced its effects in the body and vice versa, although both these forms of interaction are well-attested facts of our experience. In the case of Figar's experiments, on the other hand, the process $\psi \rightarrow \varphi$ does not take place within a single, unitary personality, but in the form of a transmission from subject (1) to subject (2), although there is no conceivable mechanism known to us by means of which such a transmission could occur. In fact we chose this example in preference to many others in which the possibility we have indicated is already presupposed. In the treatise *"De sulphure"* of the *Novum lumen chymicum* in the *Musaeum Hermeticum*, an anonymous alchemist wrote: "The soul, however, by which man is differentiated from the other animals, operates in the body but possesses a wider field of operation outside the body, since outside the body it possesses absolute power."[38]

In the terms of our diagram on p. 164, cases like Figar's experiment are examples of approach (2), in which however ψ is located outside the body (*extra corpus*).

Nowadays, phenomena of this type are described as parapsychological and are actually a greater nuisance to orthodox scientists than psychosomatic phenomena. On the other hand, Jung from the very beginning lent a ready hearing to results of this kind, for two reasons. In the first place, the majority of the human race has always been convinced that such things are possible (and in fact they still believe the same today, in defiance of all scientific enlightenment, though they often keep this secret), and such a conviction is in itself a significant psychological fact; and secondly because such findings actually fit in very well with Jung's own concept of the archetypes (which we shall be discussing shortly). He did not express his views on this subject in a systematic form until 1952.[39] However, the psychological problem which I was obliged by my subject to discuss above cannot be dealt with satisfactorily from a Jungian point of view without reference to these late reflections.

If we take as our starting point the general question of the correlation between psyche and physis, we shall be struck by the fact that we are accustomed to thinking of approach (1) in our diagram as a commonplace matter of everyday experience. It is, however, clear to us now that this approach by no means satisfies the requirements of strict causal thinking. On the other hand, approach (2) is naively regarded as just as incomprehensible or nonexistent as approach (1) is assumed to be self-evident. We find it impossible to explain *how* psyche can be supposed to produce an effect in physis, and this holds good whether physis is *intra corpus* (inside the body) or *extra corpus* (outside the body), as is the case with certain parapsychological effects.

I personally am convinced that the existence of these phenomena can no longer be seriously called in question. And here I take my stand on certain venerable procedures, known to us from of old, such as oracles and other similar methods of divination. On closer examination these are invariably found to consist of a psychic effect *extra corpus*, which cannot be accounted for in terms of any known mechanism of transmission. Let us take as an example what is probably the most ancient oracle that has come down to us, the Chinese *I Ching or Book of Changes*.[40] A heap of 49 yarrow stalks is separated into groups by a process of repeated division and sub-division, until a remainder is left over which is no longer divisible. A line is allocated to this remainder, and when this operation has been carried out six times, a group of six lines is formed; this is known as a hexagram. In accordance with certain specified principles, the individual lines can be assigned to two classes; they can be either broken or unbroken. The result is a mathematical possibility of 64 hexagrams. Each of these corresponds to a specific life situation, and the sign which is obtained from the six lines in this way represents the *diagnosis* of this situation.

The individual lines can be either moving or rigid, i.e., they can *remain* whole or broken lines or they can *change* into their opposites (hence the title "Book of Changes"). Once again, this is determined in accordance with certain specified principles. The sign of change derived from the first hexagram by this transformation represents the *prognosis* of the situation. The individual hexagrams are regarded as *images* and are given corresponding names. From the point of view of form they are, of course, geometrical in character. Our aim, then, in consulting this oracle is to obtain a characterization or typical portrait of our situation at a specific moment, and also a forecast of another typical situation into which it is likely to develop. And all this comes about as a result of our more or less random action in dividing up the yarrow stalks.

If we are prepared to take the view that a procedure of this kind may be meaningful, we can only assume, starting as we do from the presuppositions of our own Western culture, that some "method" is involved in the dividing-up operations which stands in a relationship of meaningful correlation to the 64 preexistent possibilities of the oracle. But we should have to admit, with Jung, that this relationship could only come about via the unconscious, because a connection of causal nature would be unthinkable to the conscious mind—and because, moreover, the unconscious psyche does, in fact, possess such a "method." If this is true, the image that arises could actually correspond to the outer or inner situation—all the more so in view of the fact that we presumably only consult an oracle when the real nature of our situation at a given moment is concealed from us—i.e., is unconscious.

This could imply that the act of consulting the oracle brings about a correspondence between the psyche or the real situation of the person concerned and the hexagram which has been formed by the yarrow stalks. Thus the objective matrices of the oracle would coincide with the subjective psyche of the inquirer, a phenomenon which cannot conceivably be accounted for in terms of any kind of causal dependency. To avoid using the onesided language of causality, Jung used to say in such cases that an *arrangement* had been brought about, either in the outside world (e.g., in the form of a hexagram) or in the inner world (e.g., in the form of a dream), or between these two worlds. He believed that arrangements of this kind can occur in critical situations when an *archetype* is constellated. At such times, we generally find ourselves in the grip of a powerful emotion, and then, as we have seen, effects of a psychophysical character are produced. But if it is true that the physical side of this equation can also be located *extra corpus*, then perhaps the oracles we have been considering may themselves turn out to be *synchronicity phenomena*,[41] since they involve the appearance in the outside world of arrangements of a similar type, which coincide in a meaningful way with the psychological situation of the inquirer at the same moment in time. Since, however, as we have said, no conceivable causal connection can exist in these cases, Jung speaks instead of *acausal connections*.

We have seen that this formulation also applies to normal—and indeed to disturbed—psychophysical functioning, for example to complex effects or psychosomatic symptoms. To conclude, then, I should like to repeat my suggestion that the whole subject of psychophysical relations should be reexamined from the point of view of synchronicity; for it is a fact that the problem which already plagued Plutarch as to *utrum animae an corporis sit libido* (whether libido belongs to the soul or the body) is still very much an open question. In terms of our diagram on p. 164 we should have to say that neither approach (1) or (2) nor the sum or product of them both is really adequate to cover this whole complicated situation.

CHAPTER VI

THE THEORY OF COMPLEXES

The abundance of experimental and clinical data on the many and various manifestations of complexes which we now have at our disposal should made it possible for us to summarize our conclusions by propounding a theory. The treatment of complexes naturally plays an important part in the practice of psychotherapy. Yet practitioners, as we know, often display little inclination or aptitude for theoretical formulations. Even Jung himself, the real discoverer of complexes, never gave a systematic account of their phenomenology. In his inaugural lecture to the Swiss Federal Institute of Technology, which was delivered May 5, 1934, he did, it is true, offer certain general reflections on the theory of complexes, but these once again are more in the nature of suggestions than of clear formulations.[1] An attempt will therefore be made in this final chapter (1) to summarize the contribution made by our experimental and clinical data toward the formulation of a special theory of complexes, and (2) to ascertain to what extent a theory of this kind might be extended so as to provide us with a general theory of complexes.

1. A Special Theory of Complexes

The word "complex" is derived from the Lat. deponent verb *complector* meaning to entwine, encircle, envelop, embrace, take possession of. The verb *compleo* means "to fill out completely," and also "to overfill" or "to make complete." The noun *complexus* means envelopment, embracing or mutual entwinement. We shall therefore use the technical term "complex" to designate a content of the

172

psyche which constitutes a relatively self-contained whole (the "vessel" which is filled or overfilled), and which itself consists of several parts that are held together, intertwined and mutually embracing, by the agency of a strong emotional tone (the "feeling-tone"), which is identical and common to them all. The following notes may serve to throw light on the *history* of the term "complex" in Jungian psychology.

According to H. Christoffel,[2] the word itself was introduced into oral discussion by Eugen Bleuler at the Burghölzli, and was then taken up and developed by Jung. In Jung's own writings we find the term for the first time in his dissertation "On the Psychology and Pathology of So-called Occult Phenomena,"[3] where however it only occurs in the form of the "ego-complex." In the sense in which we shall be using it in this chapter, the term first appears in Jung's paper "On Simulated Insanity,"[4] though here, too, there is no attempt at definition.

Subsequently, expressions such as "feeling-toned complex of ideas," "split-off complex," "impacted feeling-complex" and the like established themselves in conversational usage. Christoffel draws attention to the fact that the "Leipzig School" (F. Krüger, V. Volkelt, and H. Werner) were more concerned with investigating the *formal* aspect of this phenomenon (in contrast to the formulations of the "Zurich School," which concentrated more on the *content* of the complexes). Thus the Leipzig School stressed the significance of complexes for normal and developmental psychology, and as pointers in the direction of gestalt psychology.

The telegraphic dialogue of the association experiment presents us with a sequence of phenomena which—especially since the introduction of time-measurement—are susceptible to quantitative evaluation in statistical terms. This enables us to compute averages on the basis of which we can interpret deviations from the norm as disturbances. The latter are then grouped into categories and supply us with a round dozen of disturbance indicators. Experience shows that in a given case all of these disturbances are likely to share a common denominator, and this in turn can be identified by interrogating the subject. Often we can only make a diagnosis of this kind by conducting an analytical exploration along the lines inaugurated by Freud, since in most cases the common denominator is in fact a content of the unconscious. Jung originally described such a content in generic terms as a "feeling-toned complex," since it was always accompanied by emotional manifestations and represented a compound magnitude. The term complex was at once taken up by the

Vienna School, since it proved to be an adequate description of their findings in the realm of the psychology of the neuroses. Its subsequent career in Vienna in the form of the father-complex, the mother-complex, the Oedipus complex, the power complex, the inferiority complex, etc., literally made history; nor has it been confined in any way to the clinical sphere in which it originated.

Jung and his fellow-workers were now able to use their experimental research to draw attention to a number of psychic manifestations which can be explained as elements in or functions of a complex. I shall list these manifestations individually below. It should, however, be noted that in so doing I shall be compelled artificially to isolate what in reality is only found as an integral phenomenon. Actually, one of the most striking conclusions that emerge from the association experiment—and in fact from psychological experiments of any kind—is that it is simply impossible to bring about by force the isolation of a psychological function. The truth is that every psychological experiment is interpreted by the subject in a way that is characteristic and peculiar to himself. His psyche interposes itself between the intention of the experimenter and the experiment—a finding which is expressed in our technical concept of "the experimental situation." The original aim of the experiment is distorted by the subject along certain specific lines, in a way which is entirely automatic and of which the subject himself is quite unconscious.

The choice of the specific mode in which the aim of the experiment is falsified is determined by the unconscious assumptions of the subject. A comparatively unintelligent subject will be inclined to interpret the experiment as an intelligence test; a female subject of the value predicate type, vis-à-vis a male experimenter, will take advantage of this "opportunity" to impress him by her "feelings," and so on. Thus the result of the experiment must always be interpreted in relation to the experimenter.

Unconscious assumptions dictated by the complex modify the result in a specific way, which is known technically as the *assimilation* of the experiment to that particular pattern of reaction. Assimilation is an autonomous effect which has an influence on all true psychological experiments; actually, this effect can only be avoided if experimental work is confined to psycho-physiological tests in the strict sense, where the essential object of the inquiry is to study simple reflex mechanisms, uncomplicated by influence from the psyche. In psychological terms, this tendency to assimilate means that the experimental situation itself acts as a kind of danger signal that alerts certain psychic contents of which the subject is usually unconscious.

Another technical term, *constellation*, was coined to denote the process by which contents alerted in this way automatically gather together and prepare for action. The process of exploration then discloses that they are, in fact, contents of complexes.

Let us now try to define "the complex configuration of the complex" in slightly greater detail. We are clearly dealing with a representation, or as we should say with Jung an *image*, of a certain psychic situation, perhaps an experience of some kind, which always has a specific emotional tone and is, moreover, difficult to reconcile, if not incompatible, with the habitual attitude or convictions of the subject's conscious mind. It really owes its coherence and consistency precisely to this very fact, since it is obviously cut off from the conscious mind and deprived of all further opportunities for assimilation and development. Thus it forms a relatively compact structure, which lives the life of a foreign body or *corpus alienum* in the psychic organism as a whole.

Its compactness is also due to the identical emotional or feeling tone which binds its component parts together and subsumes them, as it were, under a single characteristic quality. Perhaps it was owing to this common quality that they settled together and became conglomerated on the same spot in the same place. One of the most mysterious properties of complexes is their ability to live a life of their own by automatically assimilating new experiences of the subject which are consonant with their own feeling tone. In this respect their nature is in no way different from that of living organisms, a peculiarity which undoubtedly invests them with an uncanny atmosphere. This autonomy of theirs naturally exists at the expense of the conscious mind, which is justifiably afraid of them for that reason. It is uncomfortable to feel an independent, alien and peculiar source of energy at work within your own psyche; nor is it surprising that the conscious mind should make every effort to discountenance its real existence. That is why we often hear some euphemistic remark such as "Oh! That's *only* a complex!"—though a defensive stratagem of this kind is scarcely likely to inhibit its tumor-like development.

In the association experiment the complex interferes with the intention of the experiment, which is, in this case, to ensure the unimpeded observance of the experimenter's instructions. As soon as a complex is touched by a stimulus-word, it starts to develop its autonomous effects. The subject can no longer react objectively, he assimilates everything to the complex by interpreting it as a challenge, an insult, a source of suspicion etc., and at the same time he tries consciously or unconsciously to obliterate the disturbances caused by the experiment. As a rule, only subjects with considerable verbal-motor facility are successful in this attempt.[5] But the reproduction experiment will later reveal that in those places where "cover reactions" of this type had been given, the subject's memory simply fails. There is, in fact, a momentary amnesia or gap in memory, a phenomenon which was exploited forensically in cross-examination long before its existence was scientifically confirmed by these experiments.

As with all elementary psychic processes, this effect may also be reversed and replaced by its opposite; what we have avoided so anxiously may actually persecute us in the form of a compulsive repetition of the same reaction, even in response to the most inappropriate stimulus-word. However, the stereotypes which are thrown up by this process can easily be recognized as defense mechanisms. A particularly remarkable feature is the way in which complex effects display their autonomy by coming and going as they please, in a rhythm of their own which we have yet to fathom. Altogether, the private life of complexes is a very obscure subject, and the same applies to their etiology (i.e., the way in which they come into being).

When we were considering the work of L. Binswanger (see p. 142), we noticed that an uncertainty exists about the definition of conscious and unconscious complexes. Binswanger maintains that the latter are covered by Freud's mechanism of repression. Yet at the same time he also says that unconscious complexes of this kind have *never* been conscious. So we have to ask ourselves how something which has never been a content of the conscious mind can be said to be repressed by the latter! There are of course subliminal impressions which are too weak to cross the threshold of consciousness. That these can be reproduced in certain circumstances can be established, e.g., under hypnosis. Perceptions may also be very weak or very peripheral and yet not be completely "extinguished," as we say in physiology; they may simply be below the threshold of the "vigilance" of the conscious mind. Whether in that case they are considerable enough to be able to form a complex is another question.

Many impressions are obliterated in the moment of perception on account of their incompatibility with the habitual attitude of the conscious mind; this seems to occur automatically or unconsciously, and Freud's mechanism of repression is certainly applicable to these cases. For Jung, on the other hand, the unconscious retains a spontaneity for which the censorship of the conscious mind cannot in any way be held responsible. Spontaneous complexes can be formed out of contents derived from the unconscious itself which have never reached a threshold value that could have activated the mechanism of repression.

Strictly speaking, only complexes of this kind which have never been conscious should be described as unconscious. These might be classified as Grade 1 complexes. Grade 2 would then be reserved for complexes which have been brought about by Freud's mechanism of repression, and which have therefore *become* unconscious owing to the interference of the conscious mind at an earlier stage. Finally, Grade 3 would comprise conscious complexes whose existence we consciously recognize, or at any rate accept provisionally as such unless and until the *unconscious* itself raises doubts about their claim to this title.

Here we touch on another basic problem involved in the process of becoming conscious, since this view ascribes to the unconscious a kind of spontaneity which may be either constructive or destructive in its impact. Complexes probably arise in the first place when the subject encounters difficulties in the process of adapting to, assimilating and digesting new experiences. Moral conflicts and the influences brought to bear by the subject's background and education are to be found at the roots of most of them. From the earliest years of our lives, however, there are bound to be a number of experiences which in themselves arouse fear and are therefore felt to be unacceptable and repressed; it is at such moments that the nucleus of a complex is laid down. In the course of life this nuclear element acquires the capacity for assimilation which we mentioned above; in fact it may develop an organization which behaves very much like a second integral personality, side by side with the ego. To what extent such a unified entity may be said to possess a consciousness of its own is an interesting subject for speculation. Whenever we succeed in analyzing a specific complex right back to its point of origin (which means that the secondary elements that have been assimilated over the years have to be removed like the successive skins of an onion), we finally strike upon the nuclear element; and in most cases this turns out to be a so-called "archetypal content."

2. A General Theory of Complexes

It will most likely be recalled that we have already on more than one occasion, made use of anthropomorphic expressions when we were describing the properties of complexes. As a matter of fact, this way of speaking is justified by the actual behavior of complexes, which, when they are, as it were, "fully-grown," display to a quite remarkable degree many of the characteristics of an autonomous personality. For example, if we are overwhelmed by a complex—something, incidentally, which can perfectly well happen to a "normal" person—a completely different personality will speak through us than the one which we commonly show to the world. And we should probably say of a person in this condition that he is "possessed" or "driven by the devil," or else that "a demon has got into him." But of course when we say such things we are actually *personifying the identity of the complex.* In certain circumstances a fully-developed complex may have the power to take the place of the ego and to dominate the field of consciousness. This is rendered all the more easy by the fact that on closer examination the ego itself can be seen to be a complex. Its structure possesses the kind of wholeness which we ascribed to the complex in our definition earlier on.

A state of possession of this kind is synonymous with the change in personality which can suddenly overtake us when highly emotional values have been challenged or threatened in some way. It can make us do things which nobody—not even ourselves—would have dreamed we were capable of. That in the face of effects of this order folklore has recourse to the concept of demons is entirely intelligible to anyone who has had experience of such matters. Once the emotion has subsided, the victim of such outbursts feels very much the same way about them himself and is unable to understand what has come over him.

Incidents of this type inevitably give rise to the most serious doubts about the status we normally ascribe to the will. Certainly, from the juridical standpoint the question will be raised as to whether it would not be appropriate to speak of diminished responsibility or even of nonresponsibility in such cases. Where the ego has been repressed to make way for a complex, the authority responsible for conscious decisionmaking is lacking since the ego itself has been assimilated by the complex. This of course only reinforces still further the complex's tendency to behave like a complete alternative personality, so that what we are really dealing with in such cases is nothing less than a fragmentation of the conscious mind, which is then in its turn compensated by the "wholeness" which the complex has achieved at its expense. This reminds us that the so-called *unity of the conscious mind* is in any case one of the most recent attainments of civilization; it was only achieved with great difficulty, and its position is by no means adequately consolidated even now.

Most so-called primitives firmly believe that they have *several* "souls," and their consciousness is in fact easily dissociable for this reason. The best that we ourselves can do in similar circumstances is to become conscious, with Goethe, of the "two souls" within our breast.

We are also familiar with *part personalities*, which carry on a more or less independent existence that may be inside or around us, depending on the degree of their dissociation from the ego. Janet and Morton Prince were able, by the use of experimental and clinical techniques, to produce or detect the existence of dissociations of this kind, and as many as five part personalities, each with its own distinctive character, have been known to appear in the same subject. These were all entirely coherent in themselves, but they knew nothing of each other's existence. Here we are confronted once again by the question as to whether complexes possess a consciousness of their own, and this actually poses a disturbing problem.

I have been speaking here of manifestations which exceed the boundaries of our ordinary experience and already border on the domain of psychopathology. Yet they have long been well-known in clinical practice and are also familiar to the general public in the form of the "voices" or personified hallucinations of schizophrenics. However, we have already discussed at length the effects of these dissociated part personalities on "the psychopathology of everyday life" in Chapter III of this volume, so that it should be unnecessary at this stage to draw attention once again to the "skeleton in the cupboard" which each one of us carries around with him.

Yet it is by no means without relevance to an extended general theory of complexes to recall certain significant phenomena in the field of the psychology of civilization on which such a theory throws an interesting light. Occasionally, as we know, there is an outbreak somewhere in the world of the curious phenomenon described popularly as "hauntings." The occurrence of this phenomenon is restricted to certain times or certain places, so that, for example, a particular locality may be said to be "haunted." Belief in ghosts and appearances of ghosts are subject to similar limitations. Mediumistic phenomena seem also to point to the presence of split-off personalities.[6]

Another special form which is assumed by the personification of split-off complexes is to be found in the manifestations mentioned in Chapter III under the heading of the "*mischievousness of the object.*" This expression itself bears witness to the fact that we are dealing here with an animation or vivification of objects, including inanimate objects, and if we approach this phenomenon from a psychological standpoint it is clear that it must be based on the *projection* of an autonomous complex upon the corresponding object. Thus the complex is seen in the object, is projected onto it, is to be found *extra corpus* and also produces its effects there. If these effects should turn out to be real, parapsychology would offer the only possible approach in those cases where no physical mechanism that could account for this occurrence is either demonstrable or conceivable.

Goblins, elves, "gentle folk," fairies, brownies and similar creatures (under whatever names) which are to be found in all cultures and historical periods are probably also personifications of complexes. They perform their mischievous antics in the dark (= the unconscious) and behave in a completely autonomous way which may be harmful or beneficial as the case may be, depending on the attitude of the conscious mind. It is certainly true that the "right" way of relating to them, which is not unconnected with showing them respect and practicing the kind of euphemism we have described, has amply proved its value in experience. Moreover, they can be a source of practical and illuminating suggestions to those who can interpret their allusive language (for example, we can use complex reactions to help us to become conscious of our own weaknesses).

In fact, as living units of the unconscious, complexes can render invaluable aid to the process of the unfolding of the personality (cf. Chap. III) and also to the productivity of the psyche. Jung numbers the Lares and Penates among personified complexes of this kind, though in this case they perform protective functions in the life of the individual.[7] *Family complexes*, on the other hand, seem rather to manifest themselves in a negative form (cf. "unto the third and fourth generation"[8]); particularly clear examples are to be found in such stories as the curse on the house of Atreus in ancient Greek drama. But the commonest *normal* manifestation of complexes is certainly to be found in *dreams*. Here personified complexes have free scope for action and provide us with unequaled material for investigation, a true *via regia* for our study of the problem of the extent to which the individual can be held responsible for the behavior of his complexes and what he can do to control them at the conscious level.

On the whole, complexes do belong to the realm of the unconscious. It is true that when we were studying the association experiment we did encounter conscious complexes, but this does not necessarily involve a contradiction, since I may be perfectly *aware* of the fact that in a given situation I have a specific complex, and yet this knowledge may not enable me to exert any real influence on its effects. Besides, would not our psychic life be insufferably boring if it did not harbor elements that make sure we are supplied with the indispensable ration of disturbance? To a considerable extent our educational system is designed to teach our children certain complexes, and in fact to inculcate certain complexes in them in the interests of their socialization. We should not forget that we actually have a greater need for internal than for external sources of disquiet. If we were deprived of the assistance of certain inner dominants which appear in the form of cultural and social complexes, we should probably not even have evolved to the level of so-called "primitive man."

Complexes, then, are to be regarded as a normal factor in our psychic life which should really on no account be lacking, since they are part of our basic mental constitution. In fact, they are among the principal sources of our psychological motivation—provided we know how to treat them properly. And here I should like to draw your attention to the wider prospect which is opened up before our eyes by Jung's own magisterial conception, according to which myths and great dramas, and in particular mystery plays and the stories told in certain great religious texts, show us, in dynamic and exemplary fashion, how we can come to terms with the problem of the complexes.

NOTES

NOTES TO FOREWORD

1. See, for example, her systematic exposition of Jung's psychology: "Introduction to the Basic Postulates of Complex Psychology" in *Studies in the Psychology of C. G. Jung*, C. G. Jung Foundation, New York, 1973. This was first published in *The Cultural Significance of Complex Psychology*, which was a Festschrift for Jung's sixtieth birthday (Springer Verlag, Berlin, 1935).
2. See *Psychological Types*, *CW* 6—*Trans*.
3. Kegan, Paul, French, Trubner and Co., Ltd., London, 1927.
4. *CW* 6.
5. See *CW* 8, I.

NOTES TO CHAPTER I

1. Pliny, *Natural History*, XXXV, 10, 36, par. 12.
2. The German edition of this book was originally published in 1968.—*Trans*.
3. Sextus Empiricus, *Outlines of Pyrrhonism*, II, 193 ff., and 234 ff.
4. Based on Aristotle, *Prior Analytics*, II, 23.
5. Heraclitus, *fragment* 45.
6. Kant, *Critique of Pure Reason*, Transcendental Analytic II, Chap. III, translated by J. M. D. Meiklejohn, Dent, Everyman's Library, London, 1934, p. 188.
7. Ibid.
8. The Burghölzli.—*Trans*.
9. This is a remarkable instance of the reduplication of cases. Thirty years earlier, Jung had had a similar experience, as he describes in "The Relations Between the Ego and the Unconscious" (*CW* 7), footnote 3, p. 141.

NOTES TO CHAPTER II

1. A pathological state of "puffed-upness" of the ego, in which it arrogates to itself contents of the collective unconscious which do not belong to it. There will be further references to this subject in subsequent volumes.
2. See, for example, Aristides, ed. Dindorf and August Hug, *Leben und Werke des Rhetors Aristides*.
3. Ἄνδρα μοι ἔννεπε, Μοῦσα, πολύτροπον, etc. (Homer, "Odyssey," I, 1).
4. I gratefuly acknowledge that I am indebted for some of these accounts to Otto Kankeleit's excellent book, *Die schöpferische Macht des Unbewussten*. These

I have identified by marking them with (K). A new edition of the book is now available, entitled *Das Unbewusste als Keimstätte des Schöpferischen. Selbstzeugnisse von Gelehrten, Dichtern und Künstlern*. Foreword by C. G. Jung.

5. H. Schenker, *Ein verschollener Brief von Mozart und das Geheimnis seines Schaffens. Zu Mozarts 175. Geburtstag* (A Lost Letter of Mozart's and the Secret of His Creative Activity. In honor of Mozart's 175th birthday), in "Kunstwart," VII (1931).

6. "Zahme Xenien," III.

7. He is thinking of Spinoza.

8. "Zahme Xenien," VIII.

9. Eckermann, *Conversations with Goethe*, trans. by John Oxenford, Everyman's Library, Dent, London, 1971, p. 250.

10. *Correspondence between Schiller and Goethe from 1794 to 1805*, trans. L. Dora Schmitz, G. Bell and Sons, London, 1914, Vol. II, pp. 371–372.

11. Op. cit., Vol. II, pp. 374–375.

12. See, for example, Philipp Lersch, *Der Traum in der deutschen Romantik* (Dreams in German Romanticism) and Albert Béguin, *L'Âme romantique et le rêve* (The Romantic Soul and Dreams).

13. Jean Paul, op. cit., 1804, quoted from 2nd ed., 1813.

14. Vergil, *Aeneid*, VII, 312.

15. Cf. C. A. Meier, *Einige Konsequenzen der neueren Psychologie*, p. 157.

16. Max Schulz, *The Poetic Voices of Coleridge*, Wayne State University Press, Detroit, 1963, p. 104.

17. This is really a classical example of the interesting psychological phenomenon of the splitting-off of the shadow, in the sense in which C. G. Jung used that term.

18. Robert Louis Stevenson, *Across the Plains*, Chatto and Windus, 8th ed., London, 1900, pp. 247–249.

19. Trans. Ludovici, pp. 101f.

20. Friedrich Nietzsche, *Twilight of the Idols* and *The Anti-Christ*, trans. Hollingdale, Penguin Books, London, 1968, p. 125.

21. Until 1952 Professor of Organic Chemical Technology at the Swiss Federal Institute of Technology.

22. *Gesnerus*, Aarau, I, 4 (1944), pp. 146–157ff.

23. Basle, 1945, pp. 235ff, and 241ff.

24. Originally published in *Berichte der Deutschen Chemischen Gesellschaft*, XXIII, Karlsruhe, 1890, p. 1302 and reprinted in Richard Anschütz, *August Kekulé*, II, Berlin, 1929, pp. 937–947, from which source it is quoted here.

25. Passages enclosed by single quotation marks are to be found translated in A. Findlay, *A Hundred Years of Chemistry*, Duckworth, London, 1948 (2nd ed.).

26. I have not succeeded in identifying this quotation. However, the text of it provides a welcome confirmation of the views put forward here.

27. Technical term for the fleeting visual impressions which occur just before the onset of sleep.

28. L. "e-motio" means literally "to be moved out of something."

29. H. E. Fierz, p. 151.

30. Anschütz, I, p. 19.

31. The history of this symbol is discussed by H. J. Sheppard in an article on "The Ouroboros and the Unity of Matter in Alchemy: A Study in Origins," in *Ambix* X/2 (1962), pp. 83–96.

32. For much older (i.e., prehistoric) examples, see Walter Drack, "Zum bronzenen Ringschmuck der Hallstattzeit aus dem schweizerischen Mittelland und

Jura" in Jb. Schweiz. Ges. Ur- und Frühgesch. Vol. 55, 1970, Basel, pp. 39 and 49, as well as F. A. Schaeffer, "Les tertres funéraires préhistoriques dans la forêt de Haguenau," 1930.

33. C. G. Jung, especially in *Mysterium Coniunctionis* (*CW* 14).

34. H. Hartleben, *Champollion, sein Leben und sein Werk.*

35. On leaving 28 rue Mazarine, you cross the road and you are then only a few yards from the courtyards of the Institut de France. These are open to pedestrians.

36. H. Hartleben, p. 70.

37. "Der Reiter und der Bodensee," by Gustav Schwab (1792 to 1850). This well-known German ballad tells the story of a horseman who rode right over the frozen Lake Constance, thinking it was land. When he reached the other side and discovered his mistake, he died of heart failure.—*Trans.*

38. C. G. Jung, "On the Nature of the Psyche," *CW* 8.

39. *The Book of the Great Chemists.* Ed. G. Bugge, Berlin, 1930, II, p. 248f. (P. Walden, formerly Professor of Chemistry at Riga, where he was born, spoke Russian and was a personal friend of Mendeleev's. He is known for the Walden Inversion in stereochemistry.)

40. The source of this quotation is not indicated, but it was in fact contained in private letters from Mendeleev to Walden. Unfortunately, Professor Walden, who was extremely old, was unable to give us more precise information. He died in 1957.

41. Gk. χαιρός = "right time," "opportune moment."—*Trans.*

42. In what follows, I am reproducing the substance of a lecture which I gave January 13, 1936, to the Zurich Society for Natural Science. It was entitled "Psychologische Streiflichter zur Geschichte des Energiebegriffs" (Psychological sidelights on the history of the concept of energy). Cf. the summary in *Vierteljahreschrift der Naturforschenden Gesellschaft in Zurich*, LXXXI/3 and 4 (1936), p. IIIf.

43. I have selected from the very extensive literature only those works in which emotional reactions are kept well in the background: (a) Jacob J. Weyrauch, "Die Mechanik der Wärme," in *Gesammelte Schriften von Robert Mayer.* This contains almost all the relevant documents. (b) S. Friedländer, "J. R. Mayer," in *Klassiker der Naturwissenschaften* I. (c) W. Ostwald, *Grosse Männer*, pp. 61-100, where repeated reference is made to the suddenness with which the idea of the heat equivalent appeared in Mayer and the conclusion is drawn that "it had long been present in the unconscious" (p. 89). (d) E. Jentsch, *Julius Robert Mayer. Seine Krankheitsgeschichte und die Geschichte seiner Entdeckung.* (e) B. Hell, "J. R. Mayer," in *Frommans Klassiker der Philosophie* XXIII. (f) Alwin Mittasch, *Julius Robert Mayers Kausalbegriff.* (g) A. Mühlberger, *Frankfurter Zeitung*, issue of 21st and 23rd January, 1879, Nrs. 21 and 23. (h) H. Timerding, *Robert Mayer und die Entdeckung des Energiegesetzes.* (i) H. Schmolz and H. Weckbach, *Robert Mayer, Sein Leben und Werk in Dokumenten.*

44. Griesinger later made a name for himself as a psychiatrist; he, too, worked in Zurich.

45. Gk. περιπέτεια = *bouleversement*; used by Aristotle of the sudden reversal of fortune on which the plot of a Greek tragedy hinges.—*Trans.*

46. Cf. Volume III of this series.

47. L. = the power and authority of the father. The original meaning in Roman law was "the power vested in the paterfamilias or head of the Roman family" (*Random House Dictionary of the English Language 1966*).—*Trans.*

48. He therefore devoted a special treatise to the origin of the heat of the sun,

its constancy and the "constancy of the sun's mass," in "Beiträge zur Dynamik des Himmels" (Contributions to Celestial Dynamics).

49. "Bemerkungen über die Kräfte der unbelebten Natur" (Remarks on the Forces of Inanimate Nature) in Justus Liebig's *Annalen der Chemie und Pharmacie*, Leipzig, 1842.

50. *Bemerkungen über das mechanische Äquivalent der Wärme* (Remarks on the Mechanical Equivalent of Heat).

51. See W. Lange-Eichbaum, *Genie, Irrsinn und Ruhm*.

52. J.J. Weyrauch, op. cit. I, p. 432.

53. W.R. Grove, "Lecture on the Progress of Physical Science, delivered 19th January, 1842" and "The Correlation of Physical Forces, Being the Substance of a Course of Lectures in 1843."

54. The figure of the girl represented the anima, in Jung's sense of that term; she wished to resume contact with the patient in this way. But this fact is only noted here by way of anticipation (cf. the fuller treatment of this subject in Vol. IV of this series). In the present context, the anima is the symbolic equivalent of the father image in Mayer's case.

55. Since this was written, Arthur Koestler has published in his book *The Act of Creation* (Hutchinson, London, 1964) a very impressive, though not always well-documented, collection of positive interventions made by the unconscious.

NOTES TO CHAPTER III

1. Sigmund Freud, *The Psycho-Pathology of Everyday Life, The Standard Edition of the Complete Psychological Works of Sigmund Freud*, The Hogarth Press, London 1960.

2. Freud, *Introductory Lectures on Psychoanalysis, Standard Ed.*, 15–16 (second lecture). See also *Psychopathology of Everyday Life*, p. 69.

3. Freud, *Psychopathology of Everyday Life*, p. 57. The speaker intended to say "came to light" (G. *Vorschein*). Instead he used the nonexistent word *Vorschwein* (lit. forepig). He had in his mind G. *Schweinereien* (disgusting occurrences)— *Trans.*

4. Freud, op. cit., pp. 95–96.

5. Freud, op. cit., pp. 89–90.

6. Lichtenberg, "Nachtrag zu den witzigen und satyrischen Bemerkungen," in *Vermischte Schriften*, II, p. 84.

7. Hanns Sachs, *Int. Z. (ärztl.) Psychoanal.*, IV (1916/17).

8. *Beyond Good and Evil*, IV (written in 1886/1887).

9. H. Silberer, *Der Zufall und die Koboldstreiche des Unbewussten*.

10. P. Janet, *L'État mental des hystériques*, pp. 537ff. A final summary is to be found in "Les Oscillations du niveau mental," in *Nouveau Traité de psychologie*, IV, fasc. 3. (1937).

11. Cf. Chap. VI.

12. In German-speaking countries, it is the custom for men as well as women to wear engagement and wedding rings.—*Trans*.

13. A. Maeder, "Contribution à la psychopathologie de la vie quotidienne," in *Archs. Psychol.* VI (1906).

14. "The German '*Versteigen*' would, on the analogy of '*verlesen*,' '*verschreiben*,' etc., mean 'to mis-climb'; but its normal meaning is 'to climb too

high' or, figuratively, 'to overreach oneself.'" (Translator's footnote to Freud, op. cit., p. 165.)

15. Freud, op. cit., pp. 164-165.

16. Goethe, *Faust*, Act V, trans. by Philip Wayne, Penguin Books, London, 1971, p. 264.

17. Freud, op. cit., p. 167, quoted from Silberer's excellent and pithy résumé, op. cit., pp. 8f.

18. The German proverb runs "Glück und Glas, wie leicht bricht das!" ("Luck and glass, how easily they break!"). It is derived from the Latin of Publilius Syrus: "Fortuna vitrea est, tum quum splendet, frangitur" ("Good luck is made of glass: when it shines, it breaks"). See Büchmann, *Geflügelte Worte*, Reclam, Stuttgart, p. 253.—*Trans*.

19. Goethe, *Faust*, Part II, Act V, Scene 5, trans. by Bayard Taylor, Washington Square Press, New York, 1964, p. 404.

20. Freud, op. cit., p. 191.

21. H. Silberer, op. cit., pp. 14f.

22. Lawrence Sterne, *The Life and Opinions of Tristram Shandy* (Volume VI, Chapter V). In this context, the papers by H. Hirschfeld and R. C. Behan on "The Accident Proneness," in *Journ. Amer. Med. Assoc.* CLXXXVI (1963) pp. 193-199, pp. 300-306, and CXCVII (1966), pp. 85-89, are also of great interest.

23. The historical development of this concept has recently been investigated by P. Froggatt and J. A. Smiley ("The Concept of Accident Proneness," in "A Review": *Brit. Jour. Indust. Med.* XX, pp. 1-12, 1964). On the basis of careful statistical inquiries, the authors concluded that we cannot really speak about accident-prone individuals, but rather of certain phases in life during which people fall a victim to accidents more frequently than at other times.

24. Alfred Adler, *The Practice and Theory of Individual Psychology*, IV b: *The Arrangement of the Neurosis*.

25. Schopenhauer, *Transzendente Spekulation über die anscheinende Absichtlichkeit im Schicksal des Einzelnen*, 1851.

26. Freud, op. cit., pp. 265-268.

27. Cf. pp. 156-157.

28. Charles Dickens, *Pictures from Italy*, André Deutsch, London, 1973, quoted by Ian Stevenson, in *Journ. Amer. Soc. Psychical Research*, LIV 2 (1960), pp. 59 ff. A good description of déjà vu, also from Charles Dickens, is quoted by Ian M. L. Hunter in *Memory* (Pelican Book A. 405, pp. 39ff.) Harmondsworth, 1966.

29. M. Bernstein, *The Search for Bridey Murphy*.

30. Morton Prince, *The Dissociation of a Personality*. Cf. also W. F. Prince, "The Doris Case of Multiple Personality," in *Proc. Amer. Soc. Psychical Research*, IX-XI, XIV and XVII (1915-1923).

31. English Translation by Frederick Jameson; Vocal Score by Karl Klindworth; Schott & Co., Ltd., London.

32. Vocal Score with English and German Words; English Version by Alfred Kalisch; Boosey & Hawkes Ltd., London and New York.

33. *CW* 9, Pt. I, "Concerning Rebirth."

34. These two collections are full of elements which reappear in Herodotus (e.g., VI, 130), Aesop, the Gesta Romanorum, Boccaccio, Chaucer and La Fontaine, as well as in Grimm's Fairy Tales; this represents quite a considerable problem for scholarship.

35. *CW* 3, "The Psychology of Dementia Praecox," p. 55.

36. The two passages, together with Jung's comments, are to be found in *CW* 1, "On the Psychology and Pathology of So-Called Occult Phenomena," pp. 82–84, cf. pp. 102–104. The extract from the log of the "Sphinx" was originally printed in Justinus Kerner, *Blätter aus Prevost*, Vol. IV, p. 57.

37. Cicero, *De Divinatione*, 2, 85–86, and Livy, 45, 4, 8.

38. Schopenhauer, *The World as Will and Imagination*, I.

39. Plutarch, *De Fortuna Romanorum*, 1 (Mor. 316 D).

40. "Another One". Fr. Th. Vischer was the first Professor of Literature at the Swiss Federal Polytechnic at Zurich (1855).

41. Cf. H. Werner, *Die Schutzgeister*.

42. Livy, 22, 3.

43. Seneca, *Ep.* 107.

44. Cleanthes, head of the Stoic School in succession to Zeno (c. 260 B.C.).

45. Jung, *CW* 4.

46. Euripides, *fr.* 956 (Nauck).

47. Epictetus, *Enchir.*, LIII.

48. Schiller, "Der Gang nach dem Eisenhammer" (1797).

NOTES TO CHAPTER IV

1. M. Fierz, "Zur physikalischen Erkenntnis" in *Eranos Yearbook XVI*, p. 433.

2. The section on "Assoziationsversuch nach C. G. Jung" ("The Association Experiment as developed by C. G. Jung") in *Handbuch der klinischen Psychologie*, I, ed. Erich Stern, on the whole does justice to the Experiment, but the treatment of it is too summary for our purposes.

3. H. Siebeck, *Geschichte der Psychologie*.

4. Zoology still recognizes the family of *psychidae*, a class of lepidoptera.

5. Freud, *The Future of an Illusion*.

6. Justinus Kerner, *Die Seherin von Prevorst* and *Blätter aus Prevorst*.

7. Nanna was the old Germanic goddess of vegetation.—*Trans.*

8. This has no connection with the sacred books of the Parsees, apart from the fact that in Fechner's view the stars are also animated by a psychic principle.

9. The titles of Fechner's books have been translated above for the convenience of the English-speaking reader. The titles of the German originals are listed in the Bibliography.

10. Brother of the eminent physicist Wilhelm Eduard Weber, one of the "Göttinger Seven."

11. "Über die psychischen Messprinzipien und das Webersche Gesetz," in *Philosophische Studien*, ed. Wilhelm Wundt, *Bd.* 4.

12. Cf., for example, Theodor Ziehen, *Leitfaden der physiologischen Psychologie*.

13. He also worked in Zurich.

14. Francis Galton, "Psychometric Experiments," in *Brain* (1879).

15. Founder of the Institut Jean-Jacques Rousseau at Geneva.

16. *Diagnostische Assoziationsstudien*; these originally appeared from 1904 to 1910 in the *Journal für Psychologie und Neurologie*. They were reprinted in two volumes, 1906 and 1909. The first English translation of this work (by Dr. M. D. Eder) was published in London in 1918, and in New York in 1919. In addition to Jung's own research, it contained papers by Eugen Bleuler, K. Wehrlin, Franz

Riklin, Emma Fürst, L. Binswanger and H. Nunberg. Jung's contributions are all to be found in the Collected Works.

In the present volume, *Diagnostic Studies* will be used as an abbreviation to denote the *original German edition*; the first English translation will be referred to under its full title of *Studies in Word Association*.

17. C. A. Meier, "Über die Bedeutung des Jungschen Assoziations-Experimentes für die Psychotherapie" ("The Significance of Jung's Association Experiment for Psychotherapy"). Report on the Congress in *Zs. ges. Neurol.*, CLXI (1937).

18. Cf. S. I. Franz, "Anomalous Reaction-Times in a Case of Manic-Depressive Depression," in *Psychol. Bull.*, II/7 (1905), and Max Isserlin, "Psychologische Untersuchungen an Manisch-Depressiven," in *Mschr. Psychiatr. Neurol.*, XXXII (1907).

19. Lucian, *De Dea Syria*, 17. The story has also been handed down to us by Plutarch, *Demetrios Poliorketes*, 38 and Appian, *Hist. Rom.*, X59.

20. Cf. C. A. Meier, "Psychomatic Medicine from the Jungian Point of View," in *The Journ. of Anal. Psychol.*, VIII (1963), p. 103.

21. In fact this is a widespread motif in folklore. Cf. *Anthol. Pal.*, IX, 745., Statius, *Silvae*, 5, 3, 153ff. and Plutarch, *Moralia*, 509ff.

22. C. G. Jung, *CW* 2, pp. 452–458.

23. C. G. Jung, *CW* 2, pp. 318–352.

24. C. G. Jung, "Zur Tatbestandsdiagnostik," in *Zs. angew. Psychol.*, I (1907), p. 163; see also *CW* 1, pp. 219–230; *CW* 2, pp. 605, n.2. and 328–332.

25. Otto Lipmann, "Die Spuren interessebetonter Erlebnisse und ihrer Symptome (Theorie, Methoden and Ergebnisse der 'Tatbestandsdiagnostik')", in Supp. to *Zs. angew. Psychol.*, I (1911), ed. William Stern and Otto Lipmann. The results of the further research by Wertheimer and Lipmann which are foreshadowed in this publication have unfortunately never been published.

26. Henry J. Watt, *Sammelbericht über die neuere Forschung in der Gedächtnis—und Assoziationspsychologie aus den Jahren 1903/1904*.

27. F. W. Kaeding, *Häufigkeitswörterbuch der deutschen Sprache*.

28. Cf. pp. 99 ff.

29. A. Eberschweiler, "Untersuchungen über die sprachlichen Komponenten der Assoziation."

30. C. G. Jung and Franz Riklin, "The Associations of Normal Subjects." German original ("Experimentelle Untersuchungen über Assoziationen Gesunder"), in *Diagnostic Studies*, contribution 1, in *Journ. Psychol. Neurol.*, III and IV (1904). First English translation (by Dr. M. E. Eder) in *Studies in Word-Association*, London 1918, New York 1919, Chap. II.

31. In this context constellation means simply the production of specific contents.

32. Emma Fürst, "Statistical Investigations on Word-Associations and on Familial Agreement in Reaction Type among Uneducated Persons." German original ("Statistische Untersuchungen über Wortassoziationen und über familiäre Übereinstimmung im Reaktionstypus bei Ungebildeten") in *Diagnostic Studies*, Contribution X, in *Journ. Psychol. Neurol. IX* (1907). First English translation in *Studies in Word-Association*, Chap. XI.

33. C. G. Jung, *CW* 2, pp. 470–472, Figs. 1, 3, 4 and 5.

34. C. G. Jung, *CW* 2, pp. 469–477.

35. Josef B. Lang, "Über Assoziationsversuche bei Schizophrenen und den Mitgliedern ihrer Familie," Zurich dissertation in *Jb. psychol. psychopathol.*

Forschgg., V. (1913). "Eine Hypothese zur psychologischen Bedeutung der Verfolgungsidee," in *Psychol. Abh.*, ed. C.G. Jung I (1914).

36. See note 53 below.

37. C.G. Jung, *CW* 1; originally published in *Journ. Psychol. Neurol., II (1903)*.

38. See note 41 below.

39. See note 30 above.

40. The subject was instructed to make pencil strokes in time with the beats of a metronome.

41. The subject was instructed to direct his attention to the immediate psychic effects of the stimulus-word (the A-phenomenon of Cordes); cf. Wundt, *Philos. St.*, XVII (1911).

42. C.G. Jung, "The Reaction-time Ratio in the Association Experiment." German original ("Über das Verhalten der Reaktionszeit beim Assoziationsexperiment") in *Diagnostic Studies*, Contribution IV, in *Journ. Psychol. Neurol.*, VI (1906). Now in *CW* 2. About the same time, "Experimental Observations on the Faculty of Memory" (German original "Experimentelle Beobachtung über das Erinnerungsvermögen") appeared in *Zbl. Nervenhlkde. Psychiatr.*, XXVIII (1905); now in *CW* 2.

43. Édouard Claparède, *L'Association des Idées*, Paris 1903.

44. C.G. Jung, *CW* 2.

45. R. Hahn, "Über die Beziehungen zwischen Fehlreaktionen und Klangassoziationen." Zurich dissertation, in Kraepelin's *Psychol. Abb.*, V/1 (1906).

46. C.G. Jung, (a) "Experimental Observations on the Faculty of Memory." German original ("Experimentelle Beobachtungen über das Erinnerungsvermögen") in *Zbl. Nervenhlkde Psychiatr.*, XXVIII (1905). Now in *CW* 2. (b) "Disturbances of Reproduction in the Association Experiment." German original ("Über die Reproduktionsstörungen beim Assoziationsexperiment") in *Diagnostic Studies*, Contribution IX in *Journ. Psychol. Neurol.*, IX (1907). First English translation in *Studies in Word-Association*, Chap. X. Now in *CW* 2.

47. G. Ch. Lichtenberg, op. cit., "Bemerkungen vermischten Inhalts. 2. Psychologische Bemerkungen," p. 112.

48. Arn. Kowalewski, *Studien zur Psychologie des Pessimismus.*

49. Wilhelm Busch, "Abenteuer eines Junggesellen."

50. W. Peters, "Gefühl und Erinnerung Beiträge zur Erinnerungsanalyse" in Kraepelin's *Psychologische Arbeiten*, VI/2 (1911); W. Peters and O. Nemecek, "Massenversuche über Erinnerungs-assoziationen," in *Fortschr. Psychol. Anw.*, ed. K. Marbe, II/IV (1914).

51. See note 46(a) above.

52. C.G. Jung, *Jb. psychoanal. psychopath. Forschgg.* II/1, p. 363 (1910).

53. Wilhelm Pfenninger, "Untersuchungen über die Konstanz und den Wechsel der psychologischen Konstellation bei Normalen und Frühdementen (Schizophrenen)," in *Jb. psychoanal. psychopathol. Forschgg.* III/2 (1912).

54. W. Hoffmann, "Über den Einfluss der Gefühlsbetonung und einiger anderer Factoren auf die Dauer und den Wechsel der Assoziationen." Zurich dissertation in Kraepelin's *Psychologische Arbeiten*, VII/1 (1915).

55. A. Eberschweiler, "Untersuchungen über die sprachliche Komponente der Assoziation." Zurich dissertation, in *Allg. Zs. Psychiatr.*, LXV (1908).

56. H. Huber, "Über den Einfluss von optischem oder akustischem Reiz und grammatikalischer Form des Reizwortes auf den Assoziationsvorgang." Zurich dissertation, in *Journ. Psychol. Neurol.*, XXIII/5/6 (1917).

57. R. Sommer, *Lehrbuch der psychopathologischen Untersuchungsmethoden.*

58. Eugen Bleuler, "Upon the Significance of Association Experiments." Foreword to *Diagnostic Studies* (1904).

I.C.G. Jung and Franz Riklin, "The Associations of Normal Subjects," originally published in 1904.

II. K. Wehrlin, "The Associations of Imbeciles and Idiots," 1904.

III. C.G. Jung, "Analysis of the Associations of an Epileptic," originally published 1905.

IV. C.G. Jung, "The Reaction-time Ratio in the Association Experiment," originally published 1905.

V. Eugen Bleuler, "Consciousness and Association," 1905.

VI. C.G. Jung, "Psychoanalysis and Association Experiments," originally published 1905.

VII. Franz Riklin, "Cases Illustrating the Phenomena of Association in Hysteria," 1906.

VIII. C.G. Jung, "Association, Dream and Hysterical Symptom," originally published in 1906.

IX. C.G. Jung, "Disturbances of Reproduction in the Association Experiment," originally published 1907.

X. Emma Fürst, "Statistical Investigations on Word-Associations and on Familial Agreement in Reaction Type among Uneducated Persons," 1907.

XI. Ludwig Binswanger, "On the Psychogalvanic Phenomenon in Association Experiments," 1907/1908.

XII. Hermann Nunberg, "On the Physical Accompaniment of Association Processes," 1910.

Note: All these papers appeared in *Studies in Word-Association*, the first English translation of the Diagnostic Studies. Jung's contributions to this series (Nos. I (with Riklin), III, IV, VI, VIII and IX) are now to be found in *CW* 2.

59. Cf. note 18 above.

60. Grace Helen Kent and A.J. Rosanoff, "A Study of Association in Insanity," in *Amer. Journ. Insanity*, LXVII 1/2 (1910).

61. A. Ley and P. Menzerath, *L'Étude experimentale de l'association des idées dans les maladies mentales.*

62. Eugen Bleuler, "Über die Bedeutung von Assoziations-versuchen," in *Journ. Psychol. Neurol.*, III (1904). English translation in *Studies in Word-Association*, Chap. 1.

63. Ibid., cf. note 30.

64. Ibid., English translation in *Studies in Word-Association*, Chap. III.

65. G. Cordes, "Experimentelle Untersuchungen über Assoziationen," in Wundt, *Philosophische Studien*, Band XVII (1901).

66. *Journ. Psychol. Neurol.*, V (1905); *CW* 2.

67. Ibid., VI (1905); *CW* 2.

68. Ibid., VI (1905). English translation in *Studies in Word-Association*, Chap. VI.

69. C.G. Jung, *On the Psychology and Pathology of So-called Occult Phenomena*, *CW* 1 (orig. published Leipzig 1902).

70. J.B. Rhine, *New Frontiers of the Mind*, New York and London 1937, and *The Reach of the Mind*, London 1948. Reprinted Harmondsworth (Penguin Books), 1954.

71. Ibid., *CW* 2, see p. 288, note 1.

72. Sigmund Freud, "Bruchstück einer Hysterie-Analyse," in *Mschr. Psychiatr. Neurol.*, XXVIII, 4 (1905); Trans. *Standard Edition*, 7, 3.

73. *Journ. Psychol. Neurol.* VII (1906). English translation in *Studies in Word-Association*, Chap. VI.

74. Franz Riklin, "Die diagnostische Bedeutung des Assoziationsversuches bei Hysterischen," in *Psychiatr. Neurol. Wschr.*, 29 (1904) and "Analytische Untersuchung der Symptome und Assoziationen eines Falles von Hysterie," ibid., 46 (1905).

75. August Forel, 1848–1931, author of a famous book about ants, was Bleuler's predecessor as superintendent of the Burghölzli at Zurich.—*Trans.*

76. *Journ. Psychol. Neurol.*, VIII (1906). First English translation in *Studies in Word-Association*, Chap. IX; now in *CW* 2.

77. Bleuler, *Affektivität, Suggestibilität, Paranoia*, Halle 1906.

78. Jung, "Association, Dream and Hysterical Symptom," see note 76 above.

79. See *CW* 2, pp. 382–407.—*Trans.*

80. *CW* 2, pp. 406–407.

81. *Journ. Psychol. Neurol.*, IX (1907). English translation in *Studies in Word-Association*, Chap. XI.

82. This famous phrase (in German "des Pudels Kern") occurs in Goethe's *Faust*, Part I, Scene III, at the point when the poodle turns into Mephistopheles. It means of course the essence or heart of the matter—*Trans.*

83. Freud, *Standard Edition*, Vol. XII, pp. 9–82.

84. Daniel Paul Schreber, *Memoirs of My Nervous Illness*, trans., with introduction, notes and discussion, by Ida Macalpine and Richard Hunter. William Dawson, London 1955. It was Freud's analysis which made this case famous.

85. Eugen Bleuler and C.G. Jung, "Komplexe und Krankheitsursachen bei Dementia praecox," in *Zbl. Nervenheilkande Psychiatr.* XXXI (1908).

86. This point was already emphasized by Bleuler in his foreword to the *Diagnostic Studies*.

87. Ley and Menzerath had already recognized that emotionality is the most important criterion of the complex.

88. Breuer and Freud, *Studies in Hysteria*; orig. ed. Deuticke, Leipzig and Vienna 1895. Trans. *Standard Edition*, II.

89. Freud, *Collected Short Papers on the Theory of the Neuroses, Standard Edition*, mostly in Vol. III; orig. ed. Vienna 1906.

90. Pierre Janet, *L'Automatisme psychologique—L'État mentale des hystériques—Les Névroses*.

91. Théodore Flournoy, *From India to the Planet Mars*, Harper, New York and London 1900, and "Nouvelles Observations sur un cas de somnabulisme avec glossolalie," in *Archs. Psychol.*, I/2 (1901).

92. Lectures delivered at Fordham University, New York, in September 1912. They later appeared in German in *Jb. psychoanal. psychopathol. Forschgg.*, V/1 (1913). Now in *CW* 4.

93. Ibid., II/1 (1910), p. 336.

94. Abstracts of the psychological works of Swiss authors (to the end of 1909) in *Jb. psychoanal. psychopathol. Forschgg.*, II/1 (1910). Now in *CW* 8.

95. Cf. C.A. Meier, "C.G. Jung's Contributions to Theory and Therapy of Schizophrenia," in *Proceedings of the Second International Congress for Psychiatry in Zurich, September 1–7, 1957*, IV (1959).

96. C.G. Jung, "The Psychology of Dementia Praecox," *CW* 3.

97. Cf. note 85 above.

98. C.G. Jung, (a) "On the Importance of the Unconscious in Psychotherapy," in *Brit. Med. Journ.*, 5th Dec. 1914; now in *CW* 3. (b) "On the Problem of Psychogenesis in Mental Diseases," in *Proc. Royal Soc. Med.*, XII/9 (1919); now in *CW* 3. (c) "On the Psychogenesis of Schizophrenia," in *Journ. Ment. Sc.* (Sept. 1939); now in *CW* 3.

99. This patient was the subject of note 96 above.

100. The patient who had the hallucination of the solar phallus; in *CW* 5, pp. 101–102.

101. C.G. Jung, *CW* 3.

102. Original title *Wandlungen und Symbole der Libido*; current title in German *Symbole der Wandlung* = *Symbols of Transformation* (*CW* 5.).

103. *CW* 3, p. 206.

104. C.G. Jung, "Schizophrenia," *CW* 3, pp. 256–272; "Recent Thoughts on Schizophrenia," *CW* 3, pp. 250–255; *CW* 3, pp. 211–225; 236, 238.

105. *CW* 3, p. 217.

106. *CW* 3, p. 224.

107. *CW* 3, p. 236.

108. *CW* 3, p. 238.

109. "On the Importance of the Unconscious in Psychotherapy."

110. See *CW* 3, p. 247.

111. *CW* 4.

112. *CW* 17.

113. Cf. note 32 above.

114. *Psychol. Abhh.*, ed. C.G. Jung, I (1914).

115. Herbert Silberer, *Probleme der Mystik und ihrer Symbolik*, Vienna and Leipzig, 1914.

116. C.A. Meier, *Ancient Incubation and Modern Psychotherapy*, trans. Monica Curtis, Northwestern University Press, Evanston 1967 (original title, *Antike Inkubation und moderne Psychotherapie*, Rascher, Zurich, 1949).

117. R. Sommer, *Lehrbuch der psychopathologischen Untersuchungsmethoden*.

118. Charles Féré, "Notes sur les Modifications de la résistance électrique sous l'influence des excitations sensorielles et des émotions," in *Cpts. rends. hébd. Soc. Biol.* (1888).

R. Vigouroux, "Sur la Résistance électrique considerée comme signe clinique," in *Progr. méd.* I. sem. (1888).

A. Vigouroux, *Étude sur la Résistance électrique chez les mélancoliques*, Paris Dissertation, 1890.

J. Tarchanoff, "Über die galvanischen Erscheinungen in der Haut des Menschen bei Reizungen der Sinnesorgane und bei verschiedenen Formen der psychischen Tätigkeit," in *Arch. Ges. Physiol.*, XXXXVI (1890).

Georg Sticker, "Über Versuche einer objectiven Darstellung von Sensibilitätsstörungen," in *Wien. klin. Rdsch.* (1897).

119. E.K. Müller, *Cpt. rend. Soc. Helv. Scs. natur.*, September 1904.

120. Otto Veraguth, (a) "Das psycho-galvanische Reflex-Phänomen," I. Bericht, in *Mschr. Psychiatr. Neurol.* (1906). (b) "Das psycho-galvanische Reflexphänomen." I–VI. Bericht 1909.

121. C.G. Jung, "On the Psychophysical Relations of the Association Experiment," in *Journ. Abnorm. Psychol.*, (Boston) I (1907). Now in *CW* 2.

122. Ludwig Binswanger, "On the Psychogalvanic Phenomenon in Association Experiments," originally published as "Über des Verhalten des psychogalvanischen Phänomens beim Assoziationsexperiment," in *Journ. Psychol. Neurol.* (1907) and

(1908) (Diagnostic Studies XI). English translation in *Studies in Word-Association*, Chap. XII.

123. Author's report in *Jb. psychoanal. psychopathol. Forschgg.*, II/1 (1910).

124. C.G. Jung: see note 121 above.

125. The German word *voll* (full) can occasionally mean "completely drunk." See *CW* 2, p. 489.—*Trans.*

126. Frederick Peterson and C.G. Jung, "Psycho-physical Investigations with the Galvanometer and Pneumograph in Normal and Insane Individuals," originally published in English in *Brain*, XXX, 118 (1907); now in *CW* 2.

127. Charles Ricksher and C.G. Jung, "Further Investigations on the Galvanic Phenomenon and Respiration in Normal and Insane Individuals." Originally published in English in *Journ. Abnorm. Psychol.* (Boston), II (1907–8). Now in *CW* 2.

128. Hermann Nunberg, "On the Physical Accompaniment of Association Processes." English translation in *Studies in Word-Association*, Chap. XIII. German original ("Über körperliche Begleiterscheinungen assoziativer Vorgänge") in *Journ. Psychol. Neurol.*, XVI (1910).

129. With regard to this distinction, cf. p. 00.

130. Hermann Nunberg, *Studies in Word-Association*, p. 549.

131. See p. 00.

132. Frederick Peterson, "The Galvanometer in Psychology," in *Journ. Abnorm. Psychol.* (Boston), III (1908).

133. Morton Prince and Frederick Peterson, "Experiments in Psycho-Galvanic Reactions from Co-Conscious (Sub-Conscious) Ideas in a Case of Multiple Personality," in *Journ. Abnorm. Psychol.* (Boston) III (1908).

134. Morton Prince, *The Dissociation of a Personality*.

135. B. Sidis and H.T. Kalmus, "Study of Galvanometric Deflections due to Psycho-Physical Processes," in *Psychol. Revw.*, XV (1908), and XVI (1909).

136. Hugo Müller, *Experimentelle Beiträge zur physikalischen Entstehung des psycho-galvanischen Phänomens*. Zurich dissertation, 1909.

137. J. Aebly, *Zur Analyse der physikalischen Vorbedingungen des psychogalvanischen Reflexes mit exosomatischer Stromquelle*. Zurich dissertation, 1910.

138. See note 119.

139. B. Sidis and L. Nelson, "The Nature and Cause of the Galvanic Phenomenon," in *Psychol. Revw.*, XVII (1910).

140. B. Sidis, "The Nature and Cause of the Galvanic Phenomenon," in *Journ. Abnorm. Psychol.* (Boston) V (1910).

141. I.H. Coriat, "Certain Pulse Reactions as a Measure of Emotions," in *Journ. Abnorm. Psychol.*, (Boston) IV (1910).

142. Esther Aptekmann, *Experimentelle Beiträge zur Psychologie des psychogalvanischen Phänomens*. Zurich dissertation, 1912. Also in *Jb. psychoanal. psychopathol. Forschg.*, III/2 (1912).

143. J. Klaesi, *Über das psychogalvanische Phänomen*. Zurich dissertation, 1912. Also in *Journ. Psychol. Neurol.*, XIX (1912).

144. V. Kuhne, "Résumé des recherches psycho-galvanométriques sur l'émotivité de M. Édouard Abramowski." *Bull. Inst. gén. psychol.* 13e annee, III (1913).

145. V.J. Müller, *Zur Kenntnis der Leitungsbahnen des psycho-galvanischen Reflexphänomens*. Zurich dissertation, 1913. In *Mschr. Psychiatr. Neurol.*, XXXIII (1913).

146. E. Wittkower, *Einfluss der Gemütsbewegungen auf den Körper*.

147. Flanders Dunbar, *Emotions and Bodily Changes*.

148. (a) Frederick Peterson, "The Galvanometer as a Measurer of Emotions," in *Brit. Med. Journ.* (Sept. 1907). (b) Frederick Peterson and W.E. Scripture, "Psycho-physical Investigations with the Galvanometer," in *Journ. Nerv. Ment. Dis.* (July 1909). (c) I.H. Coriat, "Certain Pulse Reactions as a Measure of the Emotions," in *Journ. Abnorm. Psychol.* (Boston) (Oct. 1909). (d) H.C. Syz, "Psycho-Galvanic Studies on Sixty-four Medical Students," in *Brit. Journ. Psychol.* (General Section), XVII (1926). (e) id., "Observations on the Unreliability of Subjective Reports on Emotional Reactions," ibid., XVII (1926). (f) id. "Psychogalvanic Studies in Schizophrenics," in *Archives Neurol. Psychiatr.*, XVI (1926). (g) id., and E.F. Kinder, "Electrical Skin Resistance in Normal and Psychiatric Subjects," in *Archives Neurol. Psychiatr.* XIX (1928). (h) id. and E.F. Kinder, "The Galvanic Skin-Reflex," in *Archives Neurol. Psychiatr.* XXVI (1931). (i) C. Landis and W.A. Hunt, "The Conscious Correlates of the Galvanic Skin Response," in *Journ. Exp. Psychol.*, XVIII (1935).

149. Whately Smith, *The Measurement of Emotion*. Smith, alias Carington, made a decisive contribution to the basic results obtained by S.G. Soal and F. Bateman (see their book *Modern Experiments in Telepathy*). Smith drew Soal's attention to the "displacement effect." This was first discovered by the well-known American astro-physicist, C.G. Abbot. See *Journ. Parapsychol.*, II (1938) (an anonymous article) and subsequently ibid., XIII (1949). Cf. Whately Carington, "Experiments on the Paranormal Cognition of Drawings," in *Proc. Soc. Psychical Research*, CXXXXVI (1940), and simultaneously in *Journ. Parapsychol.*, IV (1940).

150. William McDougall, *Body and Mind*. Now published as a paperback by Beacon Press, Boston, Mass.

151. Ed. D.F. Candland, *Van Nostrand Insight Book*.

NOTES TO CHAPTER V

1. Constantinus Africanus, *De melancolia*, lib. I fol. 163 v. col. II 50–52, ed. M.T. Malato and V. de Martini, Rome, 1959. The translation given by these writers is misleading, unless there is a scribe's error in *Codex Vat. Lat.* 2455 or a misprint in this edition. With regard to my translation of "accidentia" by "symptoms," cf. p. 00.

2. Plutarch, *Democritus Polyorcetes*; see also Appian, *Hist. Rom.* X. 59. We have already discussed this case more briefly in another context.

3. Cf. Hugo von Hofmannsthal, *Der Rosenkavalier*, end of Act III, the Marschallin to Sophie, "And for your pallor, perhaps my nephew there has the medicine for that!"

4. Musée Condé, Chantilly, No. 432.

5. Hippolytus.

6. Cf. *The Psychological Variables in Human Cancer*, ed. J.A. Gengerelli and F.J. Kirkner.

7. H. Boerhaave, *Institutiones medicae, digestae ab Hermanno Boerhaave*, ed. Leydensis sexta, S 771 (Lugduni Batavorum 1746), p. 387. In the original Latin, the passage reads as follows: *Affectus animi violenti aut diu permanentes iidem cerebrum, nervos, spiritus, musculos mirabiliter efficacissime mutant, figunt,*

depravant, unde quoscunque fere morbos valent producere et fovere pro sua diversitate et duratione.

8. Pub. Jacobus van Eeems, Francofurti et Lipsiae 1762.

9. German original *Studien über Minderwertigkeit von Organen*, 1907; the English translation was published in 1917.—*Trans.*

10. This is the doctrine of the *causa occasionalis*, which is already to be found among the Arabian philosophers and was specifically developed by Geulincx (1625 to 1699), according to whom a direct interaction between body and soul was unthinkable on account of the total difference between the two substances, with the result that our "causes" only represented "occasions."

11. Oswald Schwarz, *Psychogenese und Psychotherapie körperlicher Symptome.*

12. Flanders Dunbar, *Emotions and Bodily Changes.*

13. Ed. Weiss and O.S. English, *Psychosomatic Medicine. Clinical Application of Psychopathology to General Medical Problems.*

14. R. Grinker and F.P. Robbins, *Psychosomatic Case Book.*

15. Franz Alexander, *Psychosomatic Medicine.*

16. The reference here is to St. Augustine's famous imperative, *ama et fac quod vis* (love and do what you like).—*Trans.*

17. The book was published in Paris in 1641. The frontispiece, which we reproduce here, is only to be found in the English translation of 1649 by Henry Earl of Monmouth and is the work of William Marshall (1591 to 1649).

18. William James, 1842 to 1910, of Harvard, the most eminent American psychologist; see his *The Principles of Psychology*, II (1890), pp. 449-450.

19. C.G. Lange, Professor of Pathology at Copenhagen, *Über Gemütsbewegungen.*

20. It is very reminiscent of Descartes' conception in *Traité des passions de l'âme*, Paris, 1649.

21. Charles Darwin, *The Expression of the Emotions in Men and Animals*, 1872, largely based on Sir Charles Bell, *Anatomy and Physiology of Expressions.*

22. Immanuel Kant, *Dreams of a Ghostseer Explained in the Light of Dreams of Metaphysics*, II/3, 1766.

23. H.G. Wolff, *Stress and Disease.* Thomas, Springfield Illinois, 1953.

24. Quoted from W.H. von Wyss, *Aufgaben und Grenzen der psychosomatischen Medizin.*

25. See pp. 128-129.

26. A summary of the previous literature is to be found in A. Hoffer and H. Osmond, *The Chemical Basis of Clinical Psychiatry.* See also Max Rinker and Herman C.B. Denber, *Chemical Concepts of Psychosis.*

27. Posidonius, *Peri Pathon.*

28. The expression is already found in Plato, *Alcib.* 130a, as I was kindly informed by H.R. Schwyzer of Zurich; it is also found in Euclid, *Elem.* VII. 5, according to a communication from A. Szabo, of Budapest.

29. Aristotle, *De caelo.*

30. Cf. E. Rousselle, "Seelische Führung im lebenden Taoismus," in *Eranos Yearbook*, 1933.

31. Paracelsus, quoted from W.H. von Wyss (cf. note 24 above).

32. Archimedes, 1. 10 al.

33. Henry Corbin, *Terre céleste et Corps de resurrection.*

34. Ibid., pp. 148ff.

35. G.R.S. Mead, *The Subtle Body.*

36. Stepan Figar, "The Application of Plethysmography to the Objective Study of So-called Extrasensory Perception," in *Jour. Soc. Psychical Research*, XL (1959), pp. 162–172.

37. The plethysmograph is an instrument used by physiologists to measure and record the fluctuations in the volume of a limb or part of a limb which are produced by fluctuations in the volume of blood in the blood vessels.

38. *Musaeum Hermeticum*, Francofurti, 1677, p. 617: *Anima autem, qua homo a ceteris animalibus differt, illa operatur in corpore, sed maiorem operationem habet extra corpus; quoniam absolute extra corpus dominatur.*

39. C. G. Jung, "Synchronicity: An Acausal Connecting Principle"; G. original "Synchronizität als ein Prinzip akausaler Zusammenhänge" in *Naturerklärung und Psyche* (Studien aus dem C. G. Jung-Institut, IV; Zurich 1952). English trans. *The Interpretation of Nature and the Psyche*. New York (Bollingen Series LI) and London (1955); now in *CW* 8.

40. *The I Ching or Book of Changes*, The Richard Wilhelm Translation rendered into English by Cary F. Baynes. Foreword by C. G. Jung. Routledge & Kegan Paul, Third Impression, London, 1965.

41. There will be more about archetypes and synchronicity phenomena in subsequent volumes.

NOTES TO CHAPTER VI

1. C. G. Jung, "A Review of the Complex Theory," *CW* 8, pp. 92–104.

2. H. Christoffel, "Der Zürcher und der Leipziger Komplex," in *Leben und Umwelt*, Jg. 4/10 (1948), pp. 223–226.

3. *CW* 1, p. 81; German orig. Leipzig 1902.

4. *CW* 1, p. 163; German orig. in *Journ. Psychol. Neurol.*, II (1903), p. 163, pp. 181–201.

5. Cf. Jung's remark, "Talleyrand's art of using words to conceal thoughts is given only to a few" (*CW* 3, p. 94).

6. Cf. C. G. Jung's dissertation "On the Psychology and Pathology of So-called Occult Phenomena," *CW* 1.

7. C. G. Jung, "A Review of the Complex Theory," *CW* 8, p. 100.

8. *Deuteronomy V, 9.—Trans.*

LITERATURE REVIEW

CHRONOLOGICAL REVIEW OF THE LITERATURE ON THE EVIDENCE-EXPERIMENT

1. Vogt, R., "Über Ablenkbarkeit und Gewöhnungsfähigkeit," *Psychol. Abb.*, III, 1901.
2. Lombroso, C., and Donelli, *Archivio psichiatr. neuropat. antropol. crim., med. leg.*, XXIII, 1902.
3. Luria, A.R., "Die Methode der abbildenden Motorik in der Tatbestandsdiagnostik," *Zs. angew. Psychol.*, XXXV, 1903.
4. Wertheimer, M., and Klein, J., "Psychologische Tatbestandsdiagnostik. Ideen zu psychologisch-experimentellen Methoden zum Zwecke der Festsellung der Anteilnahme eines Menschen au einem Tatbestande," *Arch. Kriminalanthr.*, XV, 1904.
5. Gross, Hanns, "Zur Frage des Wahrnehmungsproblems III," *Btrr. Psychol. Aussage*, II/2, 1905.
6. Wertheimer, M., "Experimentelle Untersuchungen zur Tatbestandsdiagnostik," *Arch. ges. Psychol.*, VI, 1/2, 1905.
7. Gross, A., "Zur Psychologischen Tatbestandsdiagnostik als kriminalistisches Hilfsmittel," *Btrr. Psychol. Aussage,* II/3, 1905.
8. Kraus, O., "Psychologische Tatbestandsdiagnostik," *Mschr. Kriminalpsychol.*, II, 1905.
9. Gross, Hanns, "Zur psychologischen Tatbestandsdiagnostik," *Arch. Kriminalanthr.*, XIX, 1/2, 1905.
10. Gross, A., "Zur psychologischen Tatbestandsdiagnostik," *Mschr. Kriminalpsychol.*, II/3, 1905.
11. Weygandt, W., "Zur psychologischen Tatbestandsdiagnostik," *Mschr. Kriminalpsychol.*, II, 6/7, 1905.
12. Jung, C.G., "On the Psychological Diagnosis of Facts," *CW* 1. German original, "Zur psychologischen Tatbestandsdiagnostik," *Zbl. Nervenhlkde. Psychiatr.*, XVI/200, 1905.
13. Gross, A., "Die Assoziationsmethode im Strafprozess," *Zs. ges. Strafrechtswiss.*, XXVI/1, 1905.
14. Grabowsky, A., "Psychologische Tatbestandsdiagnostik," Supp.

to *Allgemeine Zeitung* of 15.12.1905.

15. Jung, C.G., "The Reaction-time Ratio in the Association Experiment," *CW* 2. German original, "Über das Verhalten der Reaktionszeit beim Assoziations-experiment," *Journ. Psychol. Neurol.*, VI/1, 1905.

16. D'Allames, (a) *Bull. Inst. gén. psychol.*, May 1905. (b) *Ann. Psychical Sc.*, II, 1905.

17. Jung, C.G., "The Psychological Diagnosis of Evidence," *CW* 2. German original, "Die Psychologische Diagnose des Tatbestandes," *Schweiz. Zs. Strafr.*, XVIII, 5/6, 1905.

18. Lederer, M., "Zur Frage der pathologischen Tatbestandsdiagnostik," *Zs. ges. Strafrechtswiss.*, XXVI/3, 1906.

19. Claparède, Eduard, "La Psychologie judiciaire. Diagnostic constellatoire de la participation réelle d'un inculpé à un délit donné," *Année Psychol.*, XII, 1906.

20. Wertheimer, M., "Tatbestandsdiagnostische Reproduktionsversuche," *Arch. Kriminalanthr.*, XXII, 1906.

21. Steckel, Wilhelm, "Die Untersuchung der Zukunft," *Die Zeit*, 31.5.1906.

22. Lederer, M., "Die Verwendung der psychologischen Tatbestandsdiagnostik in der Strafrechtspraxis," *Mschr. Kriminalpsychol.*, III, 1906.

23. Zürcher, Emil, "Zur psychologischen Diagnose des Tatbestandes," *Mschr. Kriminalpsychol.*, III/3, 1906.

24. Freud, Sigmund, "Psycho-Analysis and the Establishment of the Facts in Legal Proceedings." Standard Edition IX, London, 1960. German original, 1906.

25. Löffler, A., "Zur psychologischen Tatbestandsdiagnostik," *Mschr. Kriminalpsychol.*, III, 1906.

26. Kramer, F., and Stern, William, "Selbstverrat durch Assoziation. Experimentelle Untersuchungen," *Btrr. Psychol. Aussage*, II/4, 1906.

27. Wright, D., *Yorkshire Post*, 16.10.1906.

28. Gross, A., "Die Assoziationsmethode im Strafprozess. Kriminalpsychologische Studie," *Zs. Strafrechtswiss.*, XXVII, 1907.

29. Altberg, L.M., "Associacionnyj metod v ugolovnom processje," *Voprosy Obščestvovjedjenija*. I.

30. Heilbronner, Karl, "Die Grundlagen der psychologischen Tatbestandsdiagnostik. Nebst einem praktischen Fall," *Zs. ges. Strafrechtswiss.*, XXVII, 1907.

31. Stöhr, "Über psychologische Tatbestandsdiagnostik," Vortrag in der österreichischen kriminalistischen Vereinigung, 1907.

32. Heegel, "Die Tatsbestandsdiagnostik im Strafverfahren," *Mschr. Kriminalpsychol.*, IV, 1907.

33. Gross, A., "Kriminalpsychologische Tatbestandsforschung," *Jur. psychiatr. Granzfragen*, V/7, 1907.

34. Specht, "Über psychologische Tatbestandsdiagnostik," Vortrag in der kriminalistischen Vereinigung Erlangen, 1907.

35. Lipmann, Otto, and Wertheimer, M., "Tatbestandsdiagnostische Kombinationsversuche," *Zs. angew. Psychol.*, I/1, 1907.

36. Seiffer, W., "Die psychologische Tatbestandsdiagnose," *Med. Klin.*, III/37, 1907.

37. Isserlin, Max, "Die diagnostische Bedeutung der Assoziationsversuche," *Münchn. Med. Wschr.*, XXVII, 1907.

38. Jung, C.G., "Disturbances of Reproduction in the Association Experiment." *CW* 2. German original "Über die Reproduktionsstörungen beim Assoziations-experiment," *Journ. Psychol. Neurol.*, IX/4, 1907.

39. Watt, Henry J., "Über den Einfluss der Geschwindigkeit der Aufeinanderfolge von Reizen auf Wortreaktionen," *Arch. ges. Psychol.*, IX, 1907.

40. Pappenheim, M., "Merkfähigkeit und Assoziationsversuch," *Zs. Psychol.*, XLVI, 1907.

41. Schnitzler, J.G., (a) *Onderzoekingen over de diagnostik van voerstellingscomplexen met behulp van het associatie-experiment*. Utrecht medical dissertation, 1907. (b) "Experimentelle Beiträge zur Tatbestandsdiagnostik," *Zs. angew. Psychol.*, II 1/2, 1908.

42. Münsterberg, Hugo, (a) *The Detective of Crime*, chapter on "The Traces of Emotion," *McClure's Magazine*, October 1907. (b) *On the Witness Stand*, chapter on "Essays on Psychology and Crime," The McClure Company, New York, 1908.

43. Wreschner, Arthur, "Die Reproduktion und Assoziation von Vorstellungen," *Zs. Psychol.*, Ergänzungsband 3, 1907–1909.

44. Schultz, Johannes H., "Assoziationsversuche zur Tatbestandsdiagnostik." Vortrag in der Göttinger forensisch-psychologischen Vereinigung, 1908.

45. Lipmann, Otto, "Tatbestandsdiagnostik," *Grundriss der Psychologie für Juristen*. Leipzig, 1908.

46. Van Der Hoeven, Jr., H., *De invloed der affectieve meerwaarde van voorstellingen in het woordreaktie-experiment. Met een aanhangsel over de bruikbaarheid van het experiment in het straf-proces*. Leiden medical dissertation, 1908.

47. Rittershaus, E., "Über Tatbestandsdiagnostik. Vorläufige Mitteilung," *Zbl. Nervenhlkde. Psychiatr.*, 1908.

48. Bolte, Richard, "Assoziationspsychologie und Assoziationsexperiment," *U.*, 12/4, 1908.

49. Gross, K., *Seelenleben des Kindes*. Berlin, 1908.

50. Lucka, E., *Die Phantasie*. Vienna and Leipzig, 1908.

51. Saling, G., "Assoziative Massenversuche," *Zs. Psychol.*, IL, 1908.

52. Scripture, E.W., "Experiments on Subconscious Ideas," *Journ. Amer. Med. Assoc.*, 1908.

53. Veraguth, Otto, "Der psychogalvanische Reflex als Mittel zum Nachweis gewisser seelischer Vorgänge," *U.*, 12/50, 1908.

54. Wulffen, Erich, *Psychologie des Verbrechers*, I., ed. Dr. P. Langenscheidt, Gross-Lichterfeld, 1908.

55. Menzerath, P., "Die Bedeutung der sprachlichen Geläufigkeit oder der formalen sprachlichen Beziehung für die Reproduktion," *Zs. Psychol.*, XLVIII, 1908.

56. Lipmann, Otto, "Eine Methode zur Vergleichung von zwei Kollektivgegenständen," *Zs. Psychol.*, XLVIII, 1908.

57. Verworn, M., *Zur Psychologie der primitiven Kunst*, Jena, 1908.

58. Gutzmann, H., (a) "Versuche über Hören und Verstehen mit Diskussionsbemerkungen von Lipmann," *Compte Rendu des travaux du Ier Congrès International de Psychiatrie, de Neurologie, de Psychologie et de l'Assistance des Aliénés*. Amsterdam, 1908. (b) "Über Hören und Verstehen," *Zs. angew. Psychol.*, I, 1908.

59. Jung, C.G., (a) "New Aspects of Criminal Psychology." *CW* 2. Italian original, "Le nuove vedute della psicologia criminale," *Riv. Psicol. Appl.*, IV/4, 1908. (b) "The Association Method." *CW* 2. German original MS, 1909. First published in *Amer. Journ. Psychol.*, XXI/2, 1910.

60. Storfer, Adolf, "Eine Gefahr der kriminalpsychologischen Tatbestandsdiagnostik," *Schweiz. Zs. Strafr.*, XXII, 1909.

61. Yerkes, R.M., and Berry, Charles S., "The Association Reaction Method of Mental Diagnosis," *Amer. Journ. Psychol.*, XX/1, 1909.

62. Stein, Philip, "Tatbestandsdiagnostische Versuche bei Untersuchungsgefangenen," (a) *Zs. Psychol.*, III, 1909; (b) offprint, 1909.

63. Montet, Charles de, "Assoziationsexperimente an einem kriminellen Fall," *Mschr. Kriminalpsychol.*, VI/1, 1909.

64. Lipmann, Otto, "Die Technik der Vernehmung vom psychologischen Standpunkte," *Mschr. Kriminalpsychol.*, VI/6, 1909.

65. Offner, M., *Gas Gedächtnis*, chapter on "Reproduktionszeit und Tatbestandsdiagnostik." Berlin, 1909.

66. Henke, F.G., and Eddy, M.W., "Mental Diagnosis by the Association Reaction Method," *Psychol. Revw.*, XVI, 1909.

67. Rittershaus, E., "Die Komplexforschung." "Tatbestandsdiagnostik," *Journ. Psychol. Neurol.*, XV, 1909; XVI, 1910.

68. Stadelmann, H., *Ärztlich pädagogische Vorschule*, Hamburg, 1909.

69. Peters, W., "Erinnerungsassoziationen." Bericht über den 3, Kongress für experimentelle Psychologie. Leipzig, 1909.

70. Leach, Hazel M., and Washburn, M.F., "Some Tests by the Association Reaction Method of Mental Diagnosis," *Amer. Journ. Psychol.*, XXI/1, 1910.

71. "Tages- und Standesfragen," Gerichtshalle, LIV/20, 1910.

72. Gregor, A., *Leitfaden der experimentellen Psychopathologie*, chapter on "Assoziationsversuche an Geisteskranken (Psychoanalyse, Tatbestandsdiagnostik, deren Wert, Erfolge und Grenzen)." Berlin, 1910.

73. Binet, Alfred, "Le Diagnostic judiciaire par la méthode des associations," *Année Psychol.*, XVI, 1910.

74. Langfeld, H.S., "Suppression with Negative Instruction," *Psychol. Bull.*, VII/6, 1910.

75. Koppen, M., and Kutzinski, Systematische Beobachtungen über die Wiedergabe kleiner Erzählungen durch Geisteskranke. Berlin, 1910.

76. Ohms, H., "Untersuchungen unterwertiger Assoziationen mittels des Worterkennungsvorgangs," *Zs. Psychol.*, LVI 1/2, 1910.

77. Huston, P.E., Shakow, D., and Erickson, M.H., "A Study of Hypnotically Induced Complexes by Means of the Luria Technique," *Journ. Gen. Psychol.*, XI, 1934.

78. Lang, J.B., "Experimentelle Beiträge zur psychologischen Diagnose des Tatbestands," *Zbl. Psychother. Grenzgebb,* IX, 1936.

BIBLIOGRAPHY OF STUDIES OF PSYCHIATRIC SUBJECTS IN WHICH USE WAS MADE OF THE ASSOCIATION EXPERIMENT

1. Jung, C.G., "The Psychopathological Significance of the Association Experiment." *CW* 2. German original, 1906.

2. Bolte, Richard, "Assoziationsversuche als diagnostisches Hilfsmittel," *Allg. Zs. Psychiatr.*, LXIV, 1907.

3. Ladame, Paul L., "L'association des idées et son utilisation comme méthode d'examen dans les maladies mentales," *L'Encéphale* 8, Paris 1908.

4. Bailey, P., "The Practical Value of the Association Test," *Amer. Journ. Med. Scs.*, 1909.

5. Henke and Eddy, "Mental Diagnosis by the Association Reaction Method," *Psychol. Revw.*, November 1909.

6. Town, "Association Tests in Practical Work for the Insane," *Psychol. Clinic*, February 1909.

7. Yerkes and Berry, "The Association Reaction Method of Mental Diagnosis," *Amer. Journ. Psychol.*, January 1909.

8. Isserlin, Max, "Assoziationsversuche bei einem forensisch begutachteten Falle von epileptischer Geistesstörung," *Mschr. Psychiatr. Neurol.*, XVIII, 1905.

9. _____, "Die diagnostische Bedeutung der Assoziations-versuche," *Münchn. Med. Wschr.*, XXVII, 1907.

10. _____, "Psychologische Untersuchung an Manisch-Depressiven," *Mschr. Psychiatr. Neurol.*, XXII, 1907.

11. Pototzky, C., "Die Verwertbarkeit des Assoziations-versuchs für die Beurteilung der traumatischen Neurosen," *Mschr. Psychiatr. Neurol.*, XXV, 1909.

12. Eitingon, Max, *Über die Wirkung des Anfalls auf die Assoziationen der Epileptischen.* Zurich dissertation. Leipzig, 1909.

13. Goett, Th., "Assoziationsversuche an Kindern," *Zs. Kinderhlkde.*, I, 1911.

14._____, "Zur Bewertung des Assoziationsversuches im Kindesalter," *Mschr. Kinderhlkde.*, XI, 1912.

15. Brunnschweiler, H., *Über Assoziationen bei organisch Dementen.* Zurich dissertation. Zurich, 1912.

16. Lang, J.B., "Eine Hypothese zur psychologischen Bedeutung der Verfolgungsidee," *Psychol. Abhh.*, ed. C.G. Jung, I, 1914.

17. Jörger, J. B., *Über Assoziationen bei Alkoholikern*. Zurich dissertation. *Mschr. Psychiatr. Neurol.*, XXXVII, 1915.

18. Sarasin, Philipp, *Assoziationen von erethischen Oligophrenen*. Zurich dissertation. *Schweiz. Arch. Neurol. Psychiatr.*, IV, 1 and 2, Zurich, 1919.

19. Volkmann, W., *Assoziationsexperimente an Schizophrenen während der Insulinschockbehandlung*. Zurich dissertation. Bruges, Zurich, 1938.

The following papers deal with the evaluation of the results of the experiment specifically from the point of view of psychotherapy:

20. Jones, Ernest, "The Practical Value of the Word-Association Method in the Treatment of the Psycho-Neuroses," *Revw. Neurol. Psychiatr.*, November 1910.

21. Lang, J. B., "Zur Bestimmung des psychoanalytischen Widerstandes," *Psychol. Abhh.*, ed. C. G. Jung, I, 1914.

22. Meier, Carl A., "Über die Bedeutung des JUNGschen Assoziationsexperimentes für die Psychotherapie," *Zs. ges. Neurol.* CLXI, 1937.

CHRONOLOGICAL REVIEW OF THE LITERATURE PUBLISHED BY THE ZURICH SCHOOL

1. Riklin, Franz, "Analytische Untersuchungen der Symptome und Assoziationen eines Falles von Hysterie (Lina H.)," *Psychiatr. Neurol. Wschr.*, XXXXVI, 1905; XXXXVII, 1905; XXXXVIII, 1905; IL, 1905; L, 1905; LI, 1905; LII, 1905.

2. Hahn, R., *Über die Beziehungen zwischen Fehlreaktionen und Klangassoziationen*. Zurich dissertation. *Psychol. Abh.*, V/1, 1906.

3. Jung, C. G., "Freud's Theory of Hysteria: A Reply to Aschaffenburgschekritik." *CW* 4. German original, 1906.

4. Maeder, Alphonse, "I. Contributions à la Psychologie de la vie quotidienne," *Arch. Psychol.*, VI, 1906.

5. _____, "Essai d'Interprétation de quelques rêves," *Arch. Psychol.*, VI, 1906.

6. Bleuler, Eugen, "Freudsche Mechanismen in der Symptomatologie von Psychosen," *Psychiatr. Neurol. Wschr.*, VIII, 1906.

7. Abraham, Karl, "Über die Bedeutung sexueller Jugendträume für die Symptomatologie der Dementia praecox," *Zbl. Nervenhlkde. Psychiatr.*, XXX, 1907.

8. Maeder, Alphonse, "II. Nouvelles Contributions à la psychopathologie," *Arch. Psychol.*, VII, 1907.

9. Bleuler, Eugen, "Sexuelle Abnormitäten der Kinder," *Jb. Schweiz Ges. Schulgesundhtspfl.*, IX, 1908.

10. Maeder, Alphonse, "Die Symbolik in den Legenden, Märchen, Gebräuchen und Träumen," *Psychiatr. Neurol. Wschr.*, X, 1908.

11. Müller, E. H., *Beiträge zur Kenntnis der Hyperemesis gravidarum.* Zurich dissertation. *Psychiatr. Neurol. Wschr.*, X, 1908.

12. Frank, Ludwig, "Zur Psychoanalyse," *Journ. Psychol. Neurol.*, Forel Festschrift, XIII, 1908.

13. Jung, C.G., "The Freudian Theory of Hysteria." *CW* 4. German original, 1908.

14. Riklin, Franz, "Wunscherfüllung und Symbolik im Märchen," *Schrr. angew. Seelenkunde*, ed. Freud, 2, 1908.

15. Eberschweiler, A., "Untersuchungen über die sprachlichen Komponenten der Assoziationen," *Allg. Zs. Psychiatrie*, LXV, 1908.

16. Maeder, Alphonse, "Sexualität und Epilepsie," *Jb. psychoanal. psychopathol. Forschgg.*, I/1, 1909.

17. Müller, H., *Experimentelle Beiträge zur physikalischen Entstehung des psycho-galvanischen Phänomens.* Zurich dissertation, 1909.

18. Chalewsky, Fanny, "Heilung eines hysterischen Bellens durch Psychoanalyse," *Zbl. Nervenhlkde. Psychiatr.*, XXXII, 1909.

19. Jung, C.G., "The Analysis of Dreams." *CW* 4. French original, 1909.

20. Pfister, Oscar, "Wahnvorstellung und Schülerselbstmord," *Schweiz. Bll. Schulgesundhtspfl.*, 1, 1909.

21. _____, "Psychoanalytische Seelsorge und experimentelle Moralpadagogik," *Protest. Mhh.*, 1, 1909.

22. _____, "Ein Fall von psychoanalytischer Seelsorge und Seelenheilung," *Evangel. Freiheit*, 3–5, 1909.

22a. Stockmayer, W., "Zur psychologischen Analyse der Dementia praecox," *Zbl. Nervenhlkd. Psychiatr.*, XXXII, 1909, pp. 699–798.

23. Eitingon, Max, *Über die Wirkung des Anfalls auf die Assoziationen der Epileptischen.* Zurich dissertation. Leipzig, 1909.

24. Müller, E. H., "Ein Fall von induziertem Irresein nebst anschliessenden Erörterungen," *Psychiatr. Neurol. Wschr.*, XI, 1909/1910.

25. Aebly, J., *Zur Analyse der physikalischen Vorbedingungen des psychogalvanischen Reflexes mit exosomatischer Stromquelle.* Zurich dissertation. Zurich, 1910.

26. Riklin, Franz, "Aus der Analyse einer Zwangsneurose," *Jb. psychoanal. psychopathol. Forschgg*, 1910.

27. Pfister, Oscar, "Analytische Untersuchungen über die Psychologie des Hasses und der Versöhnung," *Jb. psychoanal. psychopathol. Forschgg.*, II/1, 1910. (This study is based on the association experiment.)

28. Maeder, Alphonse, "Psychologische Untersuchungen an Dementia praecox-Kranken," *Jb. psychoanal. psychopathol. Forschgg.*, II/1, 1910.

29. Bleuler, Eugen, "Die Psychoanalyse Freuds," *Jb. psychoanal. psychopathol. Forschgg.*, II/2, 1910.

30. Pfister, Oscar, "Die Frömmigkeit des Grafen von Zinzendorf," *Schrr. angew. Seelenkunde*, X, 1910, ed. Sigmund Freud.

31._____, "Zur Psychologie des hysterischen Madonnenkults," *Zbl. Psychoanal.*, I/1, 1910.

32. Jung, C.G., "A Contribution to the Psychology of Rumour." *CW* 4. German original, 1910.

33. Spielrein, Sabina, *Über den psychologischen Inhalt eines Falles von Schizophrenie (Dementia praecox).* Zurich dissertation. *Jb. psychoanal. psychopathol. Forschgg.*, III/1, 1911.

34. Bertschinger, Heinrich, "Illustrierte Halluzinationen," *Jb. psychoanal. psychopathol. Forschgg.*, III/1, 1911.

35. Jung, C.G., *Symbols of Transformation. CW* 5. German original, Part 1, 1911.

36. Pfister, Oscar, "Die psychologische Enträtselung der religiösen Glossolalie und der automatischen Kryptographie," *Jb. psychoanal. psychopathol. Forschgg.*, III/1, 1911.

37. Maeder, Alphonse, "Zur Entstehung der Symbolik im Traum in der Dementia praecox etc.," *Zbl. Psychoanal.*, I/9, 1911.

38. Riklin, Franz, "Über einige Probleme der Sagendeutung," *Zbl. Psychoanal.*, I/10, 1911.

39. Jung, C.G., "On the Significance of Number Dreams." *CW* 4. German original, 1911.

40. Maeder, Alphonse, "Über zwei Frauentypen," *Zbl. Psychoanal.*, I/12, 1911.

41. Nelken, Jan, "Psychologische Untersuchungen an Dementia praecox-Kranken," *Journ. Psychol. Neurol.*, XVIII, 1911.

42. Riklin, Franz, "Eine Lüge," *Zbl. Psychoanal.*, I/5–6, 1911.

43. Aptekmann, Esther, Experimentelle Beiträge zur Psychologie des psycho-galvanischen Phänomens. Zurich dissertation, 1912. *Jb. psychoanal. psychopathol. Forschgg.*, III/2, 1912.

44. Spielrein, Sabina, "Die Destruktion als Ursache des Werdens," *Jb. psychoanal. psychopathol. Forschgg.*, IV/1, 1912.

45. Jung, C.G., *Symbols of Transformation. CW* 5. German original, Part 2, 1912.

46. Pfister, Oscar, "Die psychologische Enträtselung der religiösen Glossolalie und der automatischen Kryptographie," *Jb. psychoanal. psychopathol. Forschgg.*, III/2, 1912.

47. Bleuler, Eugen, "Das autistische Denken," *Jb. psychoanal. psychopathol. Forschgg.*, IV/1, 1912.

48. Grebelskaja, Sch., "Psychologische Analyse einer Paranoiden," *Jb. psychoanal. psychopathol. Forschgg.*, IV/1, 1912.

49. Nelken, J., "Analytische Beobachtungen über Phantasien eines Schizophrenen," *Jb. psychoanal. psychopathol. Forschgg.*, IV/1, 1912.

50. Maeder, Alphonse, "Über die Funktion des Traumes (mit Berücksichtigung der Tagesträume, des Spieles usw.)," *Jb. psychoanal. psychopathol. Forschgg.*, IV/2, 1912.

51. Nelken, J., "Über schizophrene Wortzerlegungen," *Zbl. Psychoanal.*, II/1, 1912.

52. Maeder, Alphonse, "Der Berg als Symbol. Der Zweifel eines Zwangsneurotikers," *Zbl. Psychoanal.*, II/1, 1912.

53. Spielrein, Sabina, "Beiträge zur Kenntnis der kindlichen Seele," *Zbl. Psychoanal.*, II/2, 1912.

54. Klaesi, Jakob, *Über das psychogalvanische Phänomen.* Zurich dissertation. *Journ. Psychol. Neurol.*, XIX, 1912.

55. Brunnschweiler, H., *Über Assoziationen bei organisch Dementen.* Zurich dissertation, 1912.

56. Pfenninger, Wilhelm, "Untersuchungen über die Konstanz und den Wechsel der psychologischen Konstellation bei Normalen und Frühdementen (Schizophrenen)," *Jb. Psychoanal. Psychopathol. Forschgg.*, III/2, 1912.

57. Itten, W., "Beiträge zur Psychologie der Dementia praecox," *Jb. psychoanal. psychopathol. Forschgg.*, V/1, 1913.

58. Pfister, Oscar, "Kryptolalie, Kryptographie und unbewusstes Vexierbild bei Normalen," in *Jb. psychoanal. psychopathol. Forschgg.*, V/1, 1913.

59. Bleuler, Eugen, "Der Sexualwiderstand," *Jb. psychoanal. psychopathol. Forschgg.*, V/1, 1913.

60. Mensendieck, Otto, "Zur Technik des Unterrichts und der Erziehung während der psychoanalytischen Behandlung," *Jb. psychoanal. psychopathol. Forschgg.*, V/2, 1913.

61. Maeder, Alphonse, "Über das Traumproblem," *Jb. psychoanal. psychopathol. Forschgg.*, V/2, 1913.

62. Lang, J.B., "Über Assoziationsversuche bei Schizophrenen und den Mitgliedern ihrer Familien," *Jb. psychoanal. psychopathol. Forschgg.*, V/2, 1913.

63. Jung, C.G., "Comment on Tausk's Criticism of Nelken." *CW* 18. German original, 1913.

64. Lang, J.B., "Aus der Analyse eines Zahlentraumes," *Zbl. Psychoanal.*, III/4-5, 1913.

65. Müller, V.J., *Zur Kenntnis der Leitungsbahnen des psychogalvanischen Reflexphänomens.* Zurich dissertation, 1913. *Mschr. Psychiatr. Neurol.*, XXXIII, 1913.

66. Lang, J.B., "Zur Bestimmung des psychoanalytischen Widerstandes," *Psychol. Abh.*, I, 1914, ed. C.G. Jung.

67. _____, "Eine Hypothese zur psychologischen Bedeutung der Verfolgungsidee," ibid.

68. Schmid, H., "Zur Psychologie der Brandstifter," ibid.

69. Schneiter, C., "Archaische Elemente in den Wahnideen eines Paranoiden," ibid.

70. Jörger, J.B., *Über Assoziationen bei Alkoholikern.* Zurich dissertation. *Mschr. Psychiatr. Neurol.* XXXVII, 1915.

71. Hoffmann, W., "Über den Einfluss der Gefühlsbetonung und einiger anderer Faktoren auf die Dauer und den Wechsel der Assoziationen," *Kraepelins Psychol. Abb.*, VII/1, 1915.

72. Huber, H., " Über den Einfluss von optischem oder akustischem Reiz und grammatikalischer Form des Reizwortes auf den Assoziationsvorgang." Zurich dissertation. *Journ. Psychol. Neurol.* XXIII 5/6, 1917.

73. Sarasin, Philipp, *Assoziationen von erethischen Oligophrenen.* Zurich dissertation. *Schweiz. Arch. Neurol. Psychiatr.*, IV, H 1 and 2, 1919.

74. Volkmann, W., *Assoziationsexperimente an Schizophrenen während der Insulinschockbehandlung.* Zurich dissertation, 1938.

LIST OF ABBREVIATIONS FOR JOURNALS AND YEARBOOKS ETC. QUOTED IN THIS VOLUME.

Allg. Zs. Psychiatr.	Allgemeine Zeitschrift für Psychiatrie und psychisch-gerichtliche Medizin, Berlin.
Ambix	Ambix, London.
Amer. Journ. Insanity	American Journal of Insanity, Baltimore, U.S.A.
Amer. Journ. Med. Scs.	American Journal of the Medical Sciences, Philadelphia, Pa.
Amer. Journ. Psychol.	American Journal of Psychology, Worcester, U.S.A.
Ann. Chem.	Justus Liebig's Annalen der Chemie und Pharmacie, Leipzig.
Ann. Psychical Sc.	Annals of Psychical Science, London.
Année Psychol.	Année Psychologique, Paris.
Arch. ges. Physiol.	Archiv der gesamten Physiologie des Menschen und der Tiere, Bonn.
Arch. ges. Psychol.	Archiv für die gesamte Psychologie, Leipzig, from 1961 Frankfurt a. M.
Arch. Kriminalanthr.	Archiv für Kriminal-Anthropologie und Kriminalistik, Leipzig.
Archive Neurol. Psychiatr.	Archive of Neurology and Psychiatry, Chicago.
Arch. Psychol.	Archiv für Psychologie, Heidelberg.
Archivio psichiatr. neuropat., antropol. crim., med. leg.	Archivio di Psichiatria, Neuropatia, Antropologia Criminale e Medicina Legale, Turin.
Archs. Psychol.	Archives de Psychologie, Geneva.
Berr. Dt. Chem. Ges.	Berichte der Deutschen Chemischen Gesellschaft, Karlsruhe.
Blätter aus Prevorst	Blätter aus Prevorst, Karlsruhe.
Brain	Brain. A Journal of Neurology, London.

Brit. Med. Journ.	British Medical Journal, London.
Brit. Journ. Industr. Med.	British Journal of Industrial Medicine, London.
Brit. Journ. Psychol.	The British Journal of Psychology, Cambridge, England.
Btrr. Psychol. Aussage	Beiträge zur Psychologie der Aussage, Leipzig.
Bull. Inst. gén. psychol.	Bulletin de l'Institut général psychologique, Paris.
Cpt. rend. Soc. Helv. Scs. natur.	Compte Rendu de la Société Helvétique des Sciences Naturelles, Aarau.
Cpts. rends. hebd. Biol.	Comptes Rendus Hebdomadaires des Séances et Mémoires de la Société de Biologie, Paris.
Diagnostic Studies	Diagnostische Assoziationsstudien, Leipzig.
L'Encéphale	L'Encéphale. Journal des Maladies mentales et nerveuses, Paris.
Evangel. Freiheit	Evangelische Freiheit, Tübingen.
Eranos Ybks.	*Eranos-Yearbooks*, Zürich.
Fortschrr. Psychol. Anw.	Fortschritte der Psychologie und ihrer Anwendungen, Leipzig/Berlin.
Gerichtshalle	Gerichtshalle, Vienna.
Gesnerus	Gesnerus, Aarau.
Hb. der klin. Psychol.	*Handbuch der klinischen Psychologie*, Zürich.
Hb. Psychiatr.	*Handbuch der Psychiatrie*, Leipzig/Vienna.
Intern. Zs. ärztl. Psychoanal.	Internationale Zeitschrift für ärztliche Psychoanalyse, Leipzig/Vienna.
Intern. Zs. Psychoanal.	Internationale Zeitschrift für Psychoanalyse, Leipzig/Vienna, later London.
Jb. psychoanal. psychopathol. Forschgg.	*Jahrbuch für Psychoanalytische und Psychopathologische Forschungen, Leipzig/Vienna.*
Jb. Schweiz. Ges. Schulgesundbtspfl.	*Jahrbuch der Schweizerischen Gesell schaft für Schulgesundheitspflege*, Zürich.
Journ. Abnorm. Psychol.	Journal of Abnormal and Social Psychology, Boston, Albany, N.Y.
Journ. Amer. Med. Assoc.	Journal of the American Medical Association, Chicago.
Journ. Amer. Soc. Psychical Research	Journal of the American Society for Psychical Research, New York.

Journ. Anal. Psychol.	Journal of Analytical Psychology, London.
Journ. Exp. Psychol.	Journal of Experimental Psychology, Lancaster, Pa.
Journ. Gen. Psychol.	Journal of General Psychology, Worcester, Mass.
Journ. Mental Sc.	Journal of Mental Science, London.
Journ. Nerv. Ment. Dis.	Journal of Nervous and Mental Disease, Chicago.
Journ. Neurol. (Brain)	A Journal of Neurology, London.
Journ. Parapsychol.	Journal of Parapsychology, Durham, N.C.
Journ. Psychol. Neurol.	Journal für Psychologie und Neurologie, Leipzig.
Jur. psychiatr. Grenzfragen	Juristisch-psychiatrische Grenzfragen, Halle.
Kultur-Staatswiss. Schrr. ETH	Kultur- und Staatswissenschaftliche Schriften der ETH, Zürich.
Leben und Umwelt	Leben und Umwelt, Aarau.
Leitf. experiment. Psychopathol.	Leitfaden der experimentellen Psycho pathologie, Berlin.
McClure's Mag.	McClure's Magazine, New York.
Med. Biol. Illustr.	Medical and Biological Illustrations, London.
Med. Klin.	Medinische Klinik, Berlin.
Mschr. Kinderhlkde.	Monatsschrift für Kinderheilkunde, Leipzig/Vienna.
Mschr. Kriminalpsychol.	Monatsschrift für Kriminalpsychologie und Strafrechtsreform, Heidelberg.
Mschr. Psychiatr. Neurol.	Monatsschrift für Psychiatrie und Neurologie, Berlin.
Münchn. Med. Wschr.	Münchner Medizinische Wochenschrift, Munich.
Philos. St.	Philosophische Studien, ed. W. Wundt, Leipzig.
Proc. Amer. Soc. Psychical for Research	Proceedings of the American Society Psychical Research, New York.
Proc. Royal Soc. Med.	Proceedings of the Royal Society of Medicine, London.
Proc. Soc. Psychical Research	Proceedings of the Society for Psychical Research, London.
Progr. Méd.	Le Progrès Médical, Paris.
Protest. Mhh.	Protestantische Monatshefte, Leipzig.
Psychiatr. Neurol. Wschr.	Psychiatrisch-Neurologische Wochenschrift, Halle.

Psychol. Abb.	Psychologische Arbeiten, ed. E. Kraepelin, Leipzig.
Psychol. Abhh.	*Psychologische Abhandlungen*, ed. C.G. Jung, Leipzig/Vienna, later Zürich.
Psychol. Bull.	The Psychological Bulletin, Lancaster/New York.
Psychol. Clinic	Psychological Clinic, Philadelphia, Lancaster, Pa.
Psychol. Revw.	The Psychological Review, Baltimore, Pa.
Revw. Neurol. Psychiatr.	Review of Neurology and Psychiatry, Edinburgh.
Riv. Psicol. Appl.	Rivista di Psicologia Applicata, Bologna.
Schrr. angew. Seelenkde.	Schriften zur angewandten Seelenkunde, Leipzig/Vienna.
Schweiz. Arch. Neurol.	Schweizerisches Archiv für Neurologie und Psychiatrie, Zürich.
Schweiz. Bll. Schulgesundhtspfl.	Schweizerische Blätter für Schulgesundheitspflege, Zürich.
Schweiz. Zs. Strafr.	Schweizerische Zeitschrift für Strafrecht, Bern.
Studd. Word-Assn.	Studies in Word-Association, ed. C.G. Jung, London.
U.	Die Umschau, Bechhold-Verlag, Frankfurt.
Universitas	Universitas, Stuttgart.
Vjschr. natf. Ges. Zürich	Vierteljahresschrift der Naturforschenden Gesellschaft in Zürich, Zürich.
Wien. Klin. Rdsch.	Wiener Klinische Rundschau, Vienna.
Yorkshire Post	Yorkshire Post, Leeds, Yorks.
Zbl. Nervenhlkde. Psychiatr.	Zentralblatt für Nervenheilkunde und Psychiatrie, ed. R.E. Gaupp, Leipzig.
Zbl. Psychoanal.	Zentralblatt für Psychoanalyse, Wiesbaden.
Zbl. Psychother. Anwendg.	Zentralblatt für Psychotherapie und ihre Anwendung, Leipzig.
Zbl. Psychother. Grenzgebb.	Zentralblatt für Psychotherapie und ihre Grenzgebiete, Leipzig.
Die Zeit.	Die Zeit, Vienna.
Zs. angew. Psychol.	Zeitschrift für angewandte Psychologie und psychologische Sammelforschung, Leipzig.

Zs. ges. Neurol.	Zeitschrift für die gesamte Neurologie und Psychiatrie, Berlin.
Zs. ges. Strafrechtswiss.	Zeitschrift für die gesamte Strafrechtswissenschaft, Berlin.
Zs. Kinderhlkde.	Zeitschrift für Kinderheilkunde, Berlin.
Zs. Psychol.	Zeitschrift für Psychologie, Leipzig.

BIBLIOGRAPHY

Abbot, C.G., "A Scientist Tests His Own ESP Ability," *Journ. Parapsychol.*, II, 1938.
_____, "Further Evidence of Displacement in ESP Tests," *Journ. Parapsychol.*, XIII, 1949.
Abraham, Karl, "Über die Bedeutung sexueller Jugendtraumen für die Symptomatologie der Dementia praecox," *Zbl. Nervenhlkde. Psychiatr.*, XXX, 1907.
Adler, Alfred, *Study of Organic Inferiority and Its Psychical Compensation*, New York, 1917. German original, 1907.
_____, *The Practice and Theory of Individual Psychology*, London, 1925. German original, 1920.
Aebly, J., "Zur Analyse der physikalischen Vorbedingungen des psychogalvanischen Reflexes mit exosomatischer Stromquelle." Zurich dissertation, 1910.
Aesop (6th Cent. B.C.), *Fables*.
Alexander, Franz, *Psychosomatic Medicine*. London, 1952.
Anschuetz, Richard, *August Kekulé*. Berlin, 1929.
Appian (2nd Cent. B.C.), *Hist. Rom.*, X, 59.
Binswanger, Ludwig, "Über des Verhalten des psychogalvanischen Phänomens beim Assoziationsexperiment," *Journ. Psychol. Neurol.*, X, 1907, and XI, 1908; also author's reports in *Jb. psychoanal. psychopathol. Forschgg.*, II/1, 1910, and *Diagnostic Studies*, XI.
Bleuler, Eugen, "Upon the Significance of Association Experiments," in *Studd. Word-Assn.*, ed. Jung, London 1918. Original German edition, 1904.
_____, "Consciousness and Association," in *Studd. Word-Assn.*, ed. Jung, London, 1918. Original German edition, 1905.
_____, *Affektivität, Suggestibilitie, Paranoia*. Halle, 1906.
_____, *Dementia praecox oder Gruppe der Schizophrenien*, in *Hb. Psychiatr.*, ed. Aschaffenburg, 4/1, 1911.
Bleuler, Eugen, and Jung, C.G., "Komplexe und Krankheitsursachen bei Dementia praecox," *Zb. Nervenhlkde. Psychiatr.*, XXXI, 1908.
Boerhaave, H. (1668-1728), "*Institutiones medicae, digestas ab Hermanno Boerhaave*," ed. Leydensis sexta, § 771 (Lugduni Batavorum, 1746), p. 387.

215

_____, *Praelectiones Academicae de Morbis Nervorum*, ed. Jacobus van Eems, Francoforti et Lipsiae, 1762.

Breuer, Josef, and Freud, Sigmund, *Studies on Hysteria*, standard ed., 2, of the Complete Psychological Works of Sigmund Freud, London, 1960. Original German edition, Leipzig and Vienna, 1895.

Busch, Wilhelm, *Abenteuer eines Junggesellen*.

Candland, D.K., *Emotions: Bodily Change. An Enduring Problem in Psychology*. Princeton, 1962.

Carington, W., "Experiments on the Paranormal Cognition of Drawings," *Proc. Soc. Psychical Research*, XLVI, 1940, and *Journ. Parapsychol.*, IV, 1940.

Christoffel, H., "Der Zürcher und der Leipziger Komplex," *Leben und Welt*, IV/10, 1948.

Cicero, Marcus Tullius (106–43 B.C.), *De div.*, 2.85/86.

Claparède, Eduard, *L'Association des Idées*. Paris, 1903.

Constantinus Africanus (1018–1089), *De melancholia*, lib. I, fol. 163 v. col. II 50–52, ed. M.T. Malato and V. Martini. Rome, 1959.

Corbin, Henry, *Terre céleste et Corps de résurrection*. Paris, 1960.

Cordes, G., "Experimentelle Untersuchungen über Assoziationen," in *Philos. St.*, ed. W. Wundt, XVII, 1901.

Coriat, I.H., "Certain Pulse Reactions as a Measure of Emotions," *Journ. Abnorm. Psychol.*, IV, 1910.

Corrie, Joan, *ABC of Jung's Psychology*. London, 1927.

Darwin, Charles (1809–1882), *The Expression of Emotions in Men and Animals*. 1872.

Denber, H.C.B., and Rinkel, M., *Chemical Concepts of Psychosis*. New York, 1958.

Descartes, René (1596–1650), *Traité des Passions de l'âme*. Paris, 1646.

Dickens, Charles (1812–1870), *Pictures from Italy*.

Dunbar, Flanders, *Emotions and Bodily Changes*. New York, 1935 (new eds. till 1945).

Eberschweiler, A., *Untersuchungen über die sprachlichen Komponenten der Assoziation*. Zurich dissertation. *Allg. Zs. Psychiatr.*, LXV, 1908.

Empiricus, Sextus (c. 200 A.D.), *Pyrrh. hyp.*, II.

English, O.S., and Weiss, Ed., *Psychomatic Medicine. Clinical Application of Psychopathology to General Medical Problems*. Philadelphia and London, 1943.

Epictetus (50–135 A.D.), *Enchir.* LIII.

Euclid (c. 300 B.C.), *Elem.* II. 5.

Euripides (480–406 B.C.), *fr.* 956 (Nauck).

Fechner, Gustav Theodor (1801–1887), *Das Büchlein vom Leben nach dem Tod*. Leipzig, 1836.

_____, *Über das höchste Gut*. Leipzig, 1846.

_____, *Nanna oder über das Seelenleben der Pflanzen*. Leipzig, 1846.

_____, *Zend-Avesta oder Gedanken über die Dinge des Himmels und des Jenseits vom Standpunkte der Naturbetrachtung*. Leipzig, 1851.

———, *Über die Seelenfrage*. Leipzig, 1861.

———, *Elemente der Psychophysik*. Leipzig, 1860. 2 vols.

———, *Die Tagesansicht gegenüber der Nachtansicht*. Leipzig, 1879.

———, "Über die psychischen Massprinzipien und das Weber'sche Gesetz," in *Philos. St.*, ed. W. Wundt, IV, 1887.

Féré, Charles, "Notes sur des Modifications de la résistance électrique sous l'influence des Excitations sensorielles et des émotions," *Cpts. rends. hebd. Soc. Biol.*, 1888.

Fierz-David, H.E., *Die Entwicklung der Chemie*. Basle, 1945.

———, "August von Kekulé's chemische Visionen," *Gesnerus*, I/4, Aarau, 1944.

Fierz, M., "Zur physikalischen Erkenntnis," in *Eranos Yb.*, 1948. Zurich, 1949.

Figar, Stepan, "The Application of Plethysmography to the Objective Study of socalled Extrasensory Perception," *Journ. Soc. Psychical Research*, XXXX, 1959.

Flournoy, Théodore, *From India to the Planet Mars. A Study of a Case of Somnambulism with Glossolalia*. New York and London, 1900. *Archs. Psychol.*, I/2, 1901.

Franz, S.I., "Anomalous Reaction-Times in a Case of Manic-Depressive Depression," *Psychol. Bull.*, II/7, 1905.

Freud, Sigmund, *The Interpretation of Dreams*. Standard edition, IV and V, London, 1960. Original German edition, Leipzig and Vienna, 1900.

———, *The Psychopathology of Everyday Life*. Standard edition, VI, London, 1960. Original German edition, Leipzig and Vienna, 1904.

———, "Fragment of an Analysis of a Case of Hysteria." Standard edition, VII, London 1960. Original German edition, 1905.

———, "Psycho-Analysis and the Establishment of the Facts in Legal Proceedings." Standard edition, IX, London, 1960. German original, 1906.

———, *Sammlung kleiner Schriften zur Neurosenlehre*, II. Leipzig and Vienna, 1905.

———, *The Future of an Illusion*. Standard edition, XXI, London, 1960. German original, Leipzig, Vienna and Zurich, 1928.

Friedländer, S., *J.R. Mayer*. In *Klassiker der Naturwissenschafen*, I, Leipzig, 1905.

Frogatt, P., and Smiley, J.A., "The Concept of Accident Proneness: A Review," *Brit. Journ. Industr. Med.*, XXI, 1964.

Fürst, Emma, "Statistical Investigations on Word-Associations and on Familial Agreement in Reaction Type among Uneducated Persons," in *Studd. in Word-Assoc.*, ed. Jung, London, 1918. German original, 1907.

Galton, Francis (1822–1911), "Psychometric Experiments," *Brain*, 1879.

Gengerelli, J.A., and Kirkner, F.J. (eds.), *The Psychological Variables in Human Cancer*, London, 1955.

Gesta Romanorum.

Gibbs, J. W., *Elementary Principles in Statistical Mechanics*. 1902.
Goethe, Johann Wolfgang, letter to Eckermann dated 11th March, 1828.
————, "Urworte. Orphisch."
Grange, K. M., "An Allegory of the Emotions," 1649, *Med. Biol. Illustr.*, XIII/3, 1863.
Gregor, A., *Leitfaden der experimentellen Psychopathologie*. Berlin, 1910.
Grinker, R., and Robbins, F. P., *Psychosomatic Case Book*. New York, 1954.
Grove, W. R., "On the Progress of Physical Science," lecture delivered 19th January, 1842. London, 1842.
————, "The Correlation of Physical Forces." Being the Substance of a Course of Lectures in 1843. London, 1846.
Hahn, R., "Über die Beziehung zwischen Fehlreaktionen und Klangassoziationen." Zurich dissertation. *Psychol. Abb.*, ed. Kraepelin, V/1, 1906.
Hartleben, H., *Champollion, sein Leben und sein Werk*. 2 vols. Berlin, 1906.
Hell, B., *J. R. Mayer*. In *Frommanns Klassiker der Philosophie*, XXIII. Stuttgart, 1925.
Heraclitus (c. 500 B.C.), *Fragment* 45.
Herodotus (485–425 B.C.), VI, 130.
Hintermann, H., "Experimentelle Untersuchung der Bewusstseinsvorgänge mit Hülfe von Reaktionen auf Reizwörter unter Berücksichtigung auch der wichtigsten pathologischen Erscheinungen." Zurich dissertation, 1916.
Hirschfield, H., and Behan, R. C., "The Accident Process," *Journ. Amer. Med. Assoc.* , CLXXXVI, 1963, and CXCVII, 1966.
Hoffer, A., and Osmond, H., *The Chemical Basis of Clinical Psychiatry*. Springfield/Oxford/Toronto, 1960.
Hoffmann, E.T.A., *Rat Krespel*.
Hoffmann, W., "Über den Einfluss der Gefühlsbetonung und einiger anderer Faktoren auf die Dauer und den Wechsel der Assoziationen." Zurich dissertation. *Psychol. Abb.*, VII/1, 1915, ed. Kraepelin.
Hofmannsthal, Hugo von, *Der Rosenkavalier*, II/32 and II/124.
Huber, H., "Über den Einfluss von optischem und akustischem Reiz und grammatikalischer Form des Reizwortes auf den Assoziationsvorgang." Zurich dissertation. *Journ. Psychol. Neurol.*, XXIII/5/6, 1917.
Hug, A. "Leben und Werke des Rhetors Aristides." Fribourg (Switzerland) dissertation, Solothurn 1912.
Hunt, W. A., and Landis, C., "The Conscious Correlates of the Galvanic Skin Response," *Journ. Exp. Psychol.*, XVIII, 1935.
Isserlin, Max, "Psychologische Untersuchungen an Manisch-Depressiven," *Mschr. Psychiatr. Neurol.*, XXII, 1907.
James, William, *The Principles of Psychology*, II, U.S.A., 1890.
Janet, Pierre, *L'Automatisme psychologique*. Paris, 1889.
————, *L'Etat mental des Hystériques*. Paris, 1911.

————, "Les Oscillations du niveau mental," *Nouveau Traité de psychologie*, IV, fasc. 3, 1937.

Jentsch, E., *Julius Robert Mayer*. Seine Krankheitsgeschichte und die Geschichte seiner Entdeckung.

Jung, C.G., "On the Psychology and Pathology of So-called Occult Phenomena." *CW* 1. Zurich dissertation. German original, Leipzig, 1902.

————, "On Simulated Insanity." *CW* 1. German original, 1903.

————, "An Analysis of the Associations of an Epileptic." *CW* 2. German original, 1905.

————, "The Reaction-time Ratio in the Association Experiment." *CW* 2. German original, 1905.

————, "Experimental Observations on the Faculty of Memory." *CW* 2. German original, 1905.

————, "On the Psychological Diagnosis of Facts." *CW* 1. German original, 1905.

————, Psychoanalysis and Association Experiments." *CW* 2. German original, 1905.

————, "The Psychopathological Significance of the Association Experiment." *CW* 2. German original, 1906.

————, "Freud's Theory of Hysteria: a Reply to Aschaffenburg." *CW* 4. German original, 1906.

————, "The Psychological Diagnosis of Evidence." *CW* 2. German original, 1906.

————, "Association, Dream and Hysterical Symptom." *CW* 2. German original, 1906.

————, "The Psychology of Dementia Praecox." *CW* 3. German original, 1907.

————, "Disturbances of Reproduction in the Association Experiment." *CW* 2. German original, 1907.

————, "On the Psychophysical Relations of the Association Experiment." *CW* 2. English original, 1907.

————, "The Content of the Psychoses." *CW* 3. German original, 1908.

————, "The Freudian Theory of Hysteria." *CW* 4. German original, 1908.

————, "New Aspects of Criminal Psychology." *CW* 2. Italian original, 1908.

————, "The Analysis of Dreams." *CW* 4. French original, 1909.

————, "The Significance of the Father in the Destiny of the Individual." *CW* 4. German original, 1909.

————, "Abstracts of the Psychological Works of Swiss Authors (to the end of 1909)." *CW* 18. German original, 1910.

————, "Psychic Conflicts in a Child." *CW* 17. German original, 1910.

————, *Symbols of Transformation. CW* 5. German original, 1911 and 1912.

————, "A Contribution to the Psychology of Rumour." *CW* 4. German original, 1910.

———, "The Association Method." *CW* 2. Lecture originally delivered in German at Clark University, Worcester, Massachusetts, 1908. First English translation, 1910.

———, "On the Significance of Number Dreams." *CW* 4. German original, 1911.

———, "The Theory of Psychoanalysis." *CW* 4. German original, 1913.

———, "A Comment on Tausk's Criticism of Nelken." *CW* 18. German original, 1913.

———, "On the Importance of the Unconscious in Psychopathology." *CW* 3. English original, 1914.

———, "Associations d'idées familiales," *Archs. Psychol.*, VII, 1904.

———, "On the Problem of Psychogenesis in Mental Disease." *CW* 3. English original, 1919.

———, "A Review of the Complex Theory." *CW* 8. German original, 1934.

———, "Concerning Rebirth." *CW* 9, Part I. German original, 1939.

———, "On the Psychogenesis of Schizophrenia." *CW* 3. English original, 1939.

———, "On the Nature of the Psyche." *CW* 8. German original, 1947.

———, "Synchronicity: An Acausal Connecting Principle." *CW* 8. German original, 1952.

———, *Mysterium Coniunctionis. CW* 14. German original, 1955 and 1956.

———, "Schizophrenia." *CW* 3. German original, 1958.

———, "Das Unbewusste als Keimstätte des Schöpferischen" ("The Unconscious as the Birthplace of the Creative"). Introduction to Kankeleit's *Die schöpferische Macht des Unbewussten.* German original, 1959.

———, "Recent Thoughts on Schizophrenia." *CW* 3. English original, 1956.

Jung, C. G., and Bleuler, Eugen, "Complexes and Aetiology in Dementia Praecox" ("Komplexe und Krankheitsusachen bei Dementia praecox"). German original in *Zbl. Nervenhlkde. Psychiatr.*, XXXI, 1908.

Jung, C. G., and Peterson, Frederick, "Psychophysical Investigations with the Galvanometer and Pneumograph in Normal and Insane Individuals." *CW* 2. English original, 1907.

Jung, C. G., and Ricksher, Charles, "Further Investigations on the Galvanic Phenomenon and Respiration in Normal and Insane Individuals." *CW* 2. English original in *Journ. Abnorm. Psychol.*, II, 1907–1908.

Jung, C. G., and Riklin, Franz, "The Associations of Normal Subjects." *CW* 2. German original, 1904.

Kaeding, F. W., *Häufigkeitswörterbuch der deutschen Sprache.*

Kalmus, H. T., and Sidis, B., "Study of Galvanometric Deflections due to Psycho-Physical Processes," *Psychol. Revw.*, XV, 1908.

Kankeleit, Otto, *Die Schöpferische Macht des Unbewussten*. Berlin, 1933. New edition: *Das Unbewusste als Keimstätte des Schöpferischen*. With a preface by C.G. Jung. Basle and Munich, 1959.

Kant, Immanuel, *Dreams of a Spirit-seer*. New York, 1900. German original, 1766.

Kent, G. Helen, and Rosanoff, A.J., "A Study of Association in Insanity," *Amer. Journ. Insanity*, LXII I/2, 1910.

Kerner, Justinus (1786–1862), ed. *Blätter aus Prevorst* (1831–1839). Sammlung IV, p. 57. Karlsruhe, 1832.

———, *Die Seherin von Prevorst*. Stuttgart, 1829.

Kinder, E.F., and Syz, H.C., "Electrical Skin Resistance in Normal and Psychotic Subjects," *Archs. Neurol. Psychiatr.*, XIX, 1928.

———, "The Galvanic Skin-Reflex," *Archs. Neurol. Psychiatr.*, XXVI, 1931.

Kirkner, F.J., and Gengerelli, J.A. (eds.), *The Psychological Variables in Human Cancer*. Berkeley and Los Angeles, 1954.

Klaesi, J., "Über das psychogalvanische Phänomen." Zurich dissertation, 1912; also in *Journ. Psychol. Neurol.*, XIX, 1912.

Kowalewski, Arnold, "Studien zur Psychologie des Pessimismus," in *Grenzfragen des Nerven- und Seelenlebens*, ed. Löwenfeld and Kurella, Wiesbaden, 1904.

Kraepelin, Emil, "Der psychologische Versuch in der Psychiatrie," *Psychol. Abb.*, I, 1896.

Kretschmer, W., "Der Assoziationsversuch nach C.G. Jung," in *Hb. der klin. Psychol.*, I/1, ed. E. Stern, Zurich, 1954.

Kuhne, V., "Résumé des recherches psycho-galvanométriques sur l'émotivité de M. Edouard Abramowski," *Bull. Inst. gén. psychol.*, 13e année, III, 1913.

Landis, C., and Hunt, W.A., "The Conscious Correlates of the Galvanic Skin Response," *Journ. Exp. Psychol.*, XVIII, 1935.

Lang, J.B., "Über Assoziationsversuche bei Schizophrenen und den Mitgliedern ihrer Familie." Zurich dissertation in *Jb. psychoanal. psychopathol. Forschgg.*, V, 1913.

———, "Eine Hypothese zur psychologischen Bedeutung der Verfolgungsidee," in *Psychol. Abhh.* I, ed. C.G. Jung, 1914.

Lange, C.G., *Über Gemütsbewegungen*.

Lange-Eichbaum, W., *Genie, Irrsinn und Ruhm*. 2nd ed. Munich, 1935.

Lersch, Ph., *Der Traum in der deutschen Romantik*. Munich, 1923.

Ley, A., and Menzerath, P., *L'Etude expérimentale de l'association des idées dans les maladies mentales*. Gand, 1911.

Lichtenberg, G.Ch., "Nachtrag zu den witzigen und satyrischen Einfällen und Bemerkungen," *Vermischte Schriften*, II.

———, "Bemerkungen vermischten Inhalts," ibid., 2. *Psychologische Bemerkungen*.

Lipmann, Otto, "Die Spuren interessebetonter Erlebnisse und ihrer Symptome (Theorie, Methoden und Ergebnisse der 'Tatbestandsdiagnostik')," in: Supp. to *Zs. angew. Psychol.* I, 1911, ed. William Stern and Otto Lipmann.

Lucian (c. 125–180 A.D.), *De Dea Syria*, 17.

Maeder, Alphonse, "Contribution à la psychopathologie de la vie quotidienne," *Archs. Psychol.*, VI, 1906.

———, "Über das Traumproblem," *Jb. psychoanal. psychopathol. Forschgg.*, V/2, 1913.

Mayer, Julius Robert (1814–1878), "Bemerkungen über die Kräfte der unbelebten Natur," *Ann. Chem.*, 1842.

———, *Bemerkunger über das mechanische Aequivalent der Wärme.* Heilbronn, 1851.

McDougall, William, *Body and Mind.* London, 1911.

Mead, G.R.S., *The Subtle Body.* London, 1919.

Meier, Carl A., "Psychologische Streiflicher zur Geschichte des Energiebegriffs." Summary in: *Vjschr. natf. Ges. Zürich*, 81st year, Nos. 3 and 4, 1936.

———, "Über die Bedeutung des Jungschen Assoziationsexperimentes für die Psychotherapie." Congress Proceedings in *Zs. Ges. Neurol.*, CLXI, 1937.

———, *Ancient Incubation and Modern Psychotherapy*, Northwestern University Press, Evanston, 1967.

———, "C.G. Jung's Contributions to Theory and Therapy of Schizophrenia," *Proceedings of the Second International Congress for Psychiatry*, Zurich, 1957, IV.

———, "Einige Konsequenzen der neueren Psychologie," in *Studia Philosophica*, XIX, Basle, 1959.

———, "Psychosomatic Medicine from the Jungian Point of View," *Journ. Anal. Psychol.*, VIII, 1963.

Mittasch, A., *Julius Robert Mayer's Kausalbegriff.* Berlin, 1940.

Müller, H., "Experimentelle Beiträge zur physikalischen Entstehung des psycho-galvanischen Phänomens." Zurich dissertation, 1909.

Müller, V.J., "Zur Kenntnis der Leitungsbahnen des psychogalvanischen Reflexphänomens." Zurich dissertation, 1913. Also in *Mschr. Psychiatr. Neurol.*, XXXIII, 1913.

Nietzsche, Friedrich, *Beyond Good and Evil*, IV/68.

Nunberg, H., "Über körperliche Begleiterscheinungen assoziativer Vorgänge," *Journ. Psychol. Neurol.*, XVI, 1910; also in *Diagnostic Studies* XII.

Osmond, H., and Hoffer, A., *The Chemical Basis of Clinical Psychiatry.* Springfield/Oxford/Toronto, 1960.

Ostwald, Wilhelm, Grosse Männer. Leipzig, 1910.

Peters, W., "Gefühl und Erinnerung," *Psychol. Abh.*, VI/2, ed. Kraepelin, Leipzig, 1911.

Peters, W., and Nemecek, "Massenversuche über Erinnerungsassoziationen," in *Fortschr. Psychol. Anw.*, ed. K. Marbe, II/IV, 1914.

Peterson, Frederick, "The Galvanometer as a Measure of Emotions," *Brit. Med. Journ.*, September 1907.

_____, "The Galvanometer in Psychology," *Journ. Abnorm. Psychol.*, III, 1908.

Peterson, Frederick, and Jung, C.G., "Psycho-physical Investigations with the Galvanometer and Pneumograph in Normal and Insane Individuals," *Brain*, XXX/118, 1907.

Peterson, Frederick, and Prince, Morton, "Experiments in Psycho-Galvanic Reactions from Co-Conscious (Sub-Conscious) Ideas in a Case of Multiple Personality," *Journ. Abnorm. Psychol.*, III, 1908.

Peterson, Frederick, and Scripture, E.W., "Psycho-physical Investigations with the Galvanometer," *Journ. Nerv. Ment. Dis.*, July 1909.

Pfenninger, Wilhelm, "Untersuchungen über die Konstanz und den Wechsel der psychologischen Konstellation bei Normalen und Frühdementen (Schizophrenen)," *Jb. Psychoanal. Psychopathol. Forschgg.*, III/2, 1912.

Plotinus (c. 205-270 A.D.), IV.4 (28), 18, 19.

Plutarch (46-120 A.D.), *De Fortuna Romanorum, 1* (Mor. 316 D).

Prince, Morton, *The Dissociation of a Personality*. New York, 1905.

_____, *The Unconscious*. 1914.

Prince, Morton, and Peterson, Frederick, "Experiments in Psycho-Galvanic Reactions from Co-Conscious (Sub-Conscious) Ideas in a Case of Multiple Personality," *Journ. Abnorm. Psychol.*, III, 1908.

Prince, W.F., "The Doris Case of Multiple Personality," *Proc. Amer. Soc. Psychical Research*, IX, 1915; X, 1916; XVII, 1923.

Proclus (born 411 A.D.), Commentary on Plato's Timaeus, 384B.

Rhine, J.B., *New Frontiers of the Mind*. New York and London, 1937.

_____, *The Reach of the Mind*. London, 1948. Penguin Books, 1954.

Ricksher, Charles, and Jung, C.G., "Further Investigations on the Galvanic Phenomenon and Respiration in Normal and Insane Individuals," *Journ. Abnorm. Psychol.*, II, 1908.

Riese, W., *La Théorie des passions à la lumière de la pensée médicale au XVIIe siècle*. Basle, 1965.

Riklin, Franz, "Die diagnostische Bedeutung des Assoziationsversuches bei Hysterischen," *Psychiatr. Neurol. Wschr.*, XXIX, 1904.

_____, "Analytische Untersuchung der Symptome und Assoziationen eines Falles von Hysterie," *Psychiatr. Neurol. Wschr.*, XXXXVI, 1905.

_____, "Cases Illustrating the Phenomena of Association in Hysteria," in *Studd. in Word-Assn.*, ed. Jung, London, 1918. German original, 1906.

_____, "Wishfulfillment and Symbolism in Fairy Tales," *Psychoanal. Revw.*, II/1, 1915.

Riklin, Franz, and Jung, C.G., "The Associations of Normal Subjects" *CW* 2. German original, 1904.

Rinkel, M., and Denber, H.C.B. (eds.), *Chemical Concepts of Psychosis*. New York, 1958.

Robbins, F.P., and Grinker, R., *Psychosomatic Case Book*. New York, 1954.

Rosanoff, A. J., and Kent, G. Helen, "A Study of Association in Insanity," *Amer. Journ. Insanity*, LXVII 1/2, 1910.

Rousselle, E., "Seelische Führung im lebenden Taoismus," *Eranos Jb.*, 1933. Zurich, 1934.

Schenker, H., *Ein verschollener Brief von Mozart und das Geheimnis seines Schaffens.* In commemoration of the 175th anniversary of Mozart's birth. Kunstwart, VII, 1931.

Schmolz, H., and Weckbach, H., *Robert Mayer, sein Leben und Werk in Dokumenten.* Weissenhorn, 1964.

Schopenhauer, Arthur, *Transzendente Spekulationen über die anscheinende Absichtlichkeit im Schicksal des Einzelnen.* 1851.

———, *The World as Will and Imagination.* I.

Schreber, Daniel P., *Memoirs of My Nervous Illness.* London, 1955. German original, 1903.

Schulz, Max, *The Poetic Voices of Coleridge.* Detroit, 1963.

Schwarz, Oswald, *Psychogenese und Psychotherapie körperlicher Symptome.* Vienna, 1925.

Scripture, E. W., and Peterson, Frederick, "Psycho-physical Investigations with the Galvanometer," *Journ. Nerv. Ment. Dis.*, July 1909.

Senault, P.J.F., *De l'usage des Passions.* Paris, 1641.

Seneca (4–65 A.D.*), ep.* 107.

Sheppard, H. J., "The Ouroboros and the Unity of Matter in Alchemy: A Study in Origins," *Ambix*, X/2, 1962.

Sidis, B., "The Nature and Cause of the Galvanic Phenomenon," *Journ. Abnorm. Psychol.*, V, 1910.

Sidis, B., and Kalmus, H. T., "Study of Galvanometric Deflections due to Psycho-Physical Processes," *Psychol. Revw.*, XV, 1908, and XVI, 1909.

Sidis, B., and Nelson, L., "The Nature and Cause of the Galvanic Phenomenon," *Psychol. Revw.*, XVII, 1910.

Siebeck, H., *Geschichte der Psychologie.* Part 1. Gotha, 1884. Reprint Amsterdam, 1961.

Silberer, Herbert, *Probleme der Mystik und ihrer Symbolik.* Vienna and Leipzig, 1914.

———, *Der Zufall und die Koboldstreiche des Unbewussten.* Bern and Leipzig, 1921.

Smiley, J. A., and Frogatt, P., "The Concept of Accident Proneness: A Review," *Brit. Journ. Industr. Med.*, XXI, 1964.

Smith, W., *The Measurement of Emotion.* London, 1922.

Soal, S. G., and Bateman, F., *Modern Experiments in Telepathy.* London, 1954.

Sommer, Robert, *Lehrbuch der psychopathologischen Untersuchungsmethoden.* Berlin and Vienna, 1899.

Sterne, Laurence, *The Life and Opinions of Tristram Shandy.*

Stevenson, Robert Louis (1850–1894), *Treasure Island.*

———, *The Strange Case of Dr. Jekyll and Mr. Hyde.*

_____, *Across the Plains.*

Sticker, G., "Über Versuche einer objektiven Darstellung von Sensibilitätsstörungen," *Wien. Klin. Rdsch.*, 1897.

Strauss, Richard, *Der Rosenkavalier.* II/32 and II/124.

Syz, H. C., "Psycho-Galvanic Studies on Sixtyfour Medical Students," *Brit. Journ. Psychol.*(General Section), XVII, 1926.

_____, "Observations on the Unreliability of Subjective Reports on Emotional Reactions," ibid., XVII, 1926.

_____, "Psychogalvanic Studies in Schizophrenics," *Archs. Neurol. Psychiatr.*, XVI, 1926.

Syz, H. C., and Kinder, E. F., "Electrical Skin Resistance in Normal and Psychotic Subjects," *Archs. Neurol. Psychiatr.*, XIX, 1928.

Tarchanoff, J., "Über die galvanischen Erscheinungen in der Haut des Menschen bei Reizungen der Sinnesorgane und bei verschiedenen Formen der psychischen Tätigkeit," *Arch. ges. Physiol.*, XXXXVI, 1890.

Timerding, H., *Robert Mayer und die Entdeckung des Energiegesetzes.* Leipzig and Vienna, 1925.

Trautscholdt, M., "Experimentelle Untersuchungen über die Assoziationen der Vorstellungen," in *Philos. St.*, ed. Wilhelm Wundt, I, 1881.

Veraguth, Otto, "Das psycho-galvanische Reflex-Phänomen," *Mschr. Psychiatr. Neurol.*, XXI/1, 1906.

_____, *Das psychogalvanische Reflexphänomen.* Berlin 1909.

Vigouroux, A., "Etude sur la Résistance électrique chez les mélancoliques." Paris dissertation, 1890.

Vigouroux, Romain, "Sur la Résistance électrique considérée comme signe clinique," *Progr. Méd.* I. sem., 1888.

Vischer, F. Th., *Auch Einer.* 1879.

Wagner, Richard, *Tristan und Isolde,* III/1.

Walden, P., *Das Buch der grossen Chemiker*, ed. G. Bugge, Berlin, 1930.

Watt, Henry J., "Sammelbericht über die neuere Forschung in der Gedächtnis-und Assoziationspsychologie aus den Jahren 1903 und 1904," *Arch. Psychol.*, VII, 1906.

Weckbach, H., and Schmolz, H., *Robert Mayer, sein Leben und Werk in Dokumenten.* Weissenhorn, 1964.

Wehrlin, K., "Über die Assoziationen von Imbezillen und Idioten," *Journ. Psychol. Neurol.*, IV, 1904, and also *Diagnostic Studies*, II.

Weiss, Eduard, and English, O. S., *Psychosomatic Medicine. Clinical Application of Psychopathology to General Medical Problems.* Philadelphia and London, 1943.

Werner, H., *Die Schutzgeister.* Stuttgart and Tübingen, 1839.

Weyrauch, J. R., "Die Mechanik der Wärme," in *Gesammelte Schriften von Robert Mayer*, 2 vols., 3rd ed., Stuttgart, 1893.

INDEX

*See Notes to chapters beginning on page 183.

227